THE VOICE OF NEWFOUNDLAND:
A SOCIAL HISTORY OF THE BROADCASTING CORPORATION
OF NEWFOUNDLAND, 1939–1949

Similar to the CBC and BBC, the Broadcasting Corporation of Newfoundland was a public broadcaster that was at the centre of a cultural
and political change from 1939 to 1949, during which Newfoundland
faced wartime challenges and engaged in a constitutional debate about
whether to become integrated into Canada. *The Voice of Newfoundland*
studies these changes by taking a close look at the Broadcasting Corporation of Newfoundland's radio programming and the responses of
their listeners.

Making excellent use of program recordings, scripts, and letters
from listeners, as well as government and corporate archives, Jeff A.
Webb examines several innovative programs that responded to the
challenges of the Great Depression and Second World War. Webb
explores the roles that radio played in society and culture during a
vibrant and pivotal time in Newfoundland's history, and demonstrates
how the broadcaster's decision to air political debates was pivotal in
its decision to join Canada and to become part of North American consumer society.

An engaging study rich in details of some of twentieth-century
Newfoundland's most fascinating figures, *The Voice of Newfoundland* is
a remarkable history of its politics and culture and an important analysis of the influence of the media and the participation of listeners.

JEFF A. WEBB is an assistant professor in the Department of History at
Memorial University of Newfoundland.

JEFF A. WEBB

The Voice of Newfoundland

A Social History of the Broadcasting
Corporation of Newfoundland,
1939–1949

UNIVERSITY OF TORONTO PRESS
Toronto Buffalo London

© University of Toronto Press Incorporated 2008·
Toronto Buffalo London
www.utppublishing.com
Printed in Canada

ISBN 978-08020-9820-7 (cloth)
ISBN 978-08020-9553-4 (paper)

Printed on acid-free paper

Library and Archives Canada Cataloguing in Publication

Webb, Jeff A. (Jeffrey Allison), 1962–
    The voice of Newfoundland : a social history of the Broadcasting
    Corporation of Newfoundland, 1939–1949 / Jeff A. Webb.

    Includes bibliographical references and index.
    ISBN 978-0-8020-9820-7 (bound).   ISBN 978-0-8020-9553-4 (pbk.)

    1. Broadcasting Corporation of Newfoundland – History.   2. Radio
    broadcasting – Newfoundland and Labrador – History.   3. Radio
    broadcasting – Social aspects – Newfoundland and Labrador – History.
    4. Newfoundland and Labrador – Social conditions – 20th century.   I. Title.

    HE8689.9.C3W43 2008   384.54'0971809044   C2008-903469-4

University of Toronto Press acknowledges the financial assistance to its
publishing program of the Canada Council for the Arts and the Ontario
Arts Council.

University of Toronto Press acknowledges the financial support for its
publishing activities of the Government of Canada through the Book
Publishing Industry Development Program (BPIDP).

This book has been published with the help of a grant from the Canadian
Federation for the Humanities and Social Sciences, through the Aid to
Scholarly Publications Program, using funds provided by the Social
Sciences and Humanities Research Council of Canada.

Contents

Illustrations follow page 120

Acknowledgments

My debts to others are very great. I have learned much from my colleagues in the Department of History at Memorial University of Newfoundland, both past and present, and thank all of them for their support. I am especially grateful to the chair of our department, Chris Youé, for his efforts to regularize my contractual appointment. I must mention one teacher, colleague, and friend in particular, the late Ralph Pastore, who is fondly remembered for his dedication to scholarship and his unfailing humour.

Through their examples as authors and skills as editors James Hiller of Memorial and David Frank of the University of New Brunswick taught me how to write history as they supervised my MA and PhD respectively, although they are not responsible for my failings. Len Husband took an interest in this project from the moment I proposed it, and along with the other staff at the University of Toronto Press provided excellent guidance. My friends Jerry Bannister and Steve High, in particular, encouraged me to press ahead with this manuscript and I am grateful for their wise counsel. Steve's enthusiasm for the project sustained me at those moments when I wondered if anyone would be interested in a history of the BCN. I owe a debt to the scholarship, advice, and friendship of Dominique Brégent-Heald, Sean Cadigan, Philip Hiscock, and Terry Bishop-Stirling. Hiscock's fine work on early Newfoundland radio as a folk medium first whetted my appetite for this subject. My fellow media historians have also been supportive peers, especially Mary Vipond of Concordia University. I thank the anonymous readers who provided valuable feedback on an earlier draft.

This book is based upon sources scattered among many archives, but the Centre for Newfoundland Studies, the Archives and Manuscript

Division of the Queen Elizabeth II Library, and the Maritime History Archive, all of Memorial, deserve thanks for their special efforts to aid my research. The J.R. Smallwood Research Foundation, also of Memorial, covered the cost of research at the National Archives, College Park, Maryland. Chantal Ducey did newspaper research for me on a student career placement grant.

   Lastly I express my thanks and my love to my parents, Gary Webb and Edna Carter, and my wife Dale Johnson and my daughter Megan Webb. Through good times and bad they have reminded me that there are more important things than history.

THE VOICE OF NEWFOUNDLAND:
A SOCIAL HISTORY OF THE BROADCASTING CORPORATION
OF NEWFOUNDLAND, 1939–1949

Introduction

Through the hardship of the Great Depression, the destruction of the Second World War, and the fierce political debates of the late 1940s, Newfoundland families gathered around their radio receivers, straining to hear radio station VONF – the 'Voice of Newfoundland.' While radio broadcasting had similar effects around the world during its golden age of the 1940s, its reception in Newfoundland had some exceptional characteristics. That country suffered a long depression that lasted from the end of the First World War to the start of the Second, and then an economic boom during the 1940s that resulted in a revolution in people's fortunes and form of government. VONF had started life as a privately owned commercial station just as such stations were becoming established as the dominant form of radio in North America, but in 1939 was bought by the government and became a public broadcaster. Listening to the radio took similar characteristics as well. For many families the radio receiver was a sort of aural hearth, a device around which they would huddle for comfort after the end of the day's labour. Yet here too the social and geographic factors gave radio listening in Newfoundland its own character. Listeners strained to hear music and news from powerful British, American, and Canadian stations, but the St John's–based VONF had an important role in Newfoundland history. It both brought the outside world into the homes of thousands of Newfoundlanders and played a pivotal role in the confederation debate of the 1940s. Between 1939 and April 1949, the Commission of Government owned the station and operated it as the Broadcasting Corporation of Newfoundland, an equivalent to the British Broadcasting Corporation (BBC) or the Canadian Broadcasting Corporation (CBC).

This book covers a period of profound change in Newfoundland. The economic revival prompted by the Second World War allowed New-foundlanders to embrace consumerism and unequivocally choose to be integrated into North America in the post-war constitutional debate. I argue that radio broadcasting was at the centre of each of these political, social, and cultural transformations. This book does not attempt a comprehensive history of Newfoundland radio, but focuses upon the specific cultural project of state-owned broadcasting in St John's. Although the government used its radio system to change the culture and politics of listeners, both broadcasters and listeners brought their own agendas to radio and made meanings of the programming that went beyond the state's administrative agenda.

Most of the classic histories of broadcasting systems in North America develop along one of three narrative lines. Some historians relate a progression of technological inventions, celebrating the genius of individual inventors and pioneer broadcasters.[1] Others focus upon the growth of corporate networks such as the National Broadcasting Corporation (NBC) in the United States, either praising the business acumen of leaders such as David Sarnoff, the head of the Radio Corporation of America (RCA), or critically analysing the resulting corporate concentration.[2] Lastly, many historians have examined the public policy debate over public or private ownership, usually focusing upon how and why Canadian radio diverged from the American model.[3] Recently a few historians have written what they call the social history of broadcasting – an approach that offers a richer story of the interaction of the institution of radio with the culture and society.[4] This book continues in that tradition; it argues that radio broadcasting had a great effect upon Newfoundland culture and society, although never entirely in the ways that policy makers and radio broadcasters intended. Listeners used radio for their own purposes, making it impossible to discern the 'meaning' of the programming through textual analysis alone.[5] This book attempts to recover what broadcasters intended through examination of the extant programming and something of how listeners perceived what they heard. Furthermore, most historians study national broadcasting systems or large corporations. These histories of a broad scale illuminate questions of policy but cannot explore the details of individual programs. My study examines a single station, which was also a national broadcaster, so both questions of policy and daily practice can be addressed.

The mass media are not just a series of technologies such as printing presses or radios, or a set of industries such as publishing or broadcasting; the mass media are the principal way that people in the twentieth century communicated ideas, attitudes, and symbols to each other on a large scale.[6] Any history of the mass media will therefore be a history of the society of which it is part, and any history of a twentieth century society will be in large measure a history of its media. When people during the 1930s fought for public broadcasting, they often imagined their listeners as *the public* (a body they sometimes saw as synonymous with the citizens of the nation state). Commercial broadcasters, on the other hand, usually worked to create *an audience* of consumers. That audience often transcended national boundaries. This study adopts a more neutral concept and conceives of those who receive the content as *listeners*. It attempts to provide a social and cultural history of broadcasting, both producers and listeners, within a fairly small country, thus allowing a multifaceted study of programming, popular culture, and politics.[7] An understanding of the conditions under which broadcasters created content is essential before deconstructing the meaning of programming can begin. At its most basic level, this book outlines the political and administrative history of the Broadcasting Corporation of Newfoundland – an organization that has not been examined by historians. It also discusses Newfoundland's public and private broadcasting debate, which, because of the particular constitutional and social position of Newfoundland in the 1930s, had a slightly different character from what took place in other countries. Yet this case study goes beyond the institutional history of a network or a study of government policy: it places broadcasting within the social context of its society and examines how radio was used by listeners.

Newfoundland historians pay a great deal of attention to the history of their resource-based economy, social relations within the fishery, and the rise and fall of an independent nation state.[8] They have also examined the state's efforts to modernize the economy.[9] Less attention has been paid to recovering the culture of the people, except by scholars who saw it though the lens of political economy or as an example of a class struggle through symbolic means.[10] Research upon the development of Newfoundland popular culture generally, and radio programming in particular, has been pioneered by folklorists, rather than historians. These scholars realized that folk culture was a source of content for the mass media and that people integrated content from the media into their folk culture.[11] This study builds upon this insight and places Newfoundland popular culture within its historical context.

Radio broadcasting was more than a leisure distraction from the material realities of people's lives; it was at the centre of many of the social and cultural changes that occurred during a vibrant period. This book addresses the effect of radio upon Newfoundland popular culture, which is a more difficult task than tracing the history of the radio corporation.[12] There are problems with uncritically taking 'Newfoundland culture' or 'popular culture' as a unit of analysis.[13] A particular Newfoundland culture developed over the centuries, based upon the economic base and ecological niches occupied by Newfoundlanders and formed in dialogue with the other cultures of the North Atlantic. One part of that total culture was popular culture, or expressive culture – terms I use here in the narrow sense of the forms that were created by the mass media.

No culture is static, and during the decade between 1939 and 1949 Newfoundland popular culture underwent significant changes. These reflected both internal developments within Newfoundland's society and government and the influence of continual contacts with other cultures. It would be a mistake to attribute all innovations within popular culture during this period to contact with foreign media or the presence of people from other cultures in Newfoundland. Although, as we shall see, such contacts introduced new forms, and the development of mass media changed the context within which popular culture was transmitted, Newfoundlanders were themselves innovators. Like the people of any area of the world, Newfoundlanders also varied considerably across class, geography, and ethnicity, to take only three examples of many cleavages, and Newfoundland could in turn be subdivided into many smaller local regions, communities, families, and individuals. Newfoundlanders in different areas had significantly different economies and patterns of life. There was no single Newfoundland culture, nor was there a single experience with broadcasting that all listeners shared. Newfoundlanders were also integrated into social, economic, and cultural structures that extended throughout North America, the British Empire, and the Western world. When embarking upon a study of the cultural history of Newfoundland, one has to be aware that mid-twentieth-century Newfoundlanders had a culture that was their own and, very importantly, a consciousness of that culture. This book will point out that radio broadcasting played an important role in developing the awareness that a Newfoundland culture existed while giving that popular culture shape. The Newfoundland popular culture did not exist in isolation, but overlapped with that of people living in other areas. Newfoundlanders were heirs to the same Western 'civilization' as their counterparts elsewhere, and their views were shaped by being part of the British Empire and their proximity to the United States. They also had always been engaged in an international economy and culture. Radio broadcasting was a twentieth-century technology that developed in conjunction with consumer capitalism, so a facile reading might juxtapose a hypothetical isolated pre-modern Newfoundland culture with the modernity of North American business once radio develops.[14] Such a false dichotomy cannot be supported by evidence. Newfoundland popular culture had always been in dynamic conversation with forms and ideas from elsewhere in the world. Newfoundland was fully integrated into international capitalism and patterns of consumption in the 1940s; in some ways it had always been.[15]

Technological innovations such as the phonograph, the cinema, and radio broadcasting provided people with opportunities to promote the spread of popular culture across great distances and allowed performances to be preserved and transmitted at a later time.[16] They embodied another important transition within popular culture as well. To an extent, performance exclusively within communities, in which everyone was a participant at the moment that the expressive form was produced, could now be replaced by performance in which the person creating the popular culture did not live within the communities in which the product was being consumed and may have produced it at a much earlier time. In the case of broadcasting, a small group of people created the content, and a larger group of listeners, who were often at a great distance from the site of production and sometimes after a great time had passed, interpreted that content. While this change was important, this study will show that dividing culture into binary oppositions, such as Newfoundland vs American or traditional vs mass media, would obscure the diversity within the culture at any given moment. This study traces an outline of Newfoundland popular culture during a pivotal decade in the country's history and shows how that culture manifested itself in radio.

There are a number of false dichotomies that run through the historiography of public broadcasting, and Canadian historians only recently dispensed with the assumption that 'public broadcasting' served the national interest and privately owned broadcasting served personal interest. This case, in which a single station operated under both private and state ownership, reveals that, despite the rhetoric about public broadcasting, the ownership of the radio station made less difference upon the nature of programming than contemporary partisans admitted. Clearly, privately owned commercial broadcasters sometimes promoted the public good and the state usually served its own interests, which may or may not have coincided with the interest of the 'public.' At various points, the state-owned broadcaster might foster loyalty to the political regime, advance the economic interests of the national business community, or attempt to mould the culture in a particular way.[17] Furthermore, both kinds of broadcasters provided time for non-commercial 'public service' programming as well as providing a venue for businesses to advertise their wares. Whether state-owned or privately owned, financed through advertising or through licence fees, a radio broadcasting station could perform many different functions simultaneously. There was, therefore, no inherent requirement for the programming to be fundamentally different during VONF's two phases. The Newfoundland state had a political agenda that prompted and shaped its move into broadcasting, but that plan did not exclude the commercial uses of the medium. Despite the paternalistic and centralizing agenda of the British-born civil servants and their desire to make Newfoundlanders more economically self-sufficient, the officials were constrained from creating a non-commercial, state-monopoly broadcaster by financial and political considerations. In fact, rather than replacing advertising, the state extended the range and impact of commercial radio programs on VONF and on its sister stations (when the BCN expanded to operate several stations). The consistency of staff, as well as financial and political exigencies, combined to give a high degree of continuity in the kind of Newfoundland popular culture that was produced from the station's early days as a privately owned commercial station through its decade as Newfoundland's state-owned broadcaster, up to the point that it was absorbed into the Canadian Broadcasting Corporation in 1949.

Broadcasting, by definition, takes content from one point and distributes it to a multitude of points. Radio broadcasters provided listeners with cultural forms that were both invented by local broadcasters and adopted from international sources. Regardless of the point of origin, this programming became part of the cultural corpus of Newfoundlanders who were geographically disparate, slightly divided by ethnic origin, and of different classes. Listeners adopted as part of their culture those contents and forms that resonated with their existing culture, regardless of whether they were learned in a local performance by a member of one's community or learned from the radio. Furthermore,

there is little reason to assume that people favoured some news or entertainment because they acquired it as part of a commercial exchange,
such as buying a phonograph record, or within routine social relations
within their communities, such as listening to someone sing as he or she
worked. Yet broadcasting was also more of a dialogue than is suggested
by the model of broadcasters producing programming and listeners
consuming it; listeners influenced the form and content of broadcasts.
Listeners submitted material to be broadcast in some instances and frequently made their preferences known to radio stations and advertisers.
This book will also argue that the most effective radio propaganda was
not that of the Commission or its broadcasting corporation, but persuasive rhetoric that rose organically from non-governmental organizations that used the BCN as its medium to engage in a dialogue with
listeners.[18]

On the most superficial level, broadcasters and listeners were on opposite poles of creation and consumption, but that is not the whole
story. We can reconstruct a plausible understanding of what broadcasters intended to mean in their programming from the text of talks, the
correspondence of the broadcasters, and extant recordings of programming. But the other side of that equation, listeners, is equally important.
Radio receivers picked the electromagnetic signals from the air and
reconstructed sounds, but listeners had to make sense of them.[19] Dis-
cerning meaning from these sounds was a creative act, and the meaning
that listeners inferred may have been significantly different from what
the originator of the programming intended. These meanings were
determined by the conditions of listeners' lives. Listeners might misun-
derstand, accept, or reject the messages intended by the broadcaster or
make their own meaning out of the content. By attending to the few
examples of listener response we have, in a few surviving letters that
criticize programming or make suggestions, we can see that listeners
formed their own critique of radio programming. They were not blank
slates upon which broadcasters left their impression. We must bear in
mind that many different lessons may have been drawn by listeners of
even the simplest of propaganda messages, depending upon their pre-
conceptions. Listeners may well have tuned out messages that they did
not want to hear or that did not fit with their mental universe. Whether
a listener quietly attended to the program or had the radio on for 'company' while doing housework likely made a difference. And when
groups of people listened together, their interactions with each other
probably had a great effect upon their understanding and impression of

the content they heard. The consumption of radio programming always took place within a social context, and as difficult as it is for a historian to reconstruct that social context, doing so is a key to reconstructing the influence of radio.[20]

A few things must be said for readers unfamiliar with Newfoundland's remarkable history. Like other colonies of the British Empire, Newfoundland had assumed greater measures of self-government during the nineteenth century and had entered the twentieth century with a sense of optimism that prosperity and modernity were within grasp. It had tried to emulate the transportation and communications innovations of other countries to provide the infrastructure that would support industrialization. It established a transatlantic telegraphic link and a link to North America, telegraph lines, a railway, and a steamship service. Unfortunately the government's efforts to develop economic alternatives to the fishery through the modern transportation and communication industries had contributed to a debt burden that the country was unable to maintain when exports collapsed during the Great Depression. Radio broadcasting could not have arrived at a less auspicious time, yet despite the economic and political crisis, broadcasting grew and created new vibrant forms of popular culture.

During the 1930s, nearly the whole population of Newfoundland and Labrador lived within sight of the sea, most of whom were in small communities in which most families fished and bartered their catch for the imported necessities of life. This economic system, known locally as truck, was seen by those outside the fish trade as exploitative of fishing families and ruinous of the work ethic of those who caught and cured the fish. The capital, St John's, had a small middle class and many who worked for wages both manufacturing items for local consumption and supporting the international trade in fish. There were a couple of other urban centres: Bell Island was a small but vibrant mining town, and the paper-manufacturing companies employed wage-earners in Grand Falls and Corner Brook. Outports were cash-poor, but enough cash circulated during the Great Depression to enable a few peddlers and mail-order companies to operate. With the collapse of government revenue and swelling expenditure upon poor relief, the state relied nearly exclusively upon customs duties, prompting the Newfoundland legislature to suspend itself. In 1934 Newfoundland reverted to being little more than a Crown colony. The paternalistic UK government-appointed Commission of Government administered the country for the next fifteen years. An economic revival accompanied the Second World War, enabling many households to enjoy a few luxuries – often the consumer products advertised by radio and magazines that were symbols of the modern lifestyle. At war's end the country debated its future form of government, and in a hard-fought referendum voters chose to become a Canadian province.[21] Despite, as I argue, radio's central place in most of these political and social changes of the decade between 1939 and 1949, Newfoundland historians have paid little attention to thinking about the medium itself, even when using the broadcasts or newspapers as evidence of government policy or people's attitudes.[22]

The form that radio broadcasting took in Newfoundland was not created in a vacuum. Many of the Newfoundlanders who played key roles in the development of VONF had experience in the United States, and Newfoundlanders listening to American programming shaped what Newfoundlanders thought broadcasting should be and to what they wanted to listen. VONF started as a commercial station much like many others throughout North America. Its in-house programs were an eclectic mix of news and weather, recorded music, live music, and dramatic readings from the local cultural community. While early listeners valued broadcasting for the ability to listen to live programming, few stations could provide enough content out of their own resources. North American broadcast stations turned to recordings and to networks to inexpensively fill time as their broadcast schedule expanded from a few hours a week toward full daily programming seven days a week. The St John's station played phonograph music from international sources and rebroadcast programming from NBC. Listeners during radio's early days valued programming that originated from distant and exotic locations for the novelty, but quickly settled into a pattern of wanting reliable local stations to serve their day-to-day needs. It would be an error to exaggerate the role of broadcasting in changing Newfoundland culture. Popular commentators sometimes assume that twentieth-century mass media, such as radio, served the role of replacing 'folk' culture with American or Canadian mass-produced popular culture. It is falsely dichotomous to represent an 'authentic' indigenous Newfoundland culture in opposition to the North American mass-culture produced by the entertainment industry. Local broadcasters, whether state-owned or privately owned, drew upon local culture for programming at the same time that they imported cultural forms.

Throughout the continent, for-profit broadcasting dominated, so stations designed programming with an eye to creating a broad audience whose attention to the programming could be sold to advertisers. This system discouraged the creation of programming that was not 'popular' in the sense of having a large number of listeners. In the United States, a constitutional debate over jurisdiction had left the emerging broadcasting industry without state regulation during its formative period and allowed unrestricted advertising content and programming directed to the masses.[23] A vibrant popular culture had emerged out of this period. Newfoundlanders were North Americans, and during the 1930s they wanted to listen to the snappy wordplay of the American comics, the hits of the American music industry, and the melodrama of the serialized drama. Having to listen to an announcer extol the virtues of a particular product was widely, but not universally, regarded as a small price to pay for the entertainment the radio brought into one's home.

In the United States, Canada, and Britain some people objected to advertising and to programming designed to appeal to non-elite tastes, and lobbied governments to create state-owned broadcasting corporations. NBC and its compatriots succeeded in preventing the emergence of any alternative to privately owned public radio. It convinced the Federal Communications Commission that only privately owned for-profit broadcasting served the public interest.[24] Meanwhile the Canadian Radio League succeeded in convincing the Canadian government to establish a state-owned broadcaster, in large part because the government believed that there was no Canadian business able to compete with the resources held by NBC. For public broadcasting advocates the question in Canada was one of 'the state or the United States.'[25] The BBC was also designed and managed, in large measure, as a rejection of the American model of radio broadcasting.[26] No such movement for public broadcasting existed in Newfoundland, and that fact is not surprising, considering the relatively rudimentary nature of the Newfoundland state and the looming financial crisis of the government. Furthermore, while cultural critics lambasted commercial broadcasting for producing content that appealed to the lowest common denominator among listeners, commercial broadcasting in Newfoundland hardly pandered to mass tastes.[27] First, the difficulties of filling a program schedule out of limited resources meant everything from 'classical' phonograph records to the most 'popular' of the vaudevillian routines and Tin Pan Alley tunes was included. Second, in the 1920s and 1930s broadcasters throughout North America, including Newfoundland, created some upscale programming, and did so for several related reasons. Broadcasters believed 'high-brow' programming would give the new technology prestige that would aid its acceptance by the disproportionately wealthy and urban potential audience. Third, radio receivers were expensive and could hardly be purchased by 'the masses' before the Second World War, particularly in Newfoundland, which suffered from relatively low per capita incomes during the first half of the twentieth century.

This book addresses several themes. It attempts to place radio broadcasting within the political and ideological history of Newfoundland during the period when Newfoundland was administered by a British-appointed bureaucracy – the Commission of Government. It provides new perspectives upon the history of the Commission's policies and the use of the media to achieve political goals. It also examines the role radio had in forging a popular culture. It's widely accepted that whatever the intent of authors and creators of radio programming, listeners interpret the content in ways that are meaningful to themselves. The difficulty is that most radio was ephemeral and has left no traces for the historian to recover. It is even more difficult to determine what people listened to and what meaning they made of it. For that reason, this book pays particular attention to such sources as scripts of programs, extant recordings, and listeners' letters. These show what listeners liked and disliked and what they wanted radio to do for them. More provocatively, the letters sometimes show listeners resisting the readings that the programmers intended.

Radio is an aural medium. The documentary record tells us something of government policy, and scripts sometimes tell us what broadcasters intended to say, but the effect of the medium upon listeners is not apparent from these sources. This is not the least because we have little evidence to examine for the tone and inflections of voices, the character of the music, and dozens of other aspects of the content. A fraction of the programming of the Broadcasting Corporation was recorded, given the difficulties and expense of recording, and only a small portion of that has survived. Listening to the extant recordings has revealed dimensions of the broadcasts not apparent in written text – sometimes aspects of the programming that were not reflected in written accounts or in the popular memory of programs. The recordings of special event broadcasts such as the 1939 Royal Tour are available to be examined closely. Little of the 'average' daily programming on VONF was recorded, and most of what was recorded has not been preserved. This also raises the important question of how representative a single broadcast was of the daily content, and the answer is that it varies, from the typical program that has been preserved by chance, to the unique. Yet the small set of extant recordings from the 1930s and 1940s are the closest we have to an unmediated representation of what listeners in the past heard and can reveal something of the production of the station. It might, at least, reveal what the Corporation judged to be worth the trouble to preserve.

Each of the chapters that follow examines a particular facet of the story of public broadcasting in Newfoundland. Chapter 1 sets out the motives that prompted the development of a state-owned radio broadcasting system. It argues that during the 1920s and early 1930s the government was preoccupied with other issues and left the provision of public broadcasting to non-government organizations such as churches and private businesses. These stations did provide a great deal of public service. Things changed when the United Kingdom government suspended Newfoundland's democratic constitution and replaced it with government by commission. The Commission of Government created a state-owned broadcaster, which it hoped would be a tool for the economic and moral reconstruction of the Newfoundland people. Chapter 2 examines some of the practical ways that the Commission used radio as a propaganda apparatus to achieve its reconstruction goals. Before these efforts could achieve their full potential, however, the Commission lost enthusiasm for the radical reconstruction of Newfoundland culture, thanks to the start of the Second World War. While the Commission failed to use the medium to its full potential, the particular circumstances in Newfoundland encouraged broadcasters to use radio in innovative ways. Chapter 3 examines several of these programs, which served the particular needs of Newfoundlanders. The message programs, for example, created an imagined community as they simultaneously encouraged listeners to adopt a North American–style consumer culture.[28] The years of the Second World War were the height of radio's social influence. Chapter 4 examines how the state used radio to mobilize the society for the war effort, encouraging recruitment, maintaining morale, and coordinating the home front. In chapter 5 a story familiar to Newfoundlanders is told with a different emphasis. Through the broadcasts of the debates of the National Convention and the campaigning before the constitutional referendum of 1948, radio allowed people to participate in the political debate over their future and made them aware of the material effects of their decision to join Canada. Chapter 6 evaluates the efforts made by the Broadcasting Corporation to return to the goals that had been set out for it during the Depression, but had been set aside during the war. It shows that Newfoundland was a little country that was vulnerable to losing its desired radio frequency to other countries and relied upon a moral case that broadcasting had a special role to play in Newfoundland. This could have served as a warning of what would have been ahead for Newfoundland in the post-war world had it not joined Canada. But join Canada it did, and it is a testament to the Newfoundland broadcasters and the unique role that broadcasting developed in the nation that the Canadian Broadcasting Corporation agreed to maintain the Voice of Newfoundland.

1 Career of Service: The Emergence of Public Broadcasting

'Only those who have experienced it,' complained J.T. Downey, 'can conceive of the monotony of life in most of our outport communities as minister.'[1] The solution, he suggested to Deputy Colonial Secretary Mews, was to create a St John's-based radio broadcasting station that would entertain and enlighten rural people. Such a station could provide entertainment as well as a full range of information, including prices of consumer goods, notices of the availability of bait, and weather forecasts. Many people during the 1920s believed that the modern technology of radio could end the isolation of rural life. The idealism of that belief was frequently accompanied by vague business models under which such a station could work; North American broadcasters did not finance their stations through the sale of advertising time until late in that decade.[2] Downey thought that the broadcaster could be privately owned, perhaps by the Marconi Company, which operated marine communications radio in Newfoundland waters. It could recover its costs though the retail of radio receivers. He believed newspapers and government departments could furnish news and fisheries' information to the station without cost, and he imagined the city's banks might sponsor musical entertainment. But it would be a decade and a half before a government-owned station attempted to fulfil all the hopes Downey had articulated. For now, however, the colonial secretary agreed that such a station could be of great value, but reported that the government had not followed up upon similar proposals in the past.[3] In the interim, other institutions filled the need for 'public' broadcasting.

Newfoundlanders were intensely interested in communications. Marconi's successful 1901 reception of a transatlantic wireless message at Signal Hill, overlooking St John's, had demonstrated that distance could be banished. Organizations such as William Coaker's Fishermen's Protective Union had realized that information was power and used the first mass medium, its own newspaper, to empower fishing families by levelling the information gap between them and the merchants who bought their fish. The Newfoundland government enthusiastically embraced new communications technologies such as the transatlantic telegraph cable, the railway, and steamships. It had been disappointed when Marconi's experiment didn't result in a permanent transatlantic radio relay station. Capitalizing on new technologies seemed impossible, however, during the 1920s, when fundamental economic problems and a perennial fiscal shortfall preoccupied the public officials. Even basic regulatory functions seemed beyond the means of the embattled government. No Newfoundland bureaucratic apparatus regulated radio broadcasters or remedied the sources of electrical interference that impeded radio reception. The fiscal crisis of the 1920s and 1930s ensured that the creation of a state-owned broadcaster like the British Broadcasting Corporation was out of the question. Churches, volunteer groups, and businesses took up the role of public service broadcasting. Eventually the reformist Commission of Government, which administered Newfoundland and Labrador from 1934 to 1949, created a state-owned broadcaster, but such bold innovations were not on the agenda during the 1920s and early 1930s.

There is an unstated assumption in many histories of radio broadcasting that privately owned stations serve their owners' interests and state-ownership is synonymous with public broadcasting, yet the church-owned 8WMC (later renamed VOWR) was in many respects Newfoundland's first public broadcaster.[4] Churches see themselves as having a role in bringing spiritual messages to the people, and religious groups in Canada, for example, were quick to take advantage of the propaganda uses of the new technology to provide religious broadcasts on Sundays. It's not surprising, therefore, that a church should take the initiative of creating a broadcast station that fit within a broadly defined educational role. In 1924 Reverend Joseph Joyce of the Wesley United Church in St John's built a transmitter, which he intended to use to broadcast church services to shut-ins. Joyce was Newfoundland born but had been educated in Canada, where he had been influenced by the social gospel, with its concern for improving the material conditions of people's lives, not just concern for their souls. After being posted to St John's, he combined his radio hobby with a desire to spread church messages more broadly. Joyce also recognized the desire for secular programming, and a Newfoundland Broadcasting Committee soon began using the church transmitter to provide news, entertainment, and public service.

Religious sectarianism had plagued much of Newfoundland's social and political life during the nineteenth century, prompting people to maintain separateness to avoid conflict. Separate schools and sectarian cultural institutions had minimized the risk of offending other churches, but a church-run station would be heard by listeners of many denominations. These dangers were not hypothetical. In Canada the International Bible Students Association (known after 1931 as the Jehovah's Witnesses) broadcasts of the 1920s had offended many listeners of other denominations, prompting the Canadian government to refuse to renew the offending station's licence. The controversy resulted in a ban upon churches owning stations and was also one of the factors that encouraged the government to appoint a royal commission into radio broadcasting, which in turn recommended a public broadcasting system.[5] Churches in Britain had squabbled over religious doctrine over the air, before settling down and becoming content with representation on the BBC. Some religious leaders in the United States were divided between those who wanted, like the Jehovah's Witnesses, to use the microphone as a pulpit to convert listeners, and those who were anxious to present religion on the air in non-confrontational ways.[6] No such problems emerged in Newfoundland, perhaps because the Methodists were more careful to not offend other denominations. VOWR was non-sectarian and non-partisan, unlike contemporary newspapers, which were frequently affiliated with a political party or faction. There was a difference between broadcasting and publishing. With radio, one could not avoid the perhaps offensive content coming into the home where women or children might hear it, while a reader could choose to not purchase a newspaper or not attend a movie or political rally. Throughout the world, governments and broadcasters took special care during the 1920s to make broadcast content respectable. Radio broadcasting entered into the sanctum of the home, unlike the yellow journalism of newspapers or the morally suspect productions of the film industry.

VOWR relied upon donations and public subscriptions from people of many denominations to fund its activities. In addition to church services, the station supplied a range of entertainment, news (supplied by the daily newspapers), and public service announcements typical of North American stations of the day. Volunteers provided a range of live entertainment and phonograph records, including popular and classical vocal and instrumental tunes. While the station lacked a full-time staff, volunteers raised money, provided on-air talent, and in general served the need for local broadcasting. The St John's newspapers printed a schedule of the church services that were broadcast, without feeling it necessary to mention the call letters of the station.

The government did consider taking a more active role in broadcasting. Joyce's ambitions to serve the public outstripped his abilities, prompting him to apply for government money to aid his station in broadcasting 'public news' during the winter. In December 1928 the Cabinet appointed a committee to report on the proposal.[7] Hugh Le-Messurier took the opportunity to propose a public broadcasting system. He reported to the committee that he had been in contact with the British broadcaster Gerald Marcuse about a plan to take over the former Naval wireless station at Mount Pearl and use it as a broadcasting transmitter. Marcuse had risen to prominence through a series of experimental shortwave broadcasts to the empire, before the BBC established a monopoly over broadcasting in the UK. LeMessurier believed that radio would eventually come under government control but had been discouraged by the previous government's lack of interest in broadcasting. The government, he believed, had not wanted to interfere with Reverend Joyce's station. LeMessurier reported that Marcuse was interested in helping to establish a station in Newfoundland, and that the station could be financed though advertising and licence fees. Not only could a high-power station serve educational needs, but it could help the country attract tourists. 'I am frightfully interested in radio,' he admitted.[8] Unfortunately, 1929 was politically turbulent, so it is not surprising that the government did nothing to move into broadcasting, despite public enthusiasm for the new technology. Upon the transfer of Joyce to a parish in Canada during the summer of 1930, a non-sectarian committee took over the station, so that the new pastor would not be burdened with running a broadcasting station as well as serving the parish.[9]

Meanwhile, the church station continued to serve the public at times of normalcy and crisis. Despite the absence of a news-gathering staff at 8WMC, the *Daily News* praised the station for its coverage of the explosion of the sealing ship SS *Viking*, in March 1931. Amateur radio operators provided communication to coordinate the rescue attempt. 8WMC then broadcast the names of survivors and kept listeners up to date with two or three daily broadcasts.[10] This work exemplifies the way that the public service role taken on by radio broadcasting in Newfoundland emerged out of marine radio. People had been shocked by the SS *Newfoundland* disaster of 1912, in which the men of that ship had frozen to death on the ice while the captain believed that they were safely aboard another vessel. The resulting enquiry recommended sealing vessels be outfitted with radios, emphasizing the importance of weather broadcasts and communication with ships at sea. Any account of 'public' broadcasting in Newfoundland would be remiss if it did not recognize that during the 1920s it was not the state that provided public broadcasting; the Wesley United Church in St John's and its volunteers did so. It is also clear that, from its beginning, Newfoundland broadcasters took as their primary role that of providing life-saving information to people scattered along the coast and on board fishing vessels.

Widespread appreciation for the public service of the station, which adopted the call sign VOWR (Voice of Wesleyan Radio) at the end of May 1931, did not mean other broadcasters were unwelcome. The second aspirant to public broadcasting was also owned by a church, and it was launched with an ambitious manifesto. Pastor Harold Williams, an American citizen, of the Seventh Day Adventist Church had been operating at twenty-five watts under the call sign 8RA. At the end of December 1930 he announced that a new station would now be operating at 5000 watts. The station would be operated by the Radio Association of Newfoundland – a group of directors who, according to their press release, would devote all revenue to the operation of the station and to charity. A friend of Pastor Williams, George Stevens of New York, moved to St John's to build and operate the station.[11] The Radio Association announced the station would 'diffuse moral, ethical, and secular education which will mould and train the public to be better and more useful citizens and subjects of Newfoundland and of the British Empire.' It intended to be able to be heard throughout the country and on the mainland, to both 'serve the country in emergency, calamity or need and to promote good will and broadcast the talent, and spirit of Newfoundland to the world outside as far as is in our reach and power.'[12] Williams and each of the twenty-eight directors had invested in the station, as had Stevens, who owned station WMRC in New York. Both VOWR and VONA – as 8RA was renamed in May 1931 – had shown that volunteer bodies could fulfil all the functions of public broadcasting, but the Great Depression was not an easy time for charities in Newfoundland, and both stations operated on limited broadcast hours, amateur performers, and volunteer broadcasters.

While churches moved into the broadcasting vacuum left by the government and businesses, the state moved into the regulatory realm. International agreements assigned call signs and required governments to eliminate faulty electrical equipment, which generated its own unwanted radio signals. Such signals caused static, hiss, and whistles, which sometimes made listening to the radio more a source of frustration than enjoyment. The mandate to repair the electrical equipment that caused this interference combined with local pressure to prompt the government to intervene. A January 1931 editorial of the *Daily News* commented upon the interference that spoiled St John's listeners' reception. It suggested the formation of a radio association of retailers that would track down and eliminate sources of interference. The mayor of St John's indicated that such work was outside the jurisdiction of the city and was too costly, but the *Daily News* believed that listeners could bear the cost.[13] The radio retailers met at the Board of Trade rooms, and a couple of their number found two sources of interference with a jury-rigged apparatus, but the retailers failed to form any lasting organization to undertake what they all agreed was necessary.[14] A letter to the editor of the *Daily News* summed up the situation. Improvements in receivers made them more sensitive and thus more liable to interference. This was a problem that only the state had the authority and financial resources to tackle:

> The world over, Radio is controlled by the state ... Is it not a fact that a Radio Association was formed, from which we had hoped great things? We have not heard much of it of late. So much for the listeners. Next we were told that the dealers had combined, and were out for the scalps of noisemakers, but once more the story was repeated. We still have our noises and the noisemakers still have their scalps. Neither dealers nor radio associations have the authority to enforce their wishes, and furthermore, none of them are in a position to import a trouble finder which will cost in the vicinity of six or seven hundred dollars and even if they did so it would be useless without adequate laws to compel owners to remove sources of interference.[15]

Earlier that month the government, always short of revenue, had announced it would be more vigilant in collecting licence fees from those who owned receivers, prompting controversy and this anonymous proposal for state regulation. The letter went on to suggest that once funds collected from licence fees reached a sufficient sum, the government would consider building 'a first class broadcasting station, one which will reach the outermost parts of the country, and render a continuous service of news, storm warnings, weather forecasts, fish and bait news, medical instruction and other such information.'[16]

The collection of annual licence fees provoked controversy. Many listeners believed it wrong to tax 'the air,' especially since owners had paid customs duty upon their receivers when they initially purchased them. Others thought that the public benefits of broadcasting might be undermined if radio ownership were discouraged by a tax. Some rural listeners also objected to paying licence fees when the money would pay for tracking down interference in St John's, since it was largely an urban problem.[17] Large parts of rural Newfoundland remained without electric power. Despite the opposition, licence fees remained in place until Newfoundland joined Canada in 1949, even though interference continued, and during the 1930s the creation of Newfoundland programming remained in the hands of churches and businesses.

In the late 1920s privately owned for-profit radio stations developed throughout much of North America, and in the 1930s VOWR and VONA were joined by several short-lived business-owned broadcasters. VOGT began broadcasting from a movie theatre on Bell Island in May 1931 and was followed by VOAS in July.[18] The latter station existed primarily to advertise the radio receivers and phonograph records on sale at the department store Ayre and Sons. In September 1932 VOGY, owned by Earnest Ash and A. Frank Wood, signed on the air. Rather than serving up church services or retailing its own goods, the 100-watt station existed primarily to advertise other businesses, so thus could claim to be Newfoundland's first commercial station.[19] It used a studio at the Newfoundland Hotel and offered potential advertisers a full service. All they need do, the station claimed, was telephone the station and VOGY would write the advertisement and program and furnish the announcer. This station was very forward-looking, promising to keep advertisers informed of developments in television and motion pictures in people's homes.[20] VOGY contributed to public life as well, broadcasting Newfoundland Prime Minister Frederick Alderdice's 1933 budget speech, for example.[21]

That station was soon joined by what was to be the most important commercial station in Newfoundland's history, VONF, which signed on in November 1932. Each of the people involved in creating VONF had experience with American radio broadcasting, and this affected the kind of business model they adopted. The station, which ultimately became Newfoundland's state-owned broadcaster when it was taken over in 1939, had its origins in the collapse of VONA. When Pastor Williams returned to the United States, he sold his station to self-taught radio engineer Oscar Hierlihy, with the agreement that he would allow the Seventh Day Adventists to continue to use his station. Hierlihy had been struck with polio as a boy and had learned the rudiments of radio technology from men at the Heart's Content transatlantic telegraph cable relay station at which his mother worked. The former operator of VONA, George Stevens, now without work, convinced Robert J. Murphy, vice-president and general manager of the Avalon Telephone Company and United Towns Electric Company, to hire him to build and operate a subsidiary of Avalon Telephone to be called the Dominion Broadcasting Company. Murphy was Newfoundland born, had attended school in Britain, and had an engineering degree from the Massachusetts Institute of Technology. He was at the forefront of technological innovation in Newfoundland. His father, J.J. Murphy, had owned several telephone and electric power companies in Newfoundland and Nova Scotia, some of which he ran until his death in 1938.[22] R.J. Murphy hired Hierlihy to help Stevens build a commercial station. Hierlihy soon closed VONA rather than compete with Avalon Telephone, prompting the Seventh Day Adventists to build VOAC in 1933 (renamed VOAR in 1938).

Murphy chose William Fenton Galgay to manage programming and oversee the studio of the new commercial station, VONF, located at McBride's Hill, St John's. Born in the United States to Newfoundland parents, the young Galgay moved to Newfoundland when the family returned in 1912. He attended Holy Cross School in St John's and later St Mary's College in West Park, New York. Galgay returned to St John's in 1924 to teach. In 1929 he left teaching to install and service sound equipment in motion picture theatres for Northern Electric Company, not only in Newfoundland, but also Quebec and Ontario.[23] Hierlihy and Galgay soon became concerned that Stevens had not purchased a transmitter, even though the studio was under construction. On their recommendation, Murphy hired Joseph Butler, a fellow Newfoundlander who had earlier in his career worked as a radio operator for Canadian Marconi Company and was then home on holiday from his job teaching radio for RCA in Boston. Butler returned to the United States to purchase a commercially built transmitter, and with Hierlihy's help got the station on the air on 14 November 1932.[24] Murphy later fired Stevens, who was subsequently awarded damages in his wrongful dismissal suit against Avalon Telephone.[25]

While VONF was a privately owned station that existed to earn a

profit, it devoted much of its efforts to public service. After a few weeks
of experimental broadcasts, the station's official inaugural broadcast
started with a statement of welcome by Galgay, followed by Murphy
addressing listeners with an outline of the station's plans. Murphy
promised VONF would have a 'career of service' to the people of Newfoundland. It would serve the whole island, he said, even if that later
required establishing a transmitter on the west coast. Murphy com-
mended Reverend Joyce and the Newfoundland Broadcasting Committee for their public service, yet he suggested that it was unfair for 'a
private station operated solely for broadcasting religious services ...
[to] be expected to meet all the demands placed upon it without operating as a commercial station.' Businesses that operated stations
'chiefly to advertise their wares' he said, also 'deserve considerable
praise for their foresight,' but Murphy thought it impossible for every
business that wanted to advertise to operate its own broadcasting station. VONF would adopt the business model that had made broadcasting a success in the United States and Canada. The station would
provide a medium through which all businesses could advertise.[26]

Murphy promised a higher quality of service than the other local stations had achieved. He suggested that VONF would not only reach the
whole of the country with local and foreign news, but would rebroadcast foreign programs at sufficient volume that interference and static
would be eliminated. He also assured listeners that the station would
provide better quality music than was available on foreign stations.
Nine tenths of the music requests from both city and outport to the
station during its test phase, he claimed, had been for classical selections. Murphy said that electrical transcriptions would be used, as well
as local musicians, since 'there is an indefinable something about the
broadcasting of a musical programme given by living, breathing,
skilled musical technicians direct from the studio at the moment that
each note is played or sung, a something that cannot be approached
by the best recorded music in existence.' 'Newfoundland might lack
world-class virtuosos,' he admitted, 'but we certainly have artists
whose performance would put to shame the discordant rasping jazz
renditions of so-called musicians which reach us from many of the foreign stations – Newfoundland artists who love their art and who will
give voluntarily of their best for the entertainment and benefit of their
fellow Newfoundlanders.'[27] Among Murphy's British and American
contemporaries there was a complex discourse surrounding jazz; it
seemed to embody sexuality, abandonment of hierarchical social order,

and the African race. Some people embraced these characteristics. Others like Murphy felt profoundly threatened by the music.[28] Murphy also shared the British objection that American popular culture was 'foreign.'

In addition to the better quality of music, Murphy promised VONF would take on a public service role. It would broadcast occasional educational lectures on the country's industries, and he concluded,

> Thus will VONF become in time truly what its initials stand for. THE VOICE OF NEWFOUNDLAND, a friendly voice crying its wares, carrying the news of the capital and of the world to its remotest village, bringing high-class entertainment into the homes of its listeners, instilling therein an appreciation of good music, providing instruction in matters vitally affecting the temporal welfare of its people and finally, by means of its Sunday broadcasts, carrying the voices of their churches to the shut-ins. Carry on VONF, may you have a long and successful life in the service of Newfoundland.[29]

It is worth noting that Murphy's conception of the system worked in one direction: content from the centre would be broadcast to passive listeners. After Murphy's ten-minute address, the station turned to a musical broadcast by Allan Pittman's Dominion Orchestra, the Ridgway Tea Programme, and a piano recital by Miss Penelope Ganou. The inaugural broadcast then ended with the debut of a program that would over the next couple of decades become nearly synonymous with Newfoundland radio – the *Gerald S. Doyle News Bulletin*, which will be discussed in a subsequent chapter. It had been on the air from 8:00 p.m. to 10:00 p.m.[30]

Historians often use the inauguration of the Commission of Government, in February 1934, as a convenient date at which to end or begin their narratives; yet in many areas of political and cultural life, including radio broadcasting, there was more continuity than change. A fiscal crisis had left the Newfoundland government nearly bankrupt and appealing to the United Kingdom government for aid. The British Treasury wanted to avoid a Newfoundland default but was unwilling to give money to the beleaguered Dominion without exercising control over how it was spent. The price for British aid was therefore the suspension of responsible government and the creation of a Commission of Government consisting of six commissioners appointed by and responsible to the Dominions Office in London. Three of the commissioners were British civil servants and were given the portfolios of Finance, Public Utilities, and Natural Resources – in other words the areas responsible for reconstructing the economy and society. The best of these commissioners came to Newfoundland with a reform agenda and had greater resources than the preceding responsible government to make necessary improvements in public administration. The other three commissioners were Newfoundlanders, one for each of the three principal Christian denominations, who took responsibility for Justice, Health and Welfare, and Home Affairs and Education.[31] As we have seen, state ownership of broadcasting was not necessary for public service radio, and as we will see the Commission tried to use broadcasting as a tool to promote its agenda.

The commissioners found both the commercial broadcasting stations VONF and VOGY willing to broadcast a variety of government programs, from a regular series of public health broadcasts to occasional addresses by commissioners upon matters of policy. The Commission thus used the commercial stations to communicate its messages to a widely dispersed rural population. This task was especially important since the non-elected government had no rural representatives who could inform people of government policy or build a consensus among the public. As useful as the privately owned stations were for this role, two weaknesses were apparent. First, public service sometimes took a back seat to entertainment, and the newly arrived British civil servants found that the quality of that entertainment did not live up to the aesthetic or technical standards to which they had grown accustomed from the BBC. There was undoubtedly some degree of repetition of phonograph records on VONF and VOGY and other examples of second-rate programming, but the very much larger and well-financed BBC may not have been a fair basis of comparison.[32] During the 1920s, conservative critics in Britain had condemned the commercial dynamic they saw in America as encouraging culture of the lowest common denominator and argued that North American broadcasters were pandering to common taste. The BBC created 'wireless' programming that its founder John Reith thought listeners 'should like and will in time come to like' rather than try to pander to their wants.[33] On the whole, British programming during the 1930s was more formal in style and elitist in taste than what emerged in the heavily commercialized North American media industry, which the Newfoundlanders had been trying to emulate. Those Newfoundland listeners who owned commercially built radio receivers that had built-in amplifiers, rather than the home-built crystal sets, were able to listen to eastern Canadian and American stations as well as British stations. Their expectations of radio content were shaped by that experience. On the other hand, the British civil servants sent to Newfoundland had as their agenda the reform of the public administration. They found Newfoundland's North American–style commercial broadcasting different from the BBC, and in many areas the commissioners routinely saw the differentness of Newfoundland as inferiority to the advanced bureaucratic structure of Whitehall.

The commissioners' centralizing bureaucratic instinct, their desire to enhance broadcasting as an educational tool, and dissatisfaction among listeners, were all factors that prompted state intervention in radio. Listeners who had paid both duty upon their receivers and an annual licence fee complained that they were getting nothing for their money, and that was a source of embarrassment to the Commission. Talks between the Department of Posts and Telegraphs and the owners of VONF and VOGY encouraged the two privately owned broadcasters to combine their programming efforts and to undertake some of the state's responsibility to find and eliminate sources of electrical interference. The stations negotiated a deal to simultaneously broadcast the same content, with one station's transmitter being used to broadcast long wave (on an AM radio frequency) and the other short wave. The two stations proposed to continue to carry Newfoundland commercial programming and hoped to rebroadcast programming from the BBC and the Canadian Radio Broadcasting Commission.[34] J. O'Halloron, secretary of posts and telegraphs, who had been seconded from the British General Post Office, drafted a plan to use VONF and VOGY more effectively. Seven months into the Commission's mandate, the energetic British-born commissioner of public utilities, Thomas Lodge, presented a proposal to establish a privately owned but state-regulated monopoly broadcaster to the Commission. It would provide educational and entertainment programming and take over the government's responsibility for preventing sources of electrical interference.[35] The plan proposed limiting advertising on the monopoly station to two hours per day and reserving the remaining hours for its own uses. The government would pay the company a fixed sum to track down and eliminate electrical interference. Unfortunately, the proposed subsidy exceeded the amount the Commission had authority to spend, and the plan had to be referred to the Dominions Office of the UK government. At the end of the year no decision had yet been made in London, and the two stations' owners found advertisers unwilling to pay the rates they had set for the new year. After four months of broadcasting the same programming, at the start of 1935 the two stations published separate advertising rates and resumed producing their own programming. The two stations would cooperate over the next few years and Murphy invested in VOGY, preparing the ground for the eventual unification of the stations. VOGY lacked the financial backing of a large enterprise such as Avalon Telephone, so the first commercial station was bought by its competitor the Dominion Broadcasting Company. VONF moved to its former competitor's studio in the government-owned Newfoundland Hotel and adapted the VOGY transmitter to broadcast on the short-wave band. VONF's studios remained in the Newfoundland Hotel for the rest of the station's life. In the meantime, Major E.E. Harper, now the new secretary for posts and telegraphs, reported to the public that the Commission continued to consider the unification of broadcasting.[36]

The Commission also endeavoured to get up-to-date information on the population and resources of the country. It conducted a census, using the Canadian census form, which asked the heads of households if they owned a radio. The results showed only a small portion of households had radios at the nadir of the Depression. Not surprisingly, ownership of radios was highest in St John's, the paper mill towns of Corner Brook and Grand Falls, and the mining town of Bell Island.[37] One measure of the new government's interest in radio was its compilation of a list, based upon the census of 1935, of the name and address of the 7,240 owners of receivers, as well as a list of total numbers of radios in hundreds of Newfoundland communities.[38] (Most small communities had only one or two receivers.) Urban communities had higher portions of workers who earned wages rather than being paid in kind for their fish or wood, and electric power upon which to power their radio receiver. Those rural listeners who were in most need of the Commission's reconstruction efforts were the least likely to own receivers. Those who did, had battery-powered radios, sometimes with wind-powered rechargers. This meant that rural listeners marshalled their power carefully, listening to only important programming such as news and weather. Radios that operated on alternating current had been available since 1927, but battery-operated radios remained the only choice for many of those who lived in fishing communities. Many people who owned receivers did invite friends and neighbours into their homes to listen to the radio, especially when some special event was being broadcast. A woman in Cannings Cove, Bonavista Bay, wrote in 1938 that she owned the only radio in her community and had a crowd of people in her home every night to listen to the children's program, *Aunt Kate*, the *Newfoundland Butter Company News Commentator*, and the *Barrelman*.[39] Fred Bursey of St Lunaire, on the Strait of Belle Isle, reported that there were only two radios in his town, but that on some occasions nearly the whole community, about 150 people, gathered in the two houses to listen to the radio.[40] So listening to the radio, at least occasionally, was more common than the statistics on radio ownership might suggest. Over time, such gatherings declined. As one scholar put it, 'More radio sets in a community meant smaller and smaller groups listening together until the experience of radio became a non-public one.'[41] This change likely had wide-ranging implications. People who listened together likely discussed the programming, affecting their understanding of what they had heard and perhaps sometimes provoking debate.

The Dominions Office and British Treasury were stalled in setting broadcasting policy by their concern with questions of governance and finance. Establishing a government presence in the industry posed administrative problems and they hesitated to write a blank cheque to fund a station that might lose money. The Dominions Office sent two BBC officials, C.G. Graves and H.L. Kirke, to Newfoundland during 1935 to report upon the administrative and technical requirements for a state-owned broadcaster. Graves, a senior official, warned that the Commission's plan for a privately owned monopoly under government control would embody the worst of both worlds, since the government would get the blame for inadequacies in programming yet lack control over the station. He advocated closing the privately owned stations and establishing a government-owned monopoly like the BBC.[42] Meanwhile, the engineer, Kirke, examined the topography in the St John's area and interviewed broadcasters to determine if one transmitter could serve the population of the whole island, or if a chain of stations would be necessary.

Public and official dissatisfaction with the existing entertainment programming and the level of protection from electrical interference were not the primary reasons the habitually tight-fisted Commission advocated using public money to create a state-owned broadcaster. The Commission accepted Graves and Kirke's view that a government-owned broadcasting monopoly could achieve two things: it could aid the Commission in publicizing its efforts to reconstruct the Newfoundland economy and get the support of the public for those efforts. It could also educate Newfoundlanders and thus aid the long-term project of making Newfoundlanders able to govern themselves. To achieve these goals, broadcasting would have to reach the people whom the Commission wanted to reform, not just the urban middle-class owners of radio receivers in St John's. The Commission considered paying for communal radio receivers in each community to which everyone could listen, which would have provided broader access to programming than leaving the provision of access up to market forces. The government accepted the fact that such a scheme was prohibitively expensive and did little beyond the token step of exempting radios intended for communal use from customs duty.[43] Other than a handful of radios in use in hospitals and the tuberculosis sanatorium, there were likely no such receivers. The Commission's decision to not provide receivers to all communities, although understandable on financial and administrative grounds, ensured that the audience for state-owned radio would initially be the same as that of commercial radio. Meanwhile, public pressure for a more active government policy continued. An editorial in the *Daily News*, for example, complained that the government collected licence fees upon receivers and gave rural listeners nothing for their money. Radio owners deserved, the editor continued, to know what the government was planning.[44]

Not surprisingly, the British-born civil servants agreed with Graves and Kirke's recommendation of a state-owned broadcaster for Newfoundland as close to the model of the BBC as the circumstances of the island allowed. The international contraction of trade of the Great Depression left Newfoundland advertisers with little money to spend on programming, and many listeners unable to afford the maintenance and licensing of their receivers. This made advertising less effective for sponsors, and VONF made little profit. The commissioners found that the commercial stations, even with their restrictive hours of operation, relied heavily upon repetitive recorded music, which they called 'mechanical music,' rather than live music, and that broadcasters were doing little to improve the musical taste of the public.[45] Some listeners agreed that the local commercial stations could be doing better:

> Would it be taking too great a liberty if we offered a criticism concerning VONF and VOGY? Let us say first that much credit is due the men who filled a long felt want of our country and thus took a step farther in its betterment. The stations have brought hours of enjoyment to hundreds of listeners in broadcasting such programmes as hockey – local, Conception

Bay and all-Newfoundland series; the board of health talks, the Rotary dinners; the Gerald S. Doyle News Bulletins, the ever popular NBC [Newfoundland Butter Company] news; the Purity Program for the younger audience and many other such programs. However we think there is room for improvement in the type of records that are broadcast. We say nothing about jazz but, to say the least, the public must be fed up on the continual diet of this type of music. These records are a poor advertisement for the firm supplying them, as they are not even the popular songs that one can listen to with some degree of pleasure. It has now reached such a stage that the majority of people do not listen to local stations at all only for such programs already mentioned. What we suggest is that the records be selected with the view of satisfying every taste. Or the time could be divided equally giving each field of music its share. What about it VONF and VOGY?[46]

Such aesthetic discussions are rare in the correspondence of Newfoundland policy makers, for whom the political and economic considerations of broadcasting policy were paramount, but more common among correspondents to the newspapers. Throughout the 1920s and 1930s many people – and Newfoundlanders were no exception – worried that the repetition of recorded music would destroy the spontaneity that real art contained. Some listeners, particularly those of older generations disliked jazz – a term they applied to a range of popular music, especially dance music, that had originated among African Americans.[47]

Policy makers did give entertainment some thought. Graves and Cedric Cliffe, another BBC executive whom the Commission consulted, were not optimistic about Newfoundland radio being able to provide entertainment.[48] Both believed that there was little talent in Newfoundland and argued that the demands of regular programming would ensure that any government-owned broadcaster would have to rely exclusively on imported entertainment. Cliffe contended that, given the resources necessary to fill a program schedule, the Commission's stated desire to eliminate mechanical music was neither desirable nor practical. He felt that a selected series of gramophone records could provide high-quality entertainment that Newfoundland artists were unable to provide. As for restrictions upon the nature of advertising on the air, Cliffe suggested that the Commission examine the rule book of the CBC.[49] He did not argue against government-ownership, however, since education and information rather than entertainment were the goals of the station.

In the spring of 1937, the Commission charged the newly appointed, British-born secretary of posts and telegraphs, G.D. (David) Frazer, with implementing the Commission's broadcasting policy.[50] Frazer condemned the existing broadcasting stations as not being fit to be on the air; he blamed this state of affairs upon their need to cater to commercial considerations. Since VONF and VOGY's money came from advertising, he argued, they 'subordinated' every consideration to making money. The alternatives he saw were to maintain the status quo, which was unacceptable, to subsidize a private broadcaster as originally envisioned by the Commission, or to establish a government system. A privately owned but government-subsidized broadcaster would open the government up to criticism, he argued, since it would still pursue advertising revenue in hope of maximizing profit, and the public would then attribute weaknesses in its programming to the inadequacy of the government grant. Frazer therefore advocated creating a Newfoundland state-owned broadcaster similar to the BBC.[51]

Unlike the experts from the BBC, Frazer was hopeful that Newfoundland musicians and performers could be used. The Commission also advised the Dominions Office against trying to impose unrealistic elitist musical tastes on listeners. Without entertainment that appealed to popular tastes, it warned, the station would not be listened to and would fail as a tool for reconstruction. The governor, Humphry Walwyn, suggested that the best way to ensure listeners would hear the government's messages was the use of Newfoundland talent to create programs with a 'character distinctive of the country.'[52] Once it had the attention of listeners, the station could perform its educational function. Despite the recognition that broadcasting had to be entertaining for its didactic role to succeed, the Commission still intended to limit the worst characteristics of commercial broadcasting. It hoped to limit 'mechanical reproductions' to times other than the coveted hours between 7:30 and 11:00 p.m., and curb the offensive 'spot' advertising by adapting the CBC rules on advertising to the Newfoundland situation.[53] Meanwhile the Commission was anxious for Dominions Office approval, especially in the face of public criticism if it were to collect licence fees due for 1938 without announcing its policy.[54]

While Newfoundland listeners waited for the Commission to announce its broadcasting policy, the government debated the measure of control over the station that it would have. It grappled with the question of maintaining arms length from its station so that the government would not be blamed for every shortcoming in the programming while simultaneously being accused of running a propaganda apparatus. The commissioner of finance, J.H. Penson, who had been seconded from the British Treasury, supported Frazer's proposal for a government-owned monopoly with its 'centralizing influence,' although he was 'alarmed' that it might be opposed by the churches, which already had a stake in broadcasting.[55] Penson consulted the heads of both the Roman Catholic Church and the Church of England in St John's and held a public meeting chaired by the mayor of St John's to gather public support for a government station. He also worried that anti-government agitators might demand access to the government-owned station. He proposed an 'independent' station with a Board of Governors appointed by the government so that critics could be denied access to the air without the Commission getting the blame.[56] The Commission had long intended that one of its members would retain control over the station.[57] The Dominions Office agreed that censorship was a sensitive matter, especially since the non-elected Commission was vulnerable to accusations that it did not represent the people. P.A.C. Clutterbuck of the Dominions Office, who in 1933 had helped draft the Amulree Report, which had justified ending responsible government, suggested banning any discussion of the form of government from the air, although he thought that allowing discussion on general matters of public policy might be helpful to the government.[58] Even this measure of free speech would be dangerous, in his view, since the Commission's critics, such as former prime minister Richard Squires, might 'be adept at smooth phrases which would meet all reasonable censorship requirements but might none-the-less have a very damaging effect among the ignorant and un-educated.'[59]

In an effort to get political cover for its policy, as it sometimes did with other sensitive matters, the Commission appointed a committee nominally independent of government to draft a broadcasting act. Penson hoped to convince the public that the broadcasting act was coming from Newfoundlanders, not the government, by appointing local men to the committee. The committee consisted of Frazer and Penson himself, as well as the Newfoundland-born Commissioner Emerson. The government also appointed the editor of the *Daily News*, J.S. Currie, who was on record as supporting a government station, the lawyers C.E. Hunt, T.H. O'Neill, and George R. Williams.[60] Williams worked in the insurance business, and as a long-standing member of the broadcasting committee that administered VOWR had the closest of anyone on the committee to public broadcasting credentials.

Behind this window dressing the British civil servants set the policy; Penson chaired the committee and Frazer took the important role as secretary. At its first meeting, on 18 June 1938, Penson circulated copies of the *CBC Act* and CBC regulations as well as a copy of the charter of the BBC. Frazer then presented a brief history of the two state-owned broadcasters. Clearly, the ground was set for Newfoundlanders to take the hint and recommend a state-owned system. At the end of their first meeting, the committee asked Frazer to prepare a draft act, and adjourned for two months.[61] Frazer copied parts of the *CBC Act* verbatim, modified it as necessary, and presented it to the committee for discussion. The *CBC Act* had been born out of accusations that the governing Liberal Party had misused the Canadian Radio Broadcasting Commission, ensuring that Parliament passed legislation that ensured the Canadian broadcaster would be independent of the governing party.[62] By copying sections of it Frazer saved the effort that might have gone into reinventing the wheel, but it meant that the weaknesses as well as the strengths of the Canadian legislation were replicated. Subsequent meetings of the committee ironed some of the bugs out of the legislation, before the Commission published the proposed act for public input.

While many people and groups supported a government-owned station for the enhanced service that it promised, a few questioned the contention that Newfoundland's national interest was best served by a government-owned broadcaster.[63] Others did not think that the state-owned broadcaster should regulate its privately owned competitors. The Board of Trade, which represented the interests of the St John's business community, favoured the creation of a centralized broadcaster but wanted provision to be made for privately owned broadcasters as well. It feared that requiring such stations to submit programming to the government station prior to going on the air would be an impediment to the privately owned stations' operations. It suggested that the act should specify the conditions under which future licences for privately owned stations could be granted. Such a change would ensure that potential entrants to the industry knew the requirements of a licence. The Broadcasting Committee decided that the Board of Trade had not made a compelling case against requiring private broadcasters to send copies of material to be broadcast to the state-owned station. To the second objection, the committee responded with the disingenuous suggestion that providing rules for new entrants into the field was outside the concern of the Broadcasting Corporation so not a matter to be specified in the act.[64] The Board of Trade also thought it undesirable that the commissioner of finance should have veto over financial decisions of the Broadcasting Corporation or that any one official should have censorship authority and power to regulate privately owned stations. At a meeting with representatives of the Board of Trade, on 19 January 1939, Commissioner Penson conceded that the governors of the Broadcasting Corporation should not be overruled by a commissioner. But Penson did not accept the Board of Trade's recommendations on either censorship or the regulation of private broadcasters. While the Board of Trade might have been expected to sympathize with private industry, in the end it approved Penson's plans.[65] The lack of provision for regulating privately owned stations is not surprising. Neither Frazer nor Penson intended to grant new licences and expected existing broadcasters to fail, leaving them with a monopoly like that enjoyed by the BBC.

Outside of public policy circles, people debated the kind of radio station and programming they wanted. A few protested the creation of a centralized government station.[66] The lawyer Leslie Curtis, for example, harshly condemned the broadcasting bill and compared Penson to 'Dr Goebbels.' In a letter to the editor of the *Daily News*, Curtis drew the distinction between public broadcasting and broadcasting that was owned by the non-elected Commission:

> Some reader may say that this is a government station, and that the government should have the right to say what may or may not be said over it. There are two answers to this question. In the first place this will be *our* radio station, supported by *our* radio tax; and, as already stated, this government does not in any way represent us, the people of this country. They represent only the British government, which because of our financial condition, claims the right to dictate to us. This form of government has *not* been requested by the people of the country ... indeed I have no hesitation in saying that it is opposed by the majority.[67]

Curtis was unimpressed by the fact that under the government's scheme the Board of Governors of the radio station would be Newfoundlanders (with the exception of the secretary of Posts and Telegraphs). Since the act provided for the commissioner of finance to have final say over all matters, he warned that the governors would be a 'rubber stamp for the Minister of Propaganda.' He also decried legislation that would discriminate against privately owned stations, which he pointed out had not been consulted by the committee drafting the legislation.[68]

Other members of the public welcomed the forthcoming state-owned station, for the educational role it could assume and the opportunity to provide an alternative to the commercialized culture of the existing stations. One anonymous correspondent to the *Daily News* argued that the station would be a 'social asset' if it were educational and worked for 'social advancement' or would be a 'social liability' 'if we merely endeavour to entertain a people, with useless babble and licentious music.' He or she objected to repetitive advertising 'plugs' and 'modern Jazz,' which damaged the morals of the young by encouraging dancing. This particular listener preferred 'the music of yesteryear' such as Schubert and Gilbert and Sullivan. The author went on to criticize quality of voice and diction of the existing radio announcers. He or she also had practical advice for the management of the station, arguing for the importance of a professional studio director who would ensure microphones would be balanced, a program director who would choose a balance of different kinds of music, and a general manager who would ensure appropriate programming without verging upon dictatorship.[69]

Once Penson had assured himself of broad public support, the governor signed the legislation on 27 January 1939 and the Commission purchased the assets of the Dominion Broadcasting Company. Most of the VONF employees accepted jobs with the government-owned station. There was one exception, however, which made the establishment of a state-owned monopoly impossible. While the Commission had been working out the details of its broadcasting policy, and well after the government intention to establish its own centralized station was known, Joseph Butler left his position as chief operator of VONF to establish his own station.[70] In 1936 he had entered into a partnership with Walter B. Williams Jr, who had operated a small home-built transmitter under the call sign VOCM. Butler purchased a new transmitter from the United States and established his own Colonial Broadcasting System Limited, making use of the existing VOCM licence.[71] Butler and Williams now rejected Frazer's offer to buy their station and hire them as operators of the government-owned station at an annual salary of $2,000, after which Frazer decided they were not 'deserving of any further consideration.'[72] At this point the Commission might have cancelled VOCM's licence, but Governor Walwyn feared public criticism that it was suppressing private enterprise.[73] As the Commission explained to the Dominions Office, it might have put VOCM out of business by refusing to renew its annual licence the next time it came up for renewal, but 'such an action would be regarded as tantamount to the suppression by the Government of a possible competitor, and would tend to give the new Central Station a bad start.'[74] A wait-and-see attitude was more prudent. Galgay, who remained as general manager of VONF under the new owners, later reported that Frazer 'made clear to Mr Butler that no increase would be permitted in the power of the station nor could he expect assistance or consideration in any form,' and 'Mr Frazer confidently expected that VOCM would eventually go out of business and no further private stations would be licensed.'[75] An antagonistic relationship between the government station and VOCM had been established even before the new station began to operate.

That potential for conflict between VOCM and the government station became evident when Penson proposed regulations under the *Newfoundland Broadcasting Act*. The regulations contained remarkable potential for meddling in the business of the privately owned station. In some respects they went farther than the CBC's rules ever had. Stations could be required to give programming to the BCN before putting it on the air, and no station could rebroadcast programs from other stations without the permission of the government station. Other clauses in the proposed regulations paralleled the Canadian regulations. Privately owned stations could not broadcast news they gathered from newspapers or rebroadcast foreign news gleaned from other broadcasting stations without their permission. Penson also endeavoured to regulate the morality of content. Broadcasters were not to mention birth control methods or advertise spirituous beverages. Should the BCN suspect a station of a violation of the regulations, the Corporation could examine the records of the station and question its employees. Violation or non-observance of a regulation could result in the station having its licence suspended for a period not exceeding three months.[76] In the end, no such regulations were enacted, perhaps because the Commission wanted to avoid provoking greater public opposition at a time when many people criticized it for its failure to have negotiated a third paper mill for the country. Furthermore, government officials believed that VOCM would likely go out of business if left alone. The state-owned and privately owned stations coexisted and often cooperated, although tensions between VONF and VOCM emerged, as we shall see.

The slogans adopted by the two stations illuminate the contrast in styles between VONF and VOCM. Even while it was owned by Murphy, VONF was the 'Voice of Newfoundland' – a St John's authoritative voice of culture and news speaking to both rural listeners and listeners in other countries who tuned in. Once it had been taken over by the government, it positioned itself as the official voice of authority to an even greater extent. By contrast, Butler took VOCM as shorthand for the 'Voice of the Common Man.' He portrayed his station as the voice of the Newfoundland people, in opposition to the British-appointed Commission of Government's station, which by implication did not speak for the people.[77]

Historians often contrast public with private radio, but there was much continuity in the programming and role of VONF between the days the station had been privately owned and when it was government-owned. Penson, Frazer, the other commissioners, and the officials from the BBC had significant roles in shaping the BCN, and yet day-to-day operations once the government took ownership were similar to the days of private ownership. First, the station continued to broadcast on the same frequency – 640 kilocycles per second (kcs). Frazer also arranged for the establishment of a second transmitter, which would carry the same programming on short wave, VONH, since the Corporation could not afford to build a series of stations that would serve the entire island. Frazer noted that this had been the solution adopted in India by its government-owned broadcaster.[78] In addition, the station continued to broadcast many of the same commercial programs and advertisements. Even with the revenue from licence fees, the Corporation still needed commercial advertisers to maintain the service. It also recognized that Newfoundland businesses needed to be able to advertise if they were to be on a level playing field with advertisers on Canadian and American radio, to which many Newfoundlanders listened.

To establish its arms-length relationship with the broadcaster yet maintain control, the Commission appointed a board in whom it had confidence, one of whom was Secretary of Posts and Telegraphs Frazer. The chairman of the Board of Governors was George R. Williams, who had helped draft the broadcasting act. He was a businessman whose judgment could be counted upon and had experience administering public service broadcasting. Joining Williams and Frazer were local lawyers Robert S. Furlong and Charles Hunt. Two rural board members were later appointed. The board directed questions of policy and provided the station's staff with someone with whom they could share the responsibility of decisions that might prove unpopular.

Frazer and the board hired the existing staff of the Dominion Broadcasting Corporation, which also encouraged continuity with the station's past as privately owned. Frazer had a low opinion of these men's abilities but wanted to avoid imposing hardship upon the staff and to take advantage of their years of broadcasting experience.[79] He believed a better candidate for general manager could be found if applicants from outside the country were sought, but since both the Commission and the BCN governors wanted the posts filled by Newfoundlanders, William Galgay was the best available. Galgay remained the Corporation's manager for all of its life, becoming manager of the Newfoundland region of the CBC when the BCN was taken over in 1949. Frazer suggested that Evan Whiteway and Mr Wood could be used as an announcer and as a transmitter operator respectively, and they too were kept on. Robert F. MacLeod, who worked for the Dominion Broadcasting Company as an announcer, could, in Frazer's view, be made musical director in light of his considerable ability.[80] No such job title was created, but MacLeod continued to perform and arrange much of the musical content of the station. Frazer accepted that the Dominion Broadcasting Company's advertising agent, Gordon Halley, could be employed as an accounts clerk and advertising agent. Frazer had the lowest opinion of the ability of sports announcer Aubrey MacDonald:

> It is understood that he has little or no technical qualifications and there are very dubious opinions as to his worth as an announcer. It is not thought that at the moment he has sufficient qualifications to warrant his being appointed as an announcer or as an operator. It is suggested, therefore that at the outset he be employed in an unestablished capacity as an assistant announcer and assistant operator at a salary of $80 per month. His future in the broadcasting service would depend upon experience of his ability as demonstrated in the service of the corporation.[81]

Even with this most unenthusiastic review, MacDonald remained on staff as an announcer. Forty years later 'Aubrey Mac' was the much-loved grand old man of Newfoundland radio.[82] Despite Frazer's luke-warm, at best, view of the staff, the Broadcasting Corporation was launched with the same staff that had managed VONF as a commercial station. The exceptions among the founders of the station were Oscar Hierlihy, who chose to work for Murphy's Avalon Telephone rather than the government broadcaster, and Joseph Butler, who had earlier left to operate VOCM.

On 13 March 1939 the Voice of Newfoundland passed into the own-ership of the Newfoundland government in a ceremony rebroadcast by the Broadcasting Corporation's sister networks, the CBC and the BBC. Commissioner Penson provided listeners with a history of the station's inception, followed by Sir William Horwood (the administrator of the country in the absence of the governor) declaring the service open. Chairman of the Board Williams, Andrew Carnell, the mayor of St John's, and Commissioner of Health and Welfare Puddester spoke of their hopes for the station. Leonard Brockington, chairman of the CBC, and F.W. Ogilvie, director general of the BBC, passed on their best wishes for the new service. Before turning the station over to its regular schedule, Secretary of State for Dominion Affairs Thomas Inskip set out the British government's hope:

> The new broadcasting station will, I hope, serve to knit together the people of Newfoundland, bringing new interests into the lives of those living in outlying parts of the country and removing their sense of isolation from each other. Newfoundland is I know going through a very difficult time. I do not want to shut my eyes to the hardships so many of the people are bearing, and we must all be aware of the serious task which confronts the Commission of Government. Yet I am glad that the erection of this broadcast station has found a place in the Commission's plan of reconstruction. It will, I believe, help to foster a new spirit of action and enterprise in Newfoundland such as can only arise out of a belief of its people in themselves and in their own ability to fight poverty and improve conditions in the island.[83]

If Newfoundlanders had not imagined their national broadcaster would be an arm of the Commission in pursuing its reconstruction agenda, Inskip's talk made the government's intention clear.

Everyone in Newfoundland recognized the potential of radio technology to overcome the problem of communicating with a population stretched thinly along a long coastline, at sea in fishing schooners, and in the woods at lumber camps. The Newfoundland government faced a financial crisis during the 1920s that prevented it from realizing that potential, leaving a gap filled by the Wesley United Church station VOWR. That amateur station presented church services to shut-ins and made use of the transmitter during other hours to serve secular needs. It fulfilled the roles one would have expected of a public broadcaster. Would-be advertisers and those looking to promote their musical careers turned to church-owned and later business-owned radio stations to create an audience for their products or services. For-profit stations took their public service seriously as well. Radio literally saved lives with timely weather forecasts and public-health broadcasts. Groups promoting adult education and churches found privately owned radio allies in public service. By 1932 businesses had worked out a model by which stations could pay for themselves through selling time to advertisers, exemplified by VONF and VOGY. These commercial stations did much to serve the public of their community, even as they created an audience for a range of entertainment. But when the Commission of Government took over in 1934, the British-born civil servants were unimpressed with these modest efforts. The commissioners hoped to create a state-owned broadcaster that would aid its reconstruction of the economy, with commercial motives taking a second priority. While the Commission lacked a specific cultural agenda (such as favouring one style of music over another), it wanted centralized administrative control of the state so that experts could take the actions necessary for the betterment of the people, even if those actions were not popular. The BCN was a part of that apparatus and was much like the BBC in that regard.[84] The BCN was an important innovation and very much consistent with the paternalism of the Commission, yet the demand for a station that served the public preceded the state-owned station, and the commercial and educational roles of broadcasting remained the same.

It would be easy to exaggerate the revolutionary effect of the Commission of Government, both because its term of office, 1934–49, makes a convenient period for historians and because the Commission's British-trained civil servants were better record-keepers than the rudimentary and hard-pressed administration that preceded it. The Commission also had a reformist agenda and the financial backing of the government of the United Kingdom, so it was able to implement ideas that had been generated by government departments and non-governmental agencies within Newfoundland, but had not been enacted before 1934 because of the lack of funds. It is worth remembering that many of these policy initiatives came from Newfoundlanders, often those in civil society, not the British civil servants. In radio broadcasting, there remained a great deal of continuity between the efforts of non-governmental institutions to serve the public and the government-owned station that followed.

The broadcaster Joseph Smallwood saw the creation of the Broadcasting Corporation of Newfoundland as a cultural milestone in the promotion of a nationalist Newfoundland culture. In his first broadcast on the newly nationalized VONF of the *Barrelman* program, which will be discussed in chapter 3, he expressed his hope for the BCN:

> It's going to provide a new medium to enable all the people of Newfoundland to get together, not just once in a while, but every day and every night throughout the year. From now on we're all going to be neighbours – all one big Newfoundland family – with the north bound together with the south, the east knit closely with the west. Our country for the first time has got a Voice: a voice that speaks the good old Newfoundland language, one that must make us clearly conscious of our common national heritage, conscious of all that we have in common, we Newfoundlanders – a common language, a common history, a common tradition, and a common destiny.[85]

Regardless of the centralizing paternalism of the Commission, and the programming the BCN purchased from outside Newfoundland, during the next decade broadcasters such as Smallwood were able to create a Newfoundland popular culture. Newfoundlanders invented forms of broadcasting that spoke to and for the Newfoundland community.

2 Addressing the Population at Large: The Government's Use of Broadcasting

Joseph Smallwood had welcomed the development of a high-power centralized radio broadcast station that could knit the county together. Ten months later, when the Commission's Department of Education began a series of educational broadcasts, Smallwood again expressed to his radio audience his hope for the role that radio could take:

> You know, I don't think there's been an item of news more fundamentally important to this country for a long time – for if there was a country in which radio broadcasting could and should be a godsend, it's Newfoundland, with its population so far-flung and so widely scattered over six thousand miles of coastline into more than thirteen hundred settlements. Of course I know that radio broadcasting shouldn't be turned into a dry and arid vehicle of dry-as-dust uplift and that sort of thing – I admit that perhaps the prime purpose of broadcasting should be that of providing entertainment: but what thoughtful Newfoundlander will fail to see that these two fine broadcast stations should also be used, at least in part, for the spread of information, the dissemination of knowledge, the formation of a sound public opinion, and anything else that helps to form the type of enlightened, well-balanced character that will enable our Newfoundland people to overcome and vanquish the present difficulties which beset them.[1]

Smallwood had his finger on the danger that faced all public broadcasters, and on the way they resolved the dilemma intrinsic to non-commercial radio. If they rejected the idea that the program's popularity among listeners was the arbiter of what made it to air and what didn't, how could they ensure that anyone listened? State-owned broadcasters existed in large part to have some criteria other than popularity determine what made it to air, but programming that was intended to have a beneficial effect on listeners had to be balanced against giving the public the entertainment it wanted. There was a public broadcasting model that people around the world could measure their own broadcaster against: the vision for the BBC held by its first director general, John Reith. This chapter sets out how the BCN compared to the Reithian ideal and examines the Commission of Government's use of VONF as a medium for communicating its policies to listeners.

The national broadcasters of Canada, Australia, New Zealand, and Newfoundland were all influenced by the example of the BBC. Reith had idealized notions of public service that were influential throughout the British world as broadcasters tried to emulate the qualities they thought the BBC exemplified. As British scholar John B. Thompson put it, Reith had defined four elements in national public broadcasting. First, commercialism (choosing programming based upon gaining the maximum number of listeners) was to be rejected in favour of selecting programming that would have a positive effect upon the listener. Second, the programs were to be made available to all citizens, not just a particular class. In practice this meant that working-class listeners would be able to listen to programming designed with middle-class tastes in mind. Third, there would be central control over programming: every citizen would hear the same programming, whatever part of the nation he or she lived in. Fourth, the public broadcaster would ensure that high standards in programming would be achieved, thus providing the best of culture and excluding material from broadcast that would harm listeners.[2] Yet Reith and many of his contemporaries saw no contradiction between this paternalism and democracy. To Reith, democracy meant equal access to the programming that the BBC thought was good for people, not the ability for people to choose what they wanted to listen to.[3] That model had its critics on both sides of the Atlantic, and neither the BBC itself nor any of the broadcasting corporations of any of the colonies or dominions in the empire that modelled themselves upon the BBC fully achieved those standards. The BCN was no exception.

The British-born officials making policy in Newfoundland not only favoured a monopoly broadcaster like the BBC, but the Commission itself consisted of men who shared a faith in experts and bureaucracy, rather than democracy, to fix problems that people could not solve for themselves.[4] They saw themselves as 'democratic' in the sense that they wanted the best for fishermen and loggers, and were suspicious of the merchant class as self-interested. But their conception of democracy did not extend to allowing people to vote on government policy or to choose radio programming. As the Royal Commission of 1933 had put it, 'Politics in Newfoundland have never been such as to inspire whole-hearted confidence in the ability of the people to govern themselves wisely.'[5] The Commission of Government might have later added that people were unable to choose radio programming wisely.

On the other side of the public/private debate, Newfoundlanders had been listening to privately owned Canadian and American stations, particularly the broadcasting networks NBC and CBS. Those networks had expanded to dominate the field by achieving economy of scale and by catering, according to their critics, to the lowest common denominator of popular taste. NBC and its counterparts had convinced the Federal Communications Commission and most of the American public that only privately owned for-profit stations were democratic, since only they had to be responsive to what the public wanted to hear, or they would lose money. Any institution that did not have a profit motive uppermost must be, in the view of the FCC, a threat to the general interest.[6]

The previous chapter pointed out how the BCN represented the Commission's desire to create a centralized bureaucratic institution that would allow it to manage the information the public had and ensure popular support for the government's agenda. This chapter examines the Commission's specific efforts to use radio as a tool for the economic reconstruction of Newfoundland. It incidentally shows how far the BCN's daily practice, although it effectively served the government's agenda, was from Reith's vision of public radio. The case here is consistent with the view of one historian of Canadian broadcasting policy, who reminds us that there is a great deal of difference between public radio that serves a democratic agenda, and state-owned radio that serves the administrative agenda of the state.[7]

The Dominions Office and the Commission of Government had been mandated to return the government to fiscal stability, so during the 1930s they had taken on new expenditures only when they believed that the money spent would be repaid with economic development. With some trepidation, the Commission had purchased and expanded VONF, and it did so not to provide entertainment like the American networks, but for the educational and propaganda uses to which the station could be put. The didactic role that radio could play took on a new urgency as the Commission realized it needed to shore up its public support. As disillusionment with the Commission set in during the last years of the 1930s, the Commission considered but rejected the idea of establishing a consultative council that could give Newfoundlanders some input into government policy and thus a sense that the policies were their own and not imposed by a group of Englishmen. As Commissioner Lodge had put it, 'It was solemnly laid down to me that the English Commissioners should regard as one of their main duties that of convincing the public of Newfoundland that their Newfoundland colleagues played an equal, if not a decisive, part in the government of the country.'[8] To take one example of this impetus to action, by 1939 the Commission was trying to select a Newfoundlander for the position of public relations officer. This person could be its voice and thus be able to sway public opinion. As the governor put it in a draft telegram for the secretary of state,

In the past, as you are aware, we have not been able to suggest any form of consultative council which would not, in our opinion, be open to grave objection. Special publicity officer also has seemed to us unnecessary in view of the fact that outside Avalon Peninsula public opinion can hardly be said to exist at all except on questions directly concerning means of livelihood and conditions of daily employment, while on the peninsula we have ourselves been able to do all that is necessary through the press, the radio and our local contacts. Recent events have led us to revise this opinion. We have been surprised at the way in which public opinion can be aroused and organized against measures of the Commission which in normal circumstances would receive considerable support. In the face of organized agitation we find our position isolated and open to attack. Those who approve of our policy remain passive. We find it difficult to put across the Government case in a way which commands popular appeal. Continuance for any considerable period of a public attitude of criticism and opposition is bound to result in a lack of cooperation from the public and to react on efficiency of government. Political forces that have been in abeyance since advent of Commission may become more active. While we still see no signs of general opposition to Commission form of Government we think that in a county so long accustomed to alternations of party system present position may become seriously embarrassing unless we take more active steps to enlist public support and to meet criticism. We hope shortly to have new State radio in operation which will supersede existing limited local system and have Island wide range. This gives us an opportunity for more effective propaganda, and we now suggest that we might try experimentally for one year system of employing Public Relations Officer to broadcast information about our measures and plans and to supply press with material for publication.[9]

This reveals not only the Commission's desire to enhance public support for its policies by having a Newfoundlander prepare press releases and radio broadcasts, but also the advantage of the island-wide transmission. The Commission ultimately hired a public relations officer, although wartime conditions meant that public agitation for the end of the Commission did not escalate as the governor had warned, and the BCN did not develop a specific propaganda program. Individual commissioners, particularly the Newfoundland-born such as Puddester, continued to have frequent access to the BCN to publicize, explain, and, if need be, defend its policies.

No public broadcaster transmitted government announcements exclusively; all networks accepted the fact that they needed to provide entertainment to maintain an audience and to maintain autonomy from the government, if they were to retain credibility. The BCN also required commercial sponsors to provide money to operate the station. Its annual one-dollar licence fee for operating a radio receiver was inadequate to fund the station's operations, so the financial demands ensured that advertising continued to have a place on VONF. In fact, the state-owned broadcaster in Newfoundland did little to restrain any but the most excessive characteristics of commercial broadcasting. Despite the rhetoric that often accompanies 'public broadcasting,' there was little difference in the kind of commercial programming during the private and public radio phase of VONF. One exception, which illustrates how trivial and capricious the differences between the two regimes could be, was the *Mammy's Bakery* program. The BCN Board of Governors objected to an advice to the lovelorn feature and to the playing of a record of Al Jolson singing 'Mammy.' The board considered these American popular culture items, which had been broadcast on VONF prior to the government takeover, to be in poor taste.[10] The more significant difference is that the Commission wanted programs to be sponsored rather than contain 'spot' announcements. This reflects a common critique of radio during its early years – in which advertisements that mentioned prices or extolled the virtues of products were thought to be an intrusion of 'business' sales tactics into the middle-class sanctum of the home. Critics of commercial radio argued that if such distasteful

messages had to be imposed upon listeners, then they should be confined to the working day and not broadcast during evening hours,
which should be reserved for middle-class family leisure.[11] Despite
these most minor of changes, the BCN thus fell short of Reith's first
requirement of public broadcasting, that commercial considerations not
affect its programming choices. The third characteristic of public radio
that Thompson identified – having one centralized voice that spoke to
citizens – was closer to being fulfilled. The BCN did allow VOWR and
VOCM to continue to broadcast at low powers to listeners in the immediate St John's area and could have done nothing about Newfoundlanders listening to high-powered Canadian and American stations
even if it had wanted to. (I have seen no evidence that anyone thought
that Newfoundlanders listening to foreign stations was a bad thing.)
But the BCN alone had a transmitter that could be heard throughout the
country.

As we have seen, dissatisfaction with the existing entertainment programming was not the primary reason the Commission created a state-
owned broadcaster. The Commission decided a government-owned
broadcasting monopoly could achieve several things. It could aid the
Commission in publicizing its efforts to reconstruct the Newfoundland
economy and get the support of the public for those efforts, and help
convince a sceptical public that the Commission was doing its best. It
could also *educate* Newfoundlanders and change their culture and thus
aid the long-term project of making Newfoundlanders able to govern
themselves. To achieve these goals, broadcasting would have to reach
the 'public,' not just commercial broadcasting's audience of consumers. Relatively few Newfoundland families owned radio receivers
compared to those of wealthier areas of North America. Low incomes
and the lack of household electric power in many areas meant that the
poorest of Newfoundland families, those who needed 'reconstruction'
the most, were the least likely to be able to own a radio receiver. The
Commission rejected paying for communal radios, as we have seen.[12]
This decision, although entirely understandable on financial grounds,
meant that the BCN did not live up to the second of Reith's elements of
public radio. It ensured that the audience for state-owned radio would
grow only as the economy improved. When, thanks to wartime conditions, income levels rose, and a greater number of families could afford
to purchase receivers, wartime rationing limited the number of Ameri-
can-built receivers that Newfoundland businesses were able to import.
The 1935 census revealed barely more than seven thousand radio

Table 2.1 Number of radio receivers in Newfoundland

Year	Licensed receivers	Estimated sets in operation
1931–1	2,240	
1932–3	2,727	
1933–4	2,767	
1934–5	1,584	
1935–6	2,937	
1937	9,887	10,941
1938	10,553	12,853
1939	11,674	16,851
1940	16,081	19,969
1941	18,308	23,039
1942	20,710	23,561
1943	28,838	36,148
1944	27,616	39,977
1945	24,820	37,676
1946	26,078	

Source: Data compiled by the National Convention's Transportation and Communications Committee, reproduced in Hiller and Harrington, The Newfoundland National Convention, 1946–1948, 2:122–3.[14]

receivers in Newfoundland, and in 1939 the Department of Posts and Telegraphs reported 10,050 licensed receivers and estimated an additional 2,500 unlicensed receivers were in operation.[13] As table 2.1 indicates, the growth in numbers of listeners remained slow and erratic as economic conditions ebbed and flowed. These figures must be taken as a general indication of the growth in the size of the listening population only. The portion of functioning receivers that were licensed in a given year deviated widely, as household finances changed the ability to pay the fee, and as the aggressiveness of enforcement varied. Postmasters and postmistresses had to add collection of licence fees to their other duties. Despite the limitations of these data, we can safely conclude that the size of the potential audience for broadcasting grew slowly during this period.

Despite the fact that many families could not afford radios, the Commission believed that radio programming could aid the Commission in its experiment in social engineering. In addition to basic information such as publicizing new regulations, radio propaganda could directly address the Amulree Report's recommendation to change Newfound-landers' culture to make them more self-reliant. The advantage that a government-owned station financed out of licence fees had over a pri-vately owned station was that it could provide a greater amount of didactic programming, rather than entertainment programming, which had broad appeal but less educational value. This difference was espe-cially important, given the limitations of newspapers and public meet-ings as tools for the Commission to communicate its goals and policies to the public. Literacy levels were low, limiting the effectiveness of pub-lished propaganda. Meanwhile, the great number of small communities stretched along the coastline made regular visits to people impossible. The only representative of the government whom many people ever had contact with was the district ranger – a combination policeman, welfare officer, and game warden, who was responsible for large terri-tories. A large portion of the population also left their homes for weeks at a time to work in the woods cutting timber, or on the Grand Banks or the coast of Labrador fishing. Radio broadcasting alone could reach some of those listeners.[15]

The government had paternalistic and administrative goals in trans-mitting radio programming to rural listeners, but the listeners had their own reasons for purchasing radio receivers. If one were to think of a national broadcasting system as two groups bearing the cost – capital invested by the government or business in transmitters, and capital invested by the listeners in receivers – then listeners invested far greater capital in the system than did those who produced the programming. One memoir of life in the Notre Dame Bay community of Salt Pans, that of Aubrey Tizzard, reported that Clayton Sansome, the owner of the first radio in his area, had paid $90 for the receiver and an additional $120 for a wind charger to replenish the battery.[16] This would have been as much as the total annual income for some families during the Great Depression, so it could not have been a purchase made lightly or one that people made so they could listen exclusively to government announcements. Tizzard captures some of the excitement of listening to entertainment from distant lands:

> The programs were mostly from the United States station KDKA and the Columbia Broadcasting Corporation (short wave). One very popular pro-gram was the Saturday night National Barn Dance, when people would crowd to Clayton's from miles around. How wonderful it was to go to Clayton's place in the evening and listen to the radio. Just to sit there and listen to people talking from far away was very thrilling indeed.[17]

Once they had listened to one, everyone wanted a receiver, Tizzard reports, but not everyone could afford it. His memoir qualifies this observation with the comment that 'there were those who thought it might interfere with their women going on flake attending to the fish in listening to some story on the radio, or interfere with the boys going out to the trap or trawl on time in the evening by listening to the *Barrelman* or the news.'[18] This reveals both the resistance to the new technology by those who thought that entertainment would take women and boys away from their work, and gendered notions of listening patterns. Tizzard implies that it was assumed that women would be distracted by 'some story,' a fictional and frivolous entertainment (he probably meant soap operas), while boys would want to listen to information and news programming, rather than attend to their chores. Yet financial hardship, not a Protestant work ethic, kept most families from owning a radio.

Understanding the history of the Commission of Government requires bearing in mind that it was non-elected and therefore had to devote attention to maintaining its legitimacy if it were to successfully achieve its goals. The Commission was answerable to the Dominions Office in London, and ultimately to the House of Commons in Westminster, but the commissioners were sensitive to seeming responsive to the Newfoundland public. It followed some forms of responsible government so as to simulate parliamentary forms. Legislation was read before the Commission several times before being signed into law by the governor, much the same as the House of Assembly had done. Drafts of legislation were published in newspapers to elicit reaction before its final version was proclaimed, and 'budget speeches' and major policy pronouncements were often made to the St John's Board of Trade or the Rotary Club, much as they might have been made to a legislature, and then were broadcast over VONF, or just read over the radio. One newspaper columnist made light of the release of the government's budget to the public through broadcasting rather than being read in the legislature. 'Little baby Budget is going to be christened at last,' wrote the Wayfarer. 'The ceremony has been set for to-night amid the somewhat chaste surroundings of a broadcasting studio.'[19] The BCN frequently recorded and broadcast such policy statements. While the legislature prior to 1934 had an opposition providing a response to the Speech from the Throne and the budget, and debates upon legislation, the government spoke to the people on radio and the people listened. There was no formal venue for debate.

The Amulree Report had recommended Newfoundland have a 'rest from politics' and a rest from elected politics it had, but not a rest from people trying to affect government policy through non-parliamentary channels. The Commission did not entirely monopolize discussion of public events. The Rotary Club invited speakers of its own choosing, as did other organizations, and these speeches were frequently broadcast. VONF carried a speech by A.B. Morine, for example, favouring an end to Commission of Government and confederation with Canada.[20] Morine's career in Newfoundland politics stretched back to the 1880s, and even though he no longer lived in Newfoundland he remained a frequent commentator on the country's affairs through letters to the *Daily News*. As a former member of the House of Assembly, Morine had some claim to be entitled to address the public, which the Commission might have accepted, and the Rotary Club addresses were routinely broadcast.

The Newfoundland government had used privately owned radio to address the public on issues during the 1920s and 1930s, and that pattern continued with the Broadcasting Corporation of Newfoundland. While the BCN generally considered discussions of labour disputes unsuitable for broadcast, Frazer had used the Dominion Broadcasting Corporation and the Colonial Broadcasting Corporation to broadcast a speech telling striking telegraph operators that their union' leadership had deceived them. A letter to the editor later complimented Frazer for his broadcast 'sermon.'[21] Frazer now contemplated weekly half-hour programs of talks by selected speakers and of discussions on international affairs. He felt 'speakers of standing and responsibility should regularly come to the microphone' to discuss matters of public importance. Round-table discussions upon international issues were a regular feature of the BBC schedule, and Frazer thought there was a large number of speakers available in St John's who could be counted on for a Newfoundland version of the round table.[22] But little came of these plans. Many individual government departments made routine broadcasts. The Department of Natural Resources sponsored the *Fisheries Programme* during 1939, for example – a program of weather reports, notices on the whereabouts of schooners, and reports on the availability of bait in various harbours.[23] Similarly, the *Library Programme* informed readers of new books available and attempted to encourage reading generally. If there was one area in which the Commission's efforts were applauded by people, it was in extending health services to many outports. As part of that initiative the series of *Health Talks*, under the direction of Dr H.M. Mosdell of the Department of Public Health and Welfare, continued as they had earlier when the station had been privately owned.[24] These public health broadcasts, which will be discussed in the next chapter, consisted of short lectures by a physician on such things as hygiene, nutrition, and the prevention of infection. There were also agricultural programs with information upon how to grow crops, forestry week broadcasts with warnings about care with fire in the woods, and soon dozens of programs devoted to specific wartime needs such as the *Air Raid Precautions* program.

From its inception, therefore, the Broadcasting Corporation was vulnerable to the charge that it was a mouthpiece of the Commission of Government, both on the grounds that it used its time to publicize its policies rather than entertain listeners and that it did not allow people critical of the Commission access to the air. The BCN portrayed VONF as the official and authoritative 'Voice of Newfoundland,' both to Newfoundlanders and to people in other countries. The stentorian voices of broadcasters such as Galgay and broadcasts by various commissioners made the case that listeners were hearing news, not gossip and rumour. There was a down side to claiming authority. As we have seen, Joseph Butler was able to portray VOCM as the people's independent alternative to the government station – the 'Voice of the Common Man.' Only a month after the establishment of the BCN, VOCM proved its willingness to give a voice to those who opposed the Commission and accused the BCN of being a government propaganda apparatus in doing so. Kenneth Brown, president of the FPU and a former member of the House of Assembly, criticized the government station over VOCM. He claimed to represent a large segment of the people of the country (in other words, contrasting his legitimacy to speak for the people to the Commission's lack of democratic legitimacy). Brown had requested the opportunity to go on VONF in reply to J.J. Thompson's claims that the newly formed Newfoundland Lumbermen's Association rather than the FPU represented loggers. The BCN turned down the request, as it had turned down Thompson's earlier request to use the station. Brown had earlier used the privately owned VONF to make a broadcast that supported the Commission's policy when it was widely being criticized for having failed to gain a third paper mill in what was known as the Gander Deal.[25] Now that he was criticizing rather than supporting the Commission and the government-owned the station, he found himself unable to get access to the air. This prompted Brown's appearance upon VOCM on 29 April 1939. In the speech he encouraged FPU members to prepare for violence against the Lumbermen's Association, which may have been the reason the BCN had declined Brown's request in the first instance. Brown went on to condemn the government-owned station in ways that challenged the BCN's claim to represent the public:

> The reason advanced for establishment of this big government station was that the interests of the Newfoundland people and the country in general should be served ... We may talk about Hitler and Mussolini, but are we under a dictatorship in this country? How much longer will the station over which I am speaking to you tonight, be extended the privilege of free speech? What would be the position if a movement were started tomorrow to bring about the restoration of some form of responsible government in Newfoundland? Would the facilities of VONF be made available to the leaders of such a movement? It is time the Broadcasting Corporation of Newfoundland made public the policy under which it is operating so we all may know where we stand in relation to radio freedom. If the station were erected for the benefit of Newfoundland and Newfoundlanders and not merely as a government propaganda bureau ...[26]

A recording of this speech is among those kept by the BCN. Presumably it was made in case the Corporation decided to take action against either Brown or VOCM. These events had broadcasting implications beyond the jurisdictional dispute between two rival unions. Since Butler claimed to have the only station independent of the government, as a rhetorical position to advance his agenda, the tensions between state-owned and privately owned radio remained unresolved throughout 1940s. Butler frequently claimed that only his station spoke for the people of Newfoundland while VONF spoke for the British-appointed Commission of Government.

It might have been having difficulty establishing acceptance of its claim to be the Voice of Newfoundland among Newfoundland listeners, but its sister national broadcasters accepted the assertion that it spoke for Newfoundland. The BBC and CBC provided advice and programming to the smaller corporation, but did not regularly rebroadcast programming that originated in St John's. Unfortunately, from Galgay's perspective, the BBC did not include a contribution from Newfoundland in its annual Christmas Day program, for example, although other dominions were represented. Despite nearly annual representations from the BCN, the BBC maintained that it selected its program for aesthetic quality, rather than territorial representation. Its officials decided they had no obligation to include content from Newfoundland.[27]

VONF had its first opportunity to have its voice listened to alongside those of the CBC and BBC during the Royal Tour of 1939. With a crisis in Europe looming, state-owned broadcasters in many countries, including Newfoundland, tried to knit the empire more closely together through radio coverage of the tour. Broadcasters endeavoured to unite the different races, ethnic groups, and classes in a common loyalty to the Crown.[28] The Broadcasting Corporation had been on the air for only three months when the King and Queen stopped in Newfoundland for part of a day on their way home after their visit to Canada. While enthusiastic crowds greeted the couple along their route, for an overwhelming majority of Newfoundlanders listening to the radio broadcast was as close to contact with the event as they came.

R.S. Furlong, a young lawyer and member of the board who had little on-air experience, covered the arrival of the royal party at Holyrood on the *Empress of Britain*. Much effort had gone into preparing for the broadcast from four remote locations – Holyrood where the couple disembarked, St John's City Hall, Government House, and Portugal Cove from which they left the island. Furlong, however, had little preparation, leaving him in Holyrood to broadcast a repetitive commentary upon what little he could see from shore. He was unable, for example, to name the music that the Church Lads Brigade Band was playing. For much of the time he was on the air, he described the weather, the crowd, the ships in the bay, and the platform upon which he stood. After listing the dignitaries within his view a couple of times, he described Mrs Carrol, the 111-year-old woman whom Joseph Smallwood had made into a public figure on the *Barrelman* program that VONF carried. Furlong wondered out loud whether Mrs Carrol would meet the King. Although he was a great distance from the dignitaries, Furlong was clearly excited and apologized for sounding 'scrappy' because of his excitement. 'I wonder if I am assisting you at all in forming a picture of what's happening here,' he admitted on air.[29] When the royal couple finally landed, Furlong's excitement became audible. 'I can see the King and the Queen,' he exclaimed. 'The King has landed! The King has landed!' Someone audibly told Furlong to 'keep the mic steady,' and Furlong related the names of the people as they were presented to the royal couple. He gushed about the beauty of the Queen and described how their majesties were dressed.[30]

After the car left Holyrood for St John's, Galgay provided a similar descriptive commentary while waiting at Cornwall Ave for the royal party to meet the mayor of St John's. There were audible cheers when the party arrived, but the microphone was too distant to pick up the mayor's address.[31] The Corporation recorded the King's address separately, so listeners heard the King's tribute to the contributions of the Newfoundland Regiment and the Newfoundland Naval Reserve to the war of 1914–18. He went on to assure listeners that, despite the country's current economic hardship, Newfoundlanders would endure.[32] Similarly, Galgay also covered waiting at Government House for the arrival of the King.[33]

Furlong was then dispatched to Portugal Cove and provided a lengthy commentary as he waited for the royal couple to disembark and the ships to make their way out of sight. He candidly confessed not knowing which ships he was looking at, nor what was happening. 'I don't know, ladies and gentlemen,' he announced at one point, 'whether there is any object in continuing this broadcast commentary very much longer because actually there is very little we can tell you.'

Neither Galgay's nor Furlong's commentary paid as much attention to the King as to the Queen, whom neither of them met. As Furlong reported,

> The last we saw of the Queen, it was rather hurried at the time, my view was obscured a little. The last we saw of the Queen was this lovely figure, in powder blue, mauve, I don't know. I've had several opinions on the colour of that costume that she wore this morning and I can't tell you whether it was powder blue, I can't tell you whether it was mauve. Somebody wanted me to find out, if I could, whether her gloves matched her costume, or whether her gloves were white or what they were. Personally I can only tell you that Her Majesty, to me, wore some sort of a bluish costume. It may have been mauve. It may have been powder blue. I am not going to enter into any sort of controversy about this at all. I have no idea if her gloves matched her costume or not, and I am afraid for information like that you will have to apply to our fashion editor. I don't know much about these things.[34]

The Broadcasting Corporation, of course, had no fashion editor. This commentary reveals that as star-struck as Furlong was, he at least had a sense of humour about the public fascination with fashion.

Galgay expressed pride in the Corporation's broadcasts of this first visit to Newfoundland by a reigning monarch. He confessed it might have been unfavourably compared to the broadcasts of the CBC and NBC of earlier legs of the tour, both of which had much more resources to bring to bear upon their coverage than VONF. But he was gratified by the BCN's technical achievement in the remote broadcasts and the quality of its commentary. 'The fact that the commentaries were unrehearsed,' he reported, gave them 'a note of sincerity and naturalness which was unmistakable.' Galgay singled out Furlong in particular for making the preparations and arrangements for the broadcasts and for his 'splendid commentaries.'[35] The broadcasts had made the connection to the Royal Family seem more personal at a time when the news from Europe was not hopeful. Special broadcasts strained the ability of the BCN and showed its limitations – the Corporation had to borrow equipment from VOWR – but also remind us of the power of the medium to create an emotional event in people's lives. This case also shows that from early on, Galgay's voice of Newfoundland radio compensated for the lack of a big budget with 'sincerity and naturalness.'

The Commission had very practical goals for the BCN that went beyond the ceremonial. Many Dominions Office officials and the British-born commissioners believed that Newfoundlanders required cultural rehabilitation as much as the country needed economic reconstruction. The *Newfoundland Royal Commission 1933 Report*, which had been chaired by Lord Amulree, had unfairly blamed politicians for pandering to voters and thus spending money unwisely. It had not compared the Newfoundland case to political corruption in other democratic countries, nor recognized that the Great Depression was a worldwide phenomenon. The Amulree Report now served as a blueprint for the Commission of Government's reconstruction effort, but was short on specifics in many areas.[36] But, following Amulree's logic, the commissioners accepted the fact that to return self-government to the country without making people self-sufficient would be to invite Newfoundland politicians to get into trouble again and return to the UK taxpayer for help. Not surprisingly, given the power of the technology to address those who lived far from St John's and those who did not read, the Commission made use of radio broadcasting as a propaganda tool for its reconstruction efforts. As Newfoundland Governor Walwyn had argued when justifying the creation of the BCN,

The task of government in this country is at present materially hampered by the lack of any sure means of addressing the population at large. It is expected that a Central Station covering the whole country will be especially valuable in connection to the programme of Rural Reconstruction, the health programme, and other schemes of development which the government has in mind. Similarly, it is felt that a station of the kind contemplated will be of particular value from an educational point of view, not only as being of assistance to schools, but also of a general cultural point of view.[37]

The Commission of Government's regularly scheduled programming, such as the Department of Natural Resources' *Cooperative Programme*, lacked the spontaneity and sensationalism of the Royal Visit, but gave the government its chance to make full use of the potential of the technology to communicate with the public. The Department of Natural Resources had an especially important role within the Commission. It undertook not only the management and development of resources but also the reconstruction of the economy. That department and Public Health used radio explicitly to achieve cultural changes that had been identified by the Amulree Report. Amulree had singled out the truck system, whereby fishing families were paid in kind for their fish rather than in cash, as one of Newfoundland's most pernicious problems. Under truck, fishing families were often permanently in debt to particular merchants and in theory at least were unable to go to another merchant for a better price as long as they owed money to the merchant who had first issued them supplies. Truck was widely blamed for ills ranging from poverty to poor-quality fish. Many people, such as the late-nineteenth- and early-twentieth-century physician Wilfred Grenfell, advocated replacing merchants with cooperatives. During the Great Depression, a few people in St John's had been aware of the Nova Scotian model of cooperation, which had been pioneered by a group of Roman Catholic priests and St Francis Xavier University. They wanted to create economic self-sufficiency within communities and turned to the Antigonish Movement as a Christian and non-Communist alternative to the excesses of capitalism. Their effort attracted the interest of many in St John's, particularly Roman Catholics, such as the young lawyer William Browne, who formed an association to develop cooperatives along the Antigonish model. The Department of Natural Resources picked up the idea and brought in both British and Nova Scotian experts. The Commission appointed Gerald Richardson, an American-citizen and graduate of St Francis Xavier, as director of cooperation on 26 May 1936; he in turn recruited four Nova Scotians to work as fieldworkers.[38] The government hoped cooperative principles could make Newfoundlanders more self-sufficient and break the injurious power of the local fish merchants. Fieldworkers in rural areas attempted to encourage cooperative credit societies and similar institutions to foster families' financial self-sufficiency and productivity and to encourage a culture of independence.

The people who would benefit most from forming a producer co-op were those whom it was most difficult for the Commission to reach. Not surprisingly, the Department of Natural Resources used its *Cooperative Programme* to inform rural listeners of the benefits of establishing producers' cooperatives and support the efforts of its fieldworkers. Broadcasting allowed the Commission to evade the monopoly that newspapers had upon the dissemination of information on the activities of the Commission. And since many listeners were unable to read, radio could effectively teach them the principles of cooperation and of the available government aid. The Department of Rural Reconstruction, under the Department of Natural Resources, had been using the privately owned VONF to carry a series of weekly programs upon 'cooperation' since 19 February 1937 and this continued after the creation of the Broadcasting Corporation.

By 1938 the Commission had run out of ideas for dealing with Newfoundland's endemic problems. In an effort to rejuvenate the Commission's policies, the government seconded John H. Gorvin from the UK Department of Agriculture and Inland Fisheries to study economic development and subsequently appointed him commissioner of natural resources. Gorvin thought that Newfoundlanders showed too much 'individualism,' in that they competed against each other to financially benefit themselves and did not work for the common good of the community. At the same time he thought they were 'dependant' upon the government to do things for their community such as building wharves.[39] Reconstructing the rural economy, Gorvin believed, would require replacing the truck system with cooperative enterprises so that people could get out from under the thumb of the merchant. Gorvin's 1938 report suggested truck had demoralized people, and 'the problem in Newfoundland is, at least, as much a moral as a material one.' He believed, therefore, that education would be 'an essential and integral part of any long term programme for reconstruction.'[40] Radio could effectively inform the public of its policies and, the commissioners hoped, change the work ethic of listeners. The commissioners' goals of changing what they saw as Newfoundlanders' individualism and making Newfoundland communities economically self-sufficient were probably unrealistic ends for radio propaganda. People were not passive receptors who were changed by the messages they heard in the ways that the government might have hoped.

In the spring of 1939 the Division of Rural Reconstruction resumed its

Cooperative Programme, which the department viewed as a success. It cited the many listeners to the preceding series who had enquired if the program was to be resumed. The inaugural broadcast of the new series, for example, consisted of musical entertainment, an address by Richardson, and a contest in which listeners submitted answers to a question he posed.[41] The *Evening Telegram* praised the use of music and drama on the broadcasts, arguing that economic recovery depended upon a rejuvenation of people's spirit and culture as well cold economics.[42]

The problem of reaching fishing families with the cooperative message remained. The department's field staff in Placentia Bay, for example, were enthusiastic about this 'phase of our propaganda machine' and encouraged local committees to buy radios jointly for the greater dissemination of information on cooperation. The assistant director for co-operation recommended the government equip the fieldworkers with radio receivers to facilitate the propaganda,[43] without result.

The tone and character of the weekly fifteen-minute program varied. The *Cooperative Programme*, which ran between 6 December 1939 and 7 July 1940, to take one phase, consisted of measures of propaganda and entertainment, the latter intended to achieve an audience for the former. The program's producer and principal performer, Whitfield Laite, was a Newfoundland-born but American-trained operatic singer who had been earning a living as a concert performer in St John's since arriving in 1937.[44] Under Laite's supervision the program adopted a 'variety show' format like many of its contemporary American radio programs, including vaudeville routines, music, and comedy.[45] Laite reported that the ratio in the *Cooperative Programme* was 60 per cent propaganda and 40 per cent songs and musical commentary.[46] The entertainment was often 'sacred' music sung by the baritone, Laite, or by another musician. Listeners contacted Laite to request particular hymns, or secular selections such as 'Down de Road,' a 'Negro song' taken from Antonin Dvorak's *New World Symphony*.[47] On at least a couple of occasions, Laite performed a song written by a listener, Charles White in Burin.[48]

Other cooperative broadcasts were more overtly propaganda. In a recording of the program from 1940, Gerald Richardson recounted the successes of the cooperatives on the west coast of Newfoundland, where the division had started its activities. Richardson discussed the successful cooperative marketing of lobster, which he predicted would one day put that fishery upon a cash basis (as opposed to fishermen being paid for their lobster in supplies).[49] In another broadcast, he expected that communities with cooperatives would no longer need the dole and emphasized the independence that resulted from people who formed cooperatives.[50] Another recording of the program has Richardson listing the towns in which lending cooperatives (credit unions) existed, reporting on some of the useful purposes to which people had put the loans they had taken out and some instruction on how a cooperative was to be organized. In this broadcast Richardson praised the efforts to create a central buying and information organization that would allow local cooperatives to combine their efforts and discussed women's producers co-ops, which gave women income and had educational value.[51] Another program consisted in large part of answers questions posed by listeners, and questions he made up, about what qualified as a genuine cooperative. He said that governments should not invest in cooperatives, other than providing information and a proper legislative framework, then went on to respond to the accusation made by some in the business community that cooperatives encouraged class warfare. Richardson told listeners to ask themselves who made such accusations, suggesting that listeners consider if they had ever heard on the radio or read in the newspaper any member of a cooperative say anything to encourage class warfare. He implied that self-interested merchants were the ones who made that accusation, and resumed his report of successes of cooperatives.[52]

Richardson's pedantic talks and lecturing vocal style lacked entertainment value. There was always a tension between the entertainment needed to achieve an audience and desire for time devoted to propaganda in each program. The department requested that Laite, who was paid per program and was not a permanent member of the staff, devise a way to 'create sensational interest' among listeners to the *Cooperative Programme*. When the program ran as high as 80 per cent direct propaganda, Laite reported, he was 'censured by the "man in the street"' for not singing more. On the other side, he reported that there were 'certain antagonistic forces ready to take up the cudgels against us should we become vendors of light entertainment.' Laite assumed that the government was interested in the program solely as a vehicle for delivering propaganda and not 'as a medium of dispensing entertainment of a frivolous and unmeaning nature.' Furthermore, in keeping with the dignity of the government, he thought many of the gimmicks used by commercial broadcasters, such as contests and comedy sketches, were out of the question. This left few mechanisms through which propaganda could be effectively delivered. For example, the program could use discussion groups, interviews with cooperators, and dramatic sketches of cooperative living. The last of these would require the employment of a professional scriptwriter, and the first required the purchase of a recording machine. Although the purchase of the recorder required the approval of the British Treasury, Laite advocated the use of recorded interviews with cooperators who were not in government employ.[53] He continued to advocate the purchase of a recording device, since 'the voice of co-operators, themselves, is the acme of propaganda' and the use of people who were not in government employ would help dispel the notion that cooperation had been inspired by 'officialdom.'[54] No such recording device was purchased. In one of the broadcasts of which a recording has survived, Richardson suggested that the only role the Co-operative Division should have was disseminating information upon cooperatives until they were up and running. He argued that cooperatives should not have government support, but stand on their own feet. He expressed the belief that by the following year the cooperative movement would be strong enough to undertake its own education activities and that there would no longer be a need for such a government division.[55]

The Commission not only used the *Cooperative Programme* to educate listeners on the benefits of cooperation, but also to counter the accusations of its critics and to publicize its policies. H.W. Quinton, the director of rural reconstruction, proposed the department undertake a series of broadcasts discussing the 'Interim Report of J.H. Gorvin' in which Gorvin advocated the development of cooperatives as a way of stimulating good work habits among fishing families while protecting them from merchants. The interim report had been read in full on the *Gerald S. Doyle News Bulletin* when it had been published, but Quinton thought there were 'many thousands of people' who 'have not had the opportunity for reading or discussing it intelligently.' He suggested a series of radio addresses taking up recommendations of the report could become a feature of the *Cooperative Programme*. Quinton argued that such addresses could counteract unfavourable comments in the local newspapers, and, he suggested to Commissioner Gorvin, could 'provide a very necessary volume of preponderating opinion in favour of your efforts.'[56] The two agreed to have the Department of Posts and Telegraphs compile a list of radio owners in rural Newfoundland, so that 'friendly' receiver owners could be asked to invite fishermen into their homes to listen to government talks on reconstruction, agriculture, cooperation, and other activities.[57] These receiver owners were presumably friendly to government policy as much as they were friendly to fishermen.

The British-born Gorvin was enthusiastic about the potential to use broadcasting as a means of mass propaganda that could overcome communications difficulties and achieve great improvement in agriculture in particular. Many commissioners hoped that cooperative farming communities would provide an alternative employment to fishing and encourage community self-sufficiency rather than, as they believed, dependence upon government to help them. Gorvin envisioned broadcasts combined with study clubs or discussion groups to provide advice and instruction in farming methods.[58] Beginning in January 1940, these broadcasts took the form of a dialogue between a farmer and an agricultural specialist – a scripted interchange that conveyed the information in a non-academic setting and included dialogue between the actors, such as 'Do you have a light?' that were intended solely to simulate a conversation rather than a lecture.[59]

Richardson had once said that the success of the cooperative movement would one day mean that the government would no longer need to employ cooperative fieldworkers. He was half right. In September 1940 the Commission ended the employment of Richardson and five of the other cooperative workers, effectively ending the government's efforts to create an alternative to capitalist industry.[60] With the start of war, the Commission decided to cut its expenditures so it would not need further grants from the UK, thus starving the economic reconstruction effort of funds, and opposition from the business community became too great for the Commission to resist. In April 1941 Gorvin himself, who had become a lightning rod for businessmen and businesswomen who felt the Commission was meddling in business, was recalled to Britain.[61] After the removal of Gorvin, the remaining commissioners were all cautious civil servants, not the sort of men to use radio in bold ways. The critics of the cooperative movement had prevailed and the Commission toned down its efforts to change Newfoundlanders into cooperators. Richardson and two other former fieldworkers later found employment with the American 'War Relocation Authority,' carrying out another sort of social engineering – relocating Americans of Japanese ancestry.[62] The *Cooperative Programme* did not end entirely. In 1943, former magistrate and schoolteacher Ted Russell became the director of cooperation, and he resumed a series of broadcasts. During 1943 and 1944 the Department of Natural Resources provided a series of talks on agriculture, providing information that ranged from proper storage of potatoes to the care of livestock.[63] Unfortunately, no measurement of the effectiveness of such programming in improving agricultural productivity was made.

The revival of trade that accompanied the end of the Great Depression caused a reversal in Newfoundland's fortunes. Soon Canadian and American servicemen and construction workers arrived, stimulating an economic recovery far greater than the modest successes the Commission had achieved. Economic revitalization no longer seemed urgent, but wartime conditions encouraged the Commission to use radio to meet new needs. The Commission wanted to sell Victory Bonds to adults and war savings stamps to children, for example. Initially the Commission saw this as a way of supporting the UK war effort, replacing grant money from Britain with locally raised funds. By 1941 the Newfoundland government had a budgetary surplus and was soon able to make loans to the British. The Commission continued to promote the sales of war bonds as a way of encouraging savings, hoping that Newfoundlanders, many of whom were earning a good income for the first time in a decade, would save some of their money for the inevitable day that the base construction was finished and the booming economy slowed. Thus the Commissioners hoped to delay the day that these families might need government assistance in the event of another post-war depression. To achieve this goal, the chief cooperative officer proposed a propaganda blitz to encourage people to join credit societies, and ensuring families saved money and giving the credit societies cash that could be invested in Victory Bonds.[64]

The division sponsored another series of the *Cooperative Programme* in 1942 and 1943, and this time engaged the listeners in the production of propaganda, much as Laite had advocated, although not through recording their voice. The Co-operative Division gave books as prizes to solicit from listeners' true stories of how credit societies benefited the life of someone of modest means. The broadcast of 21 December 1942 illustrates the pattern. The announcer expressed hopes for success in the war, and emphasized how 'cooperation' at home could aid the war effort. This was followed by advertising for credit societies, followed by a short story that illustrated the benefits of belonging to a credit society. This story had been submitted by a listener, Mrs Walter McIssac of Doyles on the island's west coast, a woman who submitted a number of such scripts that were used. Mrs McIssac's story was followed by a book review of a recent biography of Joseph Stalin, which the listener who submitted the next week's cooperative story would win. Other programs included lectures on handicrafts, and talks on the benefits of cooperatives by people such as Newfoundland novelist Margaret Duley.[65]

By using the 'voice' of members of cooperative societies, the program made use of several of Laite's earlier suggestions for making the propaganda more effective. The program attempted to make it seem that the propaganda came from the rural Newfoundland people rather than the government. This might have been an important change, since, as we have seen, some in the business community accused the British-born commissioners of fomenting class warfare through their reform efforts. The 'stories' had a narrative structure that made them entertaining and the book prize made it into a contest (a tactic often used by commercial broadcasters to elicit an audience but one that Laite had not advocated). The format was not universally successful. One of the fieldworkers, Steve O'Driscoll, who had assembled a group of people to listen to the program, expressed dissatisfaction that the previous evening's broadcast had paid less attention to the propaganda than it had the book review. In a patronizing comment, he suggested that out-of-town listeners would not be interested in the review of *Berlin Diary* since they would be unable to understand the book. Those few who could understand it, he felt, were unlikely to be the sort of people who would be clients for a loan at the credit society. O'Driscoll favoured a more popular approach, like that of American commercial radio. He advised the department to devote more time to the cooperative propaganda and to dramatize the stories by putting more 'Fibber McGee and Molly punch' into them. Then, he suggested, it could be followed by instruction on how to get a loan.[66] For all the Co-operative Division's efforts, there was no measure taken of the effect this effort to foster a cooperation had, and the pressure for its success waned as employment on the bases and a revived fishery put people back to work.

The economy had revived and the Commission had a budget surplus by 1941, but the government had made little progress in preparing citizens for the resumption of democratic government. The Commission had recognized that a citizens' advisory body might help mobilize public opinion in favour of the government's reconstruction program, but had decided against it since it might become the site of public opposition. The discussion of broadcasting by the Transportation and Communications Committee of the National Convention prompted the editor of the *Daily News* to comment upon the failure of the Commission to make good use of the educational potential of radio. He suggested that a series of radio forums could 'be a principal feature of the cultural life of the country, bringing to people in remote places just the kind of discussion they like to hear and from which they can learn a great deal.' The BCN, he wrote, had tried to organize such programs but had its plans frustrated by people's unwillingness to take part in pubic debate on the air. 'In spite of past failures,' the editor suggested, 'the hope still must remain that before long a determined effort will be made to give to radio broadcasting in Newfoundland a greater usefulness through the addition of new cultural and educational programmes.'[67] The National Convention, which is discussed in a subsequent chapter, did serve as a forum for the discussion of a range of public issues, but on the other hand the demands of broadcasting the convention prevented the Broadcasting Corporation from creating such cultural and educational programs. In October 1948, with the constitutional debate decided, a public-minded schoolteacher, Grace Sparkes, and a group of citizens prepared a series of ten discussions under the title 'Newfoundland Community Forum.' Galgay made time for the series with the proviso that it contain nothing that might offend the members of any denomination.[68]

The programming discussed so far was intended for an adult audience and represents the BCN's efforts to aid the Commission in redressing economic and social problems. Some programming was aimed at changing children's economic behaviour as well. The Department of Finance sponsored the *Children's Savings Programme* during the war in an effort to encourage children to save their nickels and dimes and purchase war savings certificates. Bob MacLeod created this children's talent program, which allowed children the opportunity to perform on air. The musician and radio host Whitefield Laite hosted the program sometimes as well. In one program, for example, a St John's schoolgirl described what children were doing to encourage war savings.[69] It was a financial success, prompting the formation of many Junior Thrift Clubs in their schools. MacLeod's idea was that a program for children should have children as entertainers, so each Thursday he had auditions for the next Saturday's broadcast. Individual singers or the one of the many choirs in St John's sang, either with their own accompanist or with MacLeod himself upon the piano or Hammond organ. A feature article in the *Evening Telegram* praised his efforts to improve the professionalism of the children, commenting that 'although he might correct their grammar and at times point out their faults in singing, he does it with such a easy manner that they love him for it and come back again when they have made some improvement.'[70] To vary the program, MacLeod ran a spelling bee for a period and had a contest in which the rural children sent in questions to be asked of St John's children. In this way outport children who could not perform on the program could be encouraged to participate by 'at least having their names mentioned and their questions used.'[71] While the wartime need to raise funds ended in 1945, the program and the Junior Thrift Clubs continued.[72]

Radio could also be used for education in the more traditional sense of supplementing teachers' lessons within the elementary and secondary school system. Starting in the fall of 1939 the Department of Education sponsored a series of weekly broadcasts titled *Widening Horizons in Education*, which consisted of 'seminars' upon teaching methodology and educational psychology. Created by the Education Department, the BCN, and Memorial University College, the series was opened by L.W. Shaw, general superintendent of education, commenting that larger broadcasters in other countries promoted listening groups, and advocating that listeners take notes as they listened so that they could reflect upon the lessons later.[73] On earlier occasions, Shaw had used the *Cooperative Programme* to promote the idea of folk schools, like that of Scandinavia and the Antigonish movement, as well as adult study groups.[74]

Despite this promising effort at using broadcasting to upgrade the expertise of teachers, less success was achieved in incorporating broadcasting in the classroom during the war years. In January 1944, Galgay proposed to the Humber River Branch of the Newfoundland Teachers Association that the BBC transcriptions of scientific talks for school children be broadcast over VOWN.[75] A former teacher himself, Galgay was interested in using radio as an educational tool, and had discussed with the officials of the Department of Education the possibility of developing a series of educational programs. The Department of Education had not taken up the proposal, and the VOWN broadcasts were Galgay's initiative. Two of the BBC's science series were used with some success – *How It Began* and *Science Lifts the Veil* – as well as a series on geography and another on music appreciation. Using the BBC programs was undoubtedly cost effective, but since these programs were not tailored to the Newfoundland school curriculum, they were bound to be disappointing. The director of adult and visual education of the Department of Education, C.W. Carter, reported,

> Teachers received these school broadcasts very enthusiastically at the beginning, but when it was found the subject matter was not completely correlated with the CHE [Council for Higher Education] syllabus, they were unwilling to make the necessary provision in the regular classroom time table, and children were compelled to listen to the programme after

school hours on Friday afternoons. Consequently, enthusiasm waned and when the music appreciation programme finally degenerated into the level of a request entertainment programme, Mr Galgay discontinued the experiment.[76]

Little happened to follow up upon Galgay's initiative. Even in the post-war years when the BCN tried to re-establish its civil role, it did little for education. In 1946, the Transportation and Communications subcommittee of the National Convention exonerated the BCN of blame for weakness in the educational programming and criticized the government's Department of Education for not having the initiative to make greater use of the available broadcasting facilities.[77] By 1948, the Broadcasting Corporation had a number of educational programs in its library that it had purchased from other broadcasters, including items such as Orson Wells's interpretation for radio of *The Merchant of Venice*, but Galgay advised that the Education Department wait until after union with Canada when the CBC's resources could be drawn upon. Galgay was also looking forward to the day that television would be installed in Newfoundland, a technology that he thought would effectively deliver educational programming.[78]

The BCN had not lived up to the Reithian ideal of public service; it was a compromise between didactic programming and commercially motivated entertainment. But it had not been established with the same agenda of the BBC. The Commission had more specific administrative goals for its broadcasting station. Governor Walwyn had originally justified the BCN by pointing out its usefulness in 'addressing the population' and its help in achieving rural reconstruction, public health, and education. Three of the most innovative and successful uses of radio to address the public are discussed in subsequent chapters: the public health broadcasts, the use of radio to coordinate the war effort, and the constitutional debates on radio. But it is clear from this chapter that although the model of the BBC was in the mind of the civil servants who created the BCN the government created a broadcasting system that met its own needs rather than the idealized view of public radio held by Reith. Rural reconstruction was a high priority of the Commission at the point when the BCN started operations. Gorvin's report advocating that cooperatives be used to revitalize the independence of Newfoundlanders and his appointment as commissioner of natural resources promised an activist government that might have used broadcasting as a tool to foster economic and cultural change. As we have seen in this chapter, VONF and the Commission of Government used broadcasting in innovative ways as they tried to rehabilitate the economic culture of rural Newfoundlanders through the cooperative movement. But by 1941 the war had revived the economy, Frazer had been replaced, and Gorvin had been sent home. On balance, radio broadcasting's effectiveness as an economic development tool did not live up to the Commission's unrealistic hope. The government did not make the sustained effort such a cultural intervention would have required, even if propaganda encouraging people to be more entrepreneurial or more cooperative could have changed the material conditions of people's lives. Within a couple of months of VONF's first broadcast, wartime needs trumped any social engineering, so Galgay was left alone to manage the station. The Commission did not make the forceful use of broadcasting, which had been the reason the Dominions Office had approved spending the money in the first place.

3 Entertainment and Enlightenment: Music and News on Newfoundland Radio

Days before the BCN signed on the air, Smallwood expressed his hope for the cultural role the station would have. He wanted it to have an 'educational' function that helped the people overcome the difficulties of the Great Depression, but he also wanted the station to create a Newfoundland popular culture:

> I certainly hope that plays, sketches, poems and other forms of literature with the 'stamp of Newfoundland' on them will begin to be written for frequent presentation on this powerful new transmitter that'll soon be covering the whole island of Newfoundland. In that way more perhaps, can be done for Newfoundland patriotism than any other medium.[1]

As Smallwood knew well, prior to the development of radio, Newfoundland culture had been largely oral. There had been a handful of poets and painters, and a novelist or two, but literacy levels remained low compared to many parts of North America. Smallwood built a radio program upon the foundation of that oral culture and recognized that radio broadcasting could be more than a venue for the transmission of the existing folk culture; it could spark the creation of a mass popular culture. As a nationalist-intellectual, Smallwood imagined this popular culture would serve as nationalist propaganda.

Over its decade of operation the BCN prompted the creation of few plays, poems, or literature, and perhaps less music of Newfoundland composition. As we have seen in the previous chapter, the educational function of the BCN did not live up to the Commission's initial hopes, and listeners wanted entertainment from their station. This chapter examines the Newfoundland cultural programs that were both the most popular with listeners and persevered in people's memories as the essential Newfoundland radio programs. These programs were cultural intervention; the broadcasters selected songs, for example, from individual Newfoundlanders and transmitted them to the mass of listeners, thus changing the repertoire of singers.[2] While listeners enjoyed different music, from classical to jazz to country-western, many valued programming that reflected the Newfoundland people to themselves, thus fulfilling Smallwood's nationalist goals for popular culture. And the most influential and unique Newfoundland radio shows originated prior to the creation of the BCN when VONF was privately owned. The bureaucratic Commission of Government invested in the transmission of Newfoundland radio, but did little to intentionally affect the entertainment or cultural programming to which people listened.

Newfoundland broadcasting had a character slightly different from that of the Canadian and American stations to which many Newfoundlanders listened during the long winter evenings. It is impossible to be precise about what foreign stations people were able to receive, but many of those who could afford more expensive receivers were able to at least occasionally hear high-powered foreign stations. A historian of Canadian radio has pointed out that the taste and expectations of radio that Canadian listeners shared had been affected by their listening to stations from the United States, but that did not mean that Canadians didn't also want Canadian broadcasting.[3] Newfoundland listeners also enjoyed foreign stations, but that did not exclude their wanting to hear their own countrymen and -women. Each of the most popular Newfoundland radio programs that this chapter examines, particularly the *Doyle News Bulletin* and the *Barrelman*, became an icon by reflecting the community of listeners to themselves.

The Commission of Government and Dominions Office policy makers who approved the creation of the BCN had given little thought to the question of entertainment before it signed on the air. It is not surprising, therefore, that the commercial programming on VONF remained relatively unchanged when the state assumed ownership. Upon opening, the BCN had thirteen program sponsors lined up, compared to the six contracts the Dominion Broadcasting Company had in force prior to the change in ownership.[4] Several companies continued to sponsor the same programs that they had prior to government ownership of the station, including Purity Factories (a candy and hardtack manufacturer), The London, New York, and Paris Association (a clothing retailer), Mammy's Bakery, and Dicks and Company (which retailed books and stationery). Mews and Dun paid for a sports program read by Aubrey MacDonald. A couple of businesses sponsored programs of live music, including one hosted by O.L. (Al) Vardy and sponsored by Terra Nova Motors (an automobile retailer), broadcast live from the Capitol Theatre.[5] Vardy was reputed to have been the highest-paid broadcaster in Newfoundland in the late 1930s. Born in Channel, Newfoundland, he had been educated in Halifax. He studied journalism at the University of Wisconsin, then worked as 'Special Feature' writer for the Hearst Syndicate. He had also lectured on political economics and social sciences for the Extension Division of the University of Wisconsin. After serving a sentence in New York State for armed robbery, he returned to Newfoundland about 1936, working in sales, then radio broadcasting. Each weekday he compiled and broadcast a fifteen-minute program of local and foreign news on behalf of the Newfoundland Butter Company. He also edited the *Fishermen's Tribune* for a time.[6]

Since they attempted to sell products to a broad cross-section of the public and thus might financially benefit from advertising, sponsors predictably represented a cross-section of Newfoundland retailers. About two thirds of the entertainment programming these companies sponsored was brought in from outside Newfoundland on transcription discs, which VONF played after and before brief statements about the company and its products. Many American radio programs were created by advertising agencies on behalf of various manufacturers and had the advertisement imbedded in the recordings themselves. A Newfoundland retailer of the products of the American company need only pay for the local station to play the recording made by the advertising agency and accompany it with a brief statement of where listeners could purchase the product.

As we have seen, during the 1930s the commissioners had found that the privately owned stations relied heavily upon repetitive recorded music rather than live music, and that broadcasters were doing little to improve the musical taste of the public.[7] Many people of the age thought that the spontaneous live performance contained artistic qualities that were lost when the music was recorded and replayed over and over again. The commissioners would have liked to eventually eliminate such 'mechanical music' and institute a public broadcasting system that produced much more live programming. Live music and drama were expensive, however, and throughout the 1930s and 1940s independent stations that lacked large audiences found it increasingly difficult to produce programs that had the high production values listeners expected. This was one of the reasons advertising agencies in the United States had taken on such a large portion of the production of programming and why American stations became affiliates of one of the large networks.

It was possible for stations in St John's to produce musical variety programs and serialized dramas. The *Irene B. Mellon*, for example, a serial musical drama about the adventures of a fictional Newfoundland schooner, had been presented upon VONF while the station had been privately owned. In many ways the program was a natural for Newfoundland. Being set on a schooner allowed it to 'visit' foreign ports and face dramatic challenges familiar to listeners, such as storms, and those not familiar, such as fighting pirates and Nazis. It included music and had advertisements for products woven into the dialogue. The *Mellon* had been created and written by Jack Withers, who incorporated music into the drama. Withers and other musicians took roles as members of the crew. The musical repertoire of the 'crew' included local compositions, traditional music, and 'hillbilly' music from America. This program began in 1934 on VOGY, which the folklore and popular culture scholar Philip Hiscock reports relied more heavily upon locally composed music and drama than its more elite culture competitor, VONF. When the two stations merged under the ownership of Avalon Telephone, the *Irene B. Mellon* program broadcast for a while on VONF but lapsed. Hiscock suggests this happened as much because of Galgay's more 'elitist' aesthetic taste as the lack of a sponsor. As we have seen, at about the same time, Butler left VONF to create a more 'popular' alternative station – VOCM. In 1936 the *Mellon* sailed again, now on Butler's station, where it continued to enjoy popularity until 1941, when its principal performers left broadcasting to pursue other, more lucrative, employment.[8] As interesting as this program was, the *Irene B. Mellon* was unusual. Other Newfoundland programming, as we will see, focused more explicitly on information.

So a Newfoundland variety or serial drama program could have been produced at the BCN, but the public broadcaster had other priorities. The preceding chapter discussed ways the government used radio to help it communicate its goals to the public, and the officials at high levels of government rarely discussed the sort of entertainment Newfoundlanders should have. The political and economic considerations of broadcasting policy were paramount in their minds, and their few discussions reveal their points of view. There were differences of opinion between the British civil servants who resided in Newfoundland, such as Frazer, and the BBC officials in the United Kingdom with whom the Dominions Office consulted, such as Cyril Graves and Cedric Cliffe. Graves and Cliffe thought that there was little talent to be found in Newfoundland and argued that the demands of regular programming would ensure that the public broadcaster would have to rely exclusively on imported entertainment. Graves had conservative musical taste; he attempted to eliminate crooning from the BBC, for example, which he referred to as a 'particularly odious form of singing.'[9] Even the production of swing music, under Graves's leadership, was centralized in London so that managers could ensure it was better than ordinary dance music and had 'the aim of inculcating a standard of taste and an appreciation of quality in jazz music.' Graves wanted swing 'to interest not to entertain.'[10] He brought this same judgment to his recommendations for Newfoundland.

The motives behind creating a public broadcaster in Newfoundland had been different from those in Britain or in Canada. Commissioners were not bothered by Newfoundlanders listening to American entertainment, as were Canadian nationalists such as the members of the Canadian Radio League, although Graves reported that foreign radio stations were popular in Newfoundland and worried about Newfoundlanders listening to German propaganda from European shortwave stations.[11] As we have seen, the potential of radio broadcasting to aid the Commission's reform agenda had been the main motive behind creating the BCN, so Frazer turned to other broadcasters to inexpensively supplement the entertainment on VONF. In a month long-trip to Canada and the United States, in April 1939, he met with officials from the CBC, NBC, and several commercial suppliers of programming. He arranged to purchase a minimum of three hours per week of the CBC's sustaining programming, which would be piped to St John's from Quebec on recently completed phone lines. Frazer also provided for the CBC to act as the BCN's agent in selling to advertisers the transmission of American commercial programming over the Newfoundland station. This programming often originated in New York or Chicago and was carried by landline to Montreal, where it was transmitted to CBC affiliates by the Canadian network. The BCN would effectively become an affiliate of the CBC for this business. Meanwhile, Frazer contracted the All Canadian Radio Facilities Ltd and its affiliates Weed and Company of New York and Whitehall Broadcasting Company of Montreal with the task of encouraging continental advertisers who wanted access to the Newfoundland market to pay for the broadcast of transcriptions.[12] Not much came of these elaborate arrangements. Soon the wartime censorship regulations in Canada required the closure of the telephone link between Quebec and St John's, restricting the live rebroadcast in St John's of CBC network programming.

The BCN was analogous to the CBC or the Australian Broadcasting Corporation. Like the others it developed its own compromise between entertainment and public service programming. As in other countries, this compromise was more the result of economic factors than any coherent philosophy. The BCN turned to local, Canadian, and American suppliers for entertainment programming and for advertising revenue. Newfoundlanders, like other North Americans, were familiar with and liked American network programming. But Newfoundland had not yet been fully integrated into the North American political structures or consumer markets, so the BCN often had to rely upon local businesses to create programming. Despite the reform agenda of the Commission, discussed in chapter 2, there was therefore significant continuity between the days when the BCN was privately owned and the period during which it was owned by the Commission. The same St John's businesses with the same cultural and commercial agendas created the programming in 1948 that had in 1938.

Entertainment programming on Newfoundland radio was also structurally different from programming in the United States. The distinctions US broadcasters made between programs that were female and male, commercial and educational, and popular and elite were not as sharply drawn in Newfoundland. The historian Michele Hilmes points out that American commercial broadcasting of the 1930s and 1940s was bifurcated: daytime consisted of programs aimed at women consumers, such as the serialized family dramas known as soap operas, while the evenings were restricted to the privileged 'male' programming such as variety shows, news, and drama. Authorship of daytime programming was obscured by the networks and the advertising agencies that created them, but evening programming, such as the comedy variety show hosted by Jack Benny or dramas such as Orson Welles's *Mercury Theatre*, or, as it was later called, *Campbell's Soup Theatre*, strove for an elite image tied to the notion of authorship and disguised its commercialism. Hilmes argues that this bifurcation allowed commercialism to be confined to daytime and the networks could counter the arguments of public radio advocates by presenting the evening fare as elite culture.[13] NBC, for example, broadcast symphony orchestras during the evening in part to establish its high culture credentials and counter the criticism of those Americans who wanted a public radio system. Like their American network counterparts, Galgay and Frazer wanted high-quality programming, but unlike the situation in the United States they recognized that in Newfoundland they had to serve all tastes during the evening. The BCN carried some women's programming during the evening, such as the soap opera *Pepper Young's Family* and the mystery drama *Beyond Reasonable Doubt*, but such an arrangement would not have occurred in the United States.[14] Perhaps because public ownership had 'won' the debate over private or state ownership in Newfoundland, the BCN did not feel the same urgency to establish its public service credentials as did the privately owned NBC in the United States. At a more practical level, radio waves travelled greater distances during the evenings than during the day, so rural Newfoundland women (and the sponsors who wanted to reach them) would not have had access to these shows had VONF broadcast them only during daylight hours.

There was another difference between broadcasting in Newfoundland and United States, one that was implicitly pointed out by a St John's listener, Hugh Lilly. American radio broadcasts were provided to listeners without direct charge, so Americans accepted the fact that listening to advertisements was their way of paying for the free entertainment. Newfoundland listeners, on the other hand, paid an annual licence fee to support the BCN. The fee was unpopular, with many listeners feeling that they got very little for their money. In a letter to the *Evening Telegram*, Lilly asked if the radio tax was being spent on educational programming or soap operas. If the latter were the case, he wrote, he did not want his tax money spent on advertising consumer products. He singled out soap operas for ridicule. Many men who wanted to distinguish the programs they liked as better than those of their wives, mothers, and daughters condemned the serialized romance drama. This was especially true of listeners and broadcasters who had elite culture aspirations. Lilly also made fun of commercialism generally.

> It is almost impossible at the present time to turn on the radio without being blasted by someone singing a mad ditty about how your hair will grow and glow with Halo, or how some new tooth paste will enable people to see one another's teeth at remote distances.[15]

Many Newfoundlanders distinguished between songs and ditties. A song was about a serious subject and contained information to which the listener should attend, perhaps a tragedy at sea or other real event, while a ditty was often a silly nonsense song, sung exclusively for fun.[16]

Soap operas and advertisements were not the only aspects of commercial broadcasting to which people objected. Another listener hoped that the creation of the BCN would mark a change in the music on the radio. The anonymous author of a letter in the *Daily News* advocated using the new station as an educational tool, and feared negative effects 'if we merely endeavour to entertain a people, with useless babble and licentious music.' This correspondent's rhetoric mirrored a common view in some quarters that dance music was a moral threat to young people:

> Why must we listen to modern Jazz, day after day? The maddening rhythm of 'Swing' 'The jitterbug' 'The yam.' We civilized beings look with horror upon a poor uncivilized tribe beating 'Tom-Toms.' They do so to amuse the passions, to hate and lust for blood of a neighbouring tribe. What think you, are our modern composers and orchestra leaders doing? The evil is not merely in jazz rather in the 'evolution of jazz' into a modern spirit of 'swing session.' This does not affect the morals of the hearers as much as it does our 'dancing youth.' Where is the music of yesteryear? Victor Herbert, Stephen Foster, Schubert, Gounod, the gems of Gilbert and Sullivan ... It is quite evident we have lost the interior sweetness of 'chamber music' and have become entangled with the outward 'tantalizing' lewd rhythm of screeching trumpets and brass. I am quite aware we cannot indefinitely impose Mozart or Schubert upon the masses, but surely we can choose a better selection of records.[17]

This letter has a rich vein of music criticism common among those who saw themselves as defending elite culture against assault. For this listener, and many more, jazz represented several overlapping threats. Its origins in the music of African Americans made it a threat to 'white culture' and inferior to the music of Europeans. The racist associations of Africans with being 'less civilized' and thus closer to nature meant that some commentators saw them as more sexualized. The beat of the music and the dancing that accompanied it, a few critics worried, would inflame young people's passions and lead to them having sex. By contrast, some people believed the music of the European tradition soothed the passions and encouraged contemplation. Newfoundlanders not only had access to the classical and jazz music, but also participated in this musical discourse.[18]

Other Newfoundland listeners liked soap operas and popular music. One self-described housewife commented upon how much women such as herself depended upon music on the radio 'for company' when children were at school and husbands at work. She complained that the restricted broadcast day was disappointing. To save money, VONF was on the air from 10:00 a.m. to 2:00 p.m. and 6:00 p.m. to 11:00 p.m., as it had been when it was privately owned. 'Mrs Fan de Radio' complained that the BCN was off the air during the afternoon and suggested that VONF and VOCM should not overlap during the day, so that listeners would be able to follow both the serial dramas and news bulletins. (She also criticized the amount of repetition of gramophone records and recommended the use of more local performers.)[19]

None of these listener reactions would have surprised the Board of Governors of the Broadcasting Corporation, and were inevitable, given the restrictions faced by the company. The inaugural program had included many of the formally trained musicians who had been the mainstays of radio during the preceding decade, such as Whitefield Laite and Stuart Godfrey, and then resumed the same commercial programming that VONF had long provided. At the end of the first month of operation, Frazer set out his views upon programs in a memorandum to his fellow board members. He pointed out that in the absence of sufficient commercial programming, the station relied too heavily upon its transcription library, risking an inordinate amount of repetition. He was enthusiastic about the forthcoming series *Concerts around the Bay*, but given Galgay's limited authority to pay artists, Frazer suggested the directors should approach artists and speakers in an effort to bolster programming. He proposed a set schedule of locally produced programming, which would then become something that listeners would look forward to each week. He suggested two weekly hour-long programs of music – one of local musicians and one of local dance bands. Several dance bands might be hired, one under the leadership of Robert MacLeod and another led by Ian Cowan, to take two examples, as well as a couple of 'Violin-Banjo four or five piece orchestras.' VONF might, he concluded, have used the St Bon's Orchestra, the Mount Cashel Band, the Church Lads Brigade Band and the Guards Band. Each of these church-sponsored youth organizations had been prominent in the musical life of the city.[20]

The BCN continued to provide the same mix of live popular and elite musical entertainment and recorded music that VONF had when it was privately owned, and the published schedule reveals that occasional

symphonic concerts from Canada and the United States were rebroadcast in St John's.[21] The program schedule of 3 May 1939 included Swing
Music at 11:30 a.m., Hill Billy Music at 8:15 p.m., Irish Tenor John Feeney
at 9:15, and the Percy Faith Orchestra (rebroadcast from the CBC) at
10:00.[22] The 27 May 1939 broadcast included 'The Kentucky Minstrels'
and 'Jackie Walsh and his string band,' presumably both country-western bands.[23] On 31 May 1939 the St Bon's Orchestra annual broadcast
included the 'Hungarian Dances' by Brahms, 'Songs of the South,'
'Danny Boy,' compositions by Schubert, and 'Ireland, Mother Ireland' a
French Horn Solo. Other music that day included a 'Hawaiian Orchestra' and 'Hill Billy' music.[24] As can be seen, the station provided a range
of popular and elite music, but rarely played Newfoundland 'traditional' music, although the schedule for 30 November reveals some
accordion solos. (The accordion being Newfoundland's 'traditional'
instrument, it is possible that this was music of Newfoundland composition.)[25] Jazz might have once been a minority taste, but by 1939 VONF
was broadcasting both local and international swing musicians nearly
daily. As jazz had evolved into swing, American musicians of European
ancestry, such as Benny Goodman and Paul Whiteman, became popular
with white audiences. Swing was no longer 'race music,' but was the
popular music of the day in Newfoundland as well as the United
States.[26]

   Not everyone in Newfoundland liked to hear music of African-Amer-
ican and Latin-American influence on the radio. Listeners criticized
recorded music on both VONF and the privately owned VOCM. A
group of listeners in Lewisporte, for example, suggested that the quality
and variety of VOCM's recorded music fell short of what it should be
and contained 'too much cheap Latin and barbaric "goo."' These listeners advocated both stations purchase some new 'English recordings.'[27]
Other listeners were disappointed that the Broadcasting Corporation
had not been a greater force for cultural improvement. A letter to the
editor complained that the BCN seemed to fear giving the impression it
was 'highbrow.' The writer claimed neither the BBC nor the American
commercial stations were timid about presenting music of all kinds, or
including programs of music appreciation. 'If the medium of broadcasting is to be a vital force within our lives,' the author continued, 'it must
surely be a source of inspiration as well as an occasional lulling of tired
senses.' The letter went on to discuss Finnish composer Jean Sibelius,
who had composed the romantic and nationalistic *Finlandia*, and suggested someone might be inspired to compose *Newfoundlandia*.[28]

In the fall of 1941 a listener prompted an angry reaction after complaining that the BCN provided too much war news and played only classical and sacred music on Sundays. He or she asked for a program of swing or popular tunes on that day.[29] The Wayfarer, the pen name of prominent businessman and journalist Albert Perlin, responded in an angry column titled 'Swing Is Tripe,' in which he referred to the author of the letter as 'moronic.'

> We don't pretend to much knowledge about music. All we do know about it is that some sounds made by musical instruments are pleasant and comforting and others are unpleasant and discomforting and even nerveracking [sic]. Swing clearly belongs to the latter class. Swing in fact is musical tripe. Better still it reflects atavistic urges among those who like it. Seen in its proper setting, under the light of a jungle moon, with a prisoner roasting slowly in a pot in the centre of a clearing while the savage captors work up a tremendous appetite for this prize delicacy by jitterbugging round in ecstatic frenzy, swing is alright. Over the air or coming from a dance band it reflects sadly upon our civilization ... But the worst crime of swing is what it does to its devotees. Men and women lose all restraint. They throw one another around like Japanese wrestlers and behave generally like jungle apes in a frolic ... They are fanatics, these jitterbugs. Only fanatics could behave in public as they do. As a consequence we expect to find ourselves shriveled in the blazing anger with which they greet this comment. That won't alter the fact that swing is a form of degeneration. It carries its devotees back to the jungle and makes a spectacle of mankind. So long as it survives, those who are working for the progress of civilization must stand aside and look with saddened eyes upon a world gone mad.[30]

This intemperate column elicited some support; another listener endorsed the idea of the BCN setting aside one day a week for only classical and sacred music.[31] The last word of the interchange went to a young person who criticized the Wayfarer for his 'prejudiced' and 'childish' attitude. This correspondent pointed out that the generation that liked swing was 'fighting the greatest battle the world has already seen.' 'We are also entitled to our fun,' the listener continued. 'Jitterbugs are not "fanatics and savages" but just healthy exuberant youth enjoying itself in approved 1941 fashion.'[32] This interchange among listeners exemplifies the fact that the aesthetic struggle over swing was in part a generational divide. And with 'the jitterbug generation' bearing the brunt of defeating Hitler, older listeners could not easily dismiss them. One might also take note that before the Canadian and American servicemen arrived in Newfoundland, the BCN and live musicians already provided Newfoundlanders with swing.

This public debate over musical taste might have taken a different shape had the BCN had a coherent music policy. The Broadcasting Corporation lacked the money to hire a full-time music director, but Robert MacLeod filled many of those duties while also working as an announcer. At the end of 1939 he prepared a memorandum on making greater use of 'local talent.' He submitted a list of thirty-seven St John's musicians who had previous radio experience and suggested there were other local musicians whose talents might be developed. MacLeod's plan would have provided listeners with a variety of styles and have given most local artists an opportunity to be heard on the air. MacLeod advocated using various church-affiliated bands, such as that of the Church Lads Brigade, and that the BCN encourage individual musicians to form duets, trios, and quartets, instrumental groups, etc., so they would have an opportunity to develop their talents. MacLeod also proposed reviving a program that had been popular earlier, in which an hour's dance music was provided by records, piano, and a vocalist.[33] Little came of these ambitious plans, in large part because the beginning of the Second World War imposed new priorities.

While MacLeod worked on developing local musicians, Frazer and Galgay tried to interest American advertising companies in bringing their shows to the BCN, but had little success, since the Newfoundland market was so small. Few American manufacturers were interested in paying for advertising in the small northern country. Lever Brothers, the soap company (which also owned the Newfoundland Butter Company, which sponsored a news program on VONF) handled its advertising from England. Patent medicine manufacturer Vick Chemical Company had a local distributor that handled its Newfoundland advertising. Some of the largest sponsors of radio programming in the United States, such as Procter and Gamble, did not even reply to the BCN's overtures. The BCN's New York agent suggested compiling a list of American products sold in Newfoundland and having the Newfoundland distributors of these products write the manufacturers asking for advertising support.[34] Frazer purchased the Lang-Worth Feature Programs from New York, which consisted of sixteen-inch double-sided disks containing 100 hours of music and 100 hours of 'continuity script.' The latter attempted to educate listeners on what to listen for, so that they would

Table 3.1 British programming purchased from the BBC

Type of program	%	Length of program (minutes)
Features	8.5	. 304
Drama	6.5	203
Comedy	4.0	152
Variety	10.0	366
Light music	38.0	1373
Folk music	7.5	271
Public affairs	11.0	394
Historical talks	8.5	308
Other	6.0	114

benefit from the music.[35] The BCN purchased the full 200 hours, and Frazer reported that the Lang-Worth music became 'the backbone of our day to day program service.'[36]

While attempting to obtain American content, Frazer also arranged for aid from the BBC. He met with BBC officials in London, telling them that the lack of money might force the Newfoundland broadcaster to 'rely almost entirely upon American Transcription material' if the BBC charged Newfoundland the standard rate for its programming. Fortunately the BBC offered the transcriptions to Newfoundland at a rate lower than the production costs, in an effort to aid the fledgling broadcaster. Frazer purchased the programming, which he believed would have a beneficial effect on Newfoundlanders.[37] For this he turned to the Empire Transcription Programmes, which had been produced by the BBC for export to the colonies.[38] In January 1939, they ordered the full seventy hours of the Empire Transcription Service.[39] W.R. Baker of the BBC requested that the BCN keep the price confidential, since other broadcasters with greater financial resources were paying more than the three pounds per hour for the first three series and five pounds for series five that was charged to the BCN.[40] Within a week after the BCN's inaugural broadcast, Frazer reported that the Empire transcriptions were 'a great success,' were 'exceedingly popular,' and were liked by the public much more than American programming. The only problem, he reported, was that BCN did not have enough of it.[41] The table 3.1 shows a breakdown of the British programming purchased under this arrangement.

Through Frazer's initiative, the BCN had bought a fair cross section of the BBC's 'middlebrow' domestic programming. They were not 'highbrow' music, which required a cultivated taste, such as the classical European repertoire, nor 'lowbrow,' which appealed to working-class tastes, such as British music hall or vaudeville. Middlebrow music attempted to gently ease listeners into appreciating elite music and educate their taste.[42] Light music and show tunes made up the largest single component of these recordings, with such programs as *Songs from the Shows: Tunes from Prewar and Present Day Musical Comedies* and the *Air-do-wells: Concert Party* featuring the BBC Variety Orchestra.[43] As one contemporary commentator upon British music put it, these were 'soothing melodies and gently undulating rhythms poured out in measured doses of soft lights and sweet music.'[44] Two British historians characterize the BBC's light music as 'a buffer zone, a no-man's land between dance music and serious music.' The BBC was not monolithic, they point out: managers saw Beethoven and Brahms as good music, and listeners who wanted radio to provide uplift agreed, but officials within the Music Department saw such music as old fashioned. They favoured chamber music, which was non-representational, or by the late 1930s, swing. Dance music was anathema, but programmers assigned canonical status to swing. The BBC added light music to the repertoire to balance out the *heavy* swing and chamber music with music that had no value other than entertainment.[45] As we can see, the aesthetic and didactic agenda behind the BBC's promotion of 'British music' defies simple characterization, but for Frazer it was a counterweight to the American popular culture.

Measuring the effect of this British programming on listeners is impossible, but it likely reinforced anglophilia in matters of taste in some listeners, even as Newfoundlanders increasingly bristled under the benign dictatorship of the Commission. When the BCN began testing the popularity of a series of school broadcasts, it used the BBC programs *How It Began*, a series on the history of technology, and *Science Lifts the Veil*.[46] The effect of these contracts was that serious music, information, and programming intended to uplift the public's taste came from Britain, while dance music, comedy, and soap operas aimed at female listeners came from the United States. A list of BBC transcriptions played during June 1948, for example, revealed that the BCN used thirty-three recorded programs, as well as the Newfoundland program of the BBC, discussed in the next chapter, *News from London*, and *BBC*

News and Analysis.[47] Excluding these 'news' programs and the rebroadcast of the BBC and Reuters, the BCN broadcast a total of sixteen hours
of BBC programming during August 1948.[48]

Before it signed on the air, Frazer had also negotiated a deal though
which a minimum of three hours of CBC programming could be transmitted over the telephone lines to the BCN each week.[49] The BCN had
adopted the CBC regulations on advertising, smoothing the way for
VONF to accept Canadian programming along the same lines as privately owned CBC affiliates in Canada. 'It would be impossible, without the aid from revenue to be derived from advertising,' Frazer wrote
to the CBC, 'to maintain a reasonable service in Newfoundland without
the help of a heavy government subsidy which, in the present state of
the finances of this country, could hardly be looked for.'[50] In return,
Canadian sponsors would acquire access to Newfoundland consumers.
Frazer was confident that the Newfoundland market would interest
these sponsors, since the number of radio receivers in operation was
increasing and the new high-powered VONF transmitter was encouraging many more people to purchase sets. Frazer seems to have been
not too far off the mark when he reported 'that nearly all Newfoundland sets are tuned into the corporation's station all the time due to the
intense interest in local affairs,' so by sponsoring news programming,
sponsors could get access to a large audience.[51] The BCN ultimately
took few CBC programs because it was expensive to carry the program
over the telegraph system through Quebec, the Maritime Provinces,
under the Cabot Strait, and across the island to St John's. Canadian
businesses that wanted to sponsor Newfoundland programming did
not materialize, so these news programs that had such an attractive
audience fell to sponsors based in St John's.

Frazer's failure to obtain contracts with large American of Canadian
sponsors encouraged the BCN to turn to local commercial sponsors.
The Newfoundland distributors of consumer products such as razors
and patent medicine, Gerald S. Doyle and Francis M. O'Leary, continued to sponsor the same programming on the state-owned Corporation
that they had when the station had been privately owned. The two
shows these men sponsored, the *Gerald S. Doyle News Bulletin* and the
Barrelman, exemplified Newfoundland radio. They had a role in Newfoundland culture and politics and because of their immense popularity tell us something of what listeners wanted from radio. Both Doyle
and O'Leary distributed many of the imported consumer items that
American and Canadian manufacturers wanted to promote. These for-

eign corporations had little reason to bother with advertising in the relatively small Newfoundland market, since their St John's–based distributors were willing to bear the cost of advertising.[52] These two programs deserve close examination for what they can tell us of the effects broadcasting had upon Newfoundland culture and social life.

As we have seen, VONF's inaugural broadcast as a privately owned station in 1932 had included the *Gerald S. Doyle News Broadcast*, which was a staple during the years that the BCN operated and continued long after VONF was taken over by the CBC. Doyle was both a successful businessman in St John's and an important cultural figure. An innovative entrepreneur, Doyle had made effective use of the mass media to advertise his wares and promote his own cultural activities. He distributed a range of Canadian and American manufactured consumer goods throughout Newfoundland, including his own brand of cod liver oil, which he advertised in a self-published *Gerald S. Doyle Song Book*. The King's Cove, Bonavista Bay, native was a traditional music enthusiast, having collected many of the folk songs in the book himself during a series of annual holidays around the coast of Newfoundland. The songbook played a large role in the folk-song revival of the 1930s and its many editions remained an influential collection of the Newfoundland folk-song canon for decades after.[53] While many of his contemporary, but more academic, folk-song collectors searched for music that had originated in the British Isles during early modern times and persisted in rural areas, Doyle's taste also included music by contemporary composers who worked within the traditional forms, such as Otto Kelland. Doyle's songbook, the radio show, and the phonograph record of Kelland's *Let Me Fish off Cape St Mary's*, which Doyle sponsored, made Kelland's compositions part of Newfoundland popular culture. Doyle's considerable innovations in print advertising were matched by his use of radio in new ways. His was credited with being the first local firm to hire musicians, the Crisco Orchestra, to provide regular broadcasts over 8RA.[54]

The *Gerald S. Doyle News Bulletin* became one of the most popular programs in Newfoundland radio history and transcended the boundaries of what was commonly accepted as 'news.'[55] The term *bulletin* provides an apt metaphor. The program was somewhat like a bulletin board in a public space upon which people could post notices of upcoming events, appeals for aid, or messages they might want to pass on to others. VONF lacked a news-gathering department so, starting in 1932, Doyle paid for the collection of local news, which could be gleaned from newspapers or contributed by the public. Doyle's staff complied these items and Galgay, under the name Frank Barkley, read the items over the air. (Broadcasters frequently used pseudonyms on the air.) It also contained personal messages to individuals of the sort that often were transmitted by telegraph or telephone. The latter ranged from notice of the arrival of vessels, to reassurances for rural listeners that their loved ones were being released from the hospital or had arrived in the capital, and occasionally more tragic news such as a death. In towns that lacked a telegraph station, in the lumber camps and at sea in fishing schooners, such messages were essential. As an *Evening Telegram* columnist put it,

> Our insularity has called for a different form of news presentation, via radio, than the accustomed form in other countries, and the Doyle bulletin has certainly filled that breach admirably. The bulletins may sound rather personal to outsiders but the people of Newfoundland like to know how their fellow villagers, if they happen to be in hospital, for example, are getting along. Everything of local significance is carried in the bulletins, from births to deaths, from law court news to general news.[56]

The *Doyle Bulletin* provided point-to-point communications at the same time that it was broadcasting information to the mass of listeners. It was also popular with many who knew none of the people whose messages were being transmitted, so we might conclude that they valued the program for its entertainment qualities as well.

The creation of the Broadcasting Corporation provided an opportunity for the station to take responsibility for collecting the news. Frazer proposed that telegraph staff in the outports gather local news and send it to St John's to be compiled into a daily 'complete national news despatch,' which could then be broadcast to the whole country.[57] This was an interesting variation upon the model of the existing *Public Despatch*, which had started in 1912. The Department of Posts and Telegraphs telegraphed daily news summaries called the *Public Despatch* to rural telegraph stations, consisting of news from St John's and the rest of the world, posted on the wall of the telegraph office or read to bystanders.[58] This one-way transmission of news evolved into two-way when people began telegraphing news to Doyle for him to include in his radio broadcast. In 1939 Doyle convinced the BCN to continue carrying his program, rather than develop its own news service. Beginning with the inauguration of the BCN, the *Doyle News* was extended from fifteen to thirty minutes.[59] Although the *Public Despatch* continued, particularly serving places where radio reception of VONF was infrequent, the *Doyle News* remained the principal source of Newfoundland news on the radio. Telegraph officers did not become news gatherers, but individual listeners submitted messages that they wanted passed on. Doyle paid an employee to collect the telegraph and telephone messages that had come in, as well as items gleaned from local newspapers, and these were passed to the BCN, to be reviewed and read by either Galgay himself or one of the announcers such as Aubrey MacDonald, who did the job more frequently, as management duties took a larger portion of Galgay's time.

People's memories of the show later in the century indicate that many listeners avidly followed such things as the well-being of people from their communities who were in St John's for health care, and sometimes followed the state of health of those whom they did not know. Given that in many cases people carefully rationed their battery power, the popularity of the program indicates a great interest among the audience for programming that reflected themselves – not just entertainment that allowed listeners to escape from the monotony of rural life during the Great Depression, like that provided in many Hollywood films. The revival of the economy that came with the Second World War did not diminish the popularity of these messages. In 1943 the Department of Posts and Telegraphs endeavoured to discourage the use of the *Doyle News* for messages that it believed should have been carried by telegraph (and paid for). Frazer's successor as secretary of the posts and telegraphs, Major Haig-Smith, instructed telegraph offices,

> In future messages directed from one individual to another for broadcasting on the radio in local news bulletins must not be accepted by postmasters unless the message is of a very urgent nature and it is known that the person or persons to whom the message is addressed cannot be reached by telegraph. A message which has as its object the saving of life or the immediate allaying of physical suffering may be regarded as very urgent and should be accepted; but messages which state that the sender is well, has recovered from an illness, is leaving for home or matters of no immediate urgency should not be accepted for inclusion in local radio news bulletins. Such messages are not news items of general interest and they absorb much broadcasting time. The telegraph system exists for the handling of these, and persons handing in these messages should be informed by the post master that they cannot be accepted and even if accepted they cannot be broadcast in future.[60]

This effort seems to have failed, since the following year Haig-Smith complained that the number of private messages seemed to have increased.[61]

In a sense, radio programs such as the *Doyle Bulletin* simulated a community; listeners from different parts of the island shared a sense of belonging to a group of people who had a common experience. Most people did not know the individual about whom the *Doyle Bulletin* spoke, but they knew that he or she had loved ones like the listener, and that those loved ones were at that same moment listening to the same message. Unintentionally, the program forged an 'imagined community,' with listeners hearing details of the lives of other people like themselves whom they would never meet but recognized as members of the same community of listeners.[62] Simulating a community could be an effective advertising strategy for Doyle. Most rural Newfoundlanders during the 1930s and early 1940s were not paid cash for the fish they caught but were paid in food, clothing, and supplies from a local merchant. Rural families and their merchants had paternalistic patron and client relationships, which Doyle lacked as a mail-order supplier of consumer products. The *Doyle News*, and his other cultural projects such as the songbook, established a social relationship between himself and listeners, encouraging them to purchase products from him beyond just listing the prices of items.

Doyle took a great interest in the program that bore his name, but Galgay found it did not live up to his notion of the sort of programming the station should provide. The program was popular with listeners and Doyle had a personal stake in it that exceeded what sponsors usually had, so Galgay could do little to change it, although he did not like the colloquialisms and non-standard English that the program unavoidably contained. Rural Newfoundland had a large number of regional dialects, none of which conformed to the BBC standard of pronunciation or the English grammar of textbooks. Galgay thought Doyle 'touchy' on the subject of the news, but maintained that the BCN staff did everything possible 'to present the news in the best possible manner.' A complaint by Doyle that his program had been cut short one evening because of technical difficulties prompted an exasperated response from Galgay to Furlong:

> The Gerald S Doyle News Bulletin is the subject of more attention than any other program on the air. It requires a great deal of re-editing and, entirely apart from the English which is generally atrocious, and which would be a

disgrace to the station if broadcast as written, on many occasions the compilation is such that the entire staff has been unable to make sense of particular items. Factual inaccuracies are numerous and many items involving persons and institutions are written in such a manner as to leave several constructions open to the listener with the possibility of interpretations which border on the libellous. The News oftentimes does not reach the studio until 6:45 or 7:00 p.m., a time when the announcers are most busy, and it is difficult enough to try and rewrite part of it without having to call Mr Doyle for an opinion. To be entirely frank there have been evenings when the Bulletin has been so badly compiled that the announcer has given up in despair and has read the News just as it was. It is frequently with extreme reluctance that the announcers have read the bulletin as they feel that its construction was such as to reflect credit neither on themselves nor on the station.[63]

Galgay wanted a more authoritative and respectable presentation style of the news. Ironically, the awkward grammatical constructions that allowed for an occasional unintentional double entendre, or perhaps an intentional double entendre on the part of the people who submitted items, became the element of the show that most entered popular memory. One famous message, which people who had not heard themselves often told as a joke decades later, was from an ill person to his or her spouse and should have read 'Not getting any better, come home' but was read as 'Not getting any, better come home.' The retelling of such humorous messages encouraged people to remember the program as if it were comedy, when the reality of the program was far more prosaic and messages were often tragic. One listener recalled that while fishing in a schooner on the Grand Banks he had heard of his own father's death on the *Doyle Bulletin*.[64]

A description of one of the broadcasts reveals that its character was not what people's memories would suggest. A 1946 recording of the *Bulletin*, read by Aubrey MacDonald, opens with an advertisement for the patent medicine Antiphlogestine, followed by an account of several Roman Catholic cardinals stopping at the Gander airbase on their way to Europe. Then there was a report that G.G. Lewis had returned to St John's from Washington where he had attended meetings of the Combined Food Board and a discussion of the implications of the meeting for salt fish prices. MacDonald then reported a drunk driving conviction in St John's, news of a tender for construction being called, notice of a forthcoming hockey tournament, the weather and ice report, and the coastal steamer report. There was one personal message, a report of a death and notice to the family that the remains would be returned home by train. Then came the train schedule, notice of jobs, a report on successful dance at Terra Nova Club and notice of another dance that evening. This was followed by notices of a Great War Veterans Association meeting, a card game, and several congratulations on births, and wedding anniversaries. The broadcast ended with an advertisement for Camay soap.[65] One might conclude that this was not much different from what would have been found in a local daily newspaper.

As indicated in the discussion of the possible uses of double entendre, people were able to turn the news and similar programs to their own purposes. An extreme case underlined the dangers of having someone outside the BCN taking control over content, although in this instance it was not Doyle's program but the Great Eastern Oil Company's *Bargain Hour* that caused the problem. The *Bargain Hour* consisted of notices of items for sale, much like the classified section of a newspaper. Galgay, or another 'responsible' member of the staff such as MacLeod, regularly read through both the *Doyle Bulletin* and the *Bargain Hour* before they were read on the air. In the spring of 1946 Galgay noticed a missing person announcement on the *Bargain Hour*, the sort of thing that would normally have been carried on the *Doyle Bulletin*, but he approved it for broadcast after deleting the mention of a reward. He worried that the offer of a reward might leave the impression that the person had done something wrong. When a few nights later a second such announcement appeared in the script, he became suspicious and instructed the announcer Aubrey MacDonald to find out the purpose of these messages. MacDonald told Galgay that the Great Eastern Oil Company used these announcements not to 'find' people but to shame those who owed the company money into paying their bill. Galgay told MacDonald that the Corporation was not going to become a bill-collecting agency, that the announcements were unethical, and that they could possibly result in the BCN being sued. MacDonald failed to tell the manager of the Great Eastern Oil Company of Galgay's decision. While Galgay was in Washington negotiating broadcasting frequencies with his other national counterparts, MacDonald read an item asking listeners to contact the Great Eastern Oil Company if they knew the whereabouts of a Mr Reginald Jones. In this instance the company had made an error, and Jones had indeed paid the money owed for the repair of his radio. Jones filed suit in the Supreme Court for damages to his reputation, naming both Great Eastern Oil and the BCN as defendants.[66] When Galgay returned to St John's and learned of the suit, MacDonald denied any recollection of Galgay telling him to not broadcast such announcements, or of having told Galgay that the manager of the oil company had been so informed. He claimed to believe that the messages were about genuinely missing persons, but later admitted that the woman at the Oil Company who compiled the program had told him the real purpose. Galgay decided upon no disciplinary action, since he was convinced that MacDonald had not intentionally violated his instructions when reading the program, but his actions 'were made in a semi automatic reaction to read anything which is placed in front of him without any reference to content.'[67] The BCN had inadvertently defamed a person because its announcer read copy provided by a sponsor. The BCN apologized to Jones, who then withdrew his action against the Broadcasting Corporation. He proceeded to sue Great Eastern Oil, even though Justice Brian Dunfield pointed out that Jones was unlikely to prevail because the law had not kept up with technology:

> I gather he [the plaintiff] proposes to try to show that to announce the matter over the air is libel, though I do not know how he can do so. (I may observe that it seems to me that the publication of defamatory matter by broadcasting ought to be put by statute into the category of libel ... It may have been the case once that the spoken word was trivial compared with the written word; but science has outstripped the law, and the word spoken by radio to thousands or millions outstrip the written word in efficacy. We are unlikely to get precedent from Great Britain, where broadcasting is public and carefully controlled; but where private stations exist the question may well arise.) But what is said over the air is in the nature of things ephemeral and passes in a moment; the hearers may or may not get the words correctly.[68]

While the BCN was off the hook for damages, Dunfield's words seem prophetic, given the case of libel that would be brought against Peter Cashin the following year.

Both the Great Eastern Oil Company's *Bargain Hour* and the *Doyle News* were created by sponsors and broadcast by the BCN. This allowed Doyle to put a very put a very personal stamp upon the national news, and the *Green Label News* sponsored by the Newfoundland Butter Company also had a local flavour. The *NBC News Commentary* by Al Vardy was a fifteen-minute program that relied upon copy from the US-based Trans-Radio News Service. Vardy's rapid delivery style emphasized the urgency of wartime news and seemed more 'American' in style when contrasted with the slower, more stentorian delivery of Galgay or one of the other BCN announcers. Smallwood later praised Vardy's program as 'the first real newscast in Newfoundland.'[69] A recording of Vardy's program opened and closed with street noise and boy calling out, 'Paper, paper, extra ... Paper, get your paper here' (perhaps an odd choice for a radio news program). Vardy went on to describe political events in Romania, the invasion of Poland by Germany and the USSR, a discussion of US Congress discussions on the *Neutrality Act*, and summary of President Roosevelt's speech. Vardy reported the warning by Premier Deladier of France that war would spread beyond Europe and involve the United States. He also reported that the media speculation about the end of the career of 'club-footed Nazi chief' Joseph Goebbels was unfounded. Vardy followed his report on a heat wave in Los Angles that had killed seventeen people, with a remark that Newfoundland weather was delightful, and the following:

> What a grand feeling it is to get up in the morning and to sit down to a breakfast where crispy, crunchy toast is placed in a conspicuous spot and right next to that toast is a dish of Green Label, that outstanding spread from the Butter Company. Believe me, that's when a person really feels fit and ready to tackle all the complex problems of the day. So why not start your day off right with delicious Green Label. In London today ... [70]

Such interweaving of content with the advertisements for the sponsor's products was common among entertainment programs in North American radio, although less so on news broadcasts. A second extant program had the advertising content confined to only the sign-on and sign-off of the program.[71]

Some listeners objected to advertising on the radio news, particularly when the program added the voices of 'Terry Parker' and 'Mother Wilkins' to the news. One listener wrote the *Daily News*, asking, 'Who wants butter and cooking recipes mixed with the allied advance in Europe' and requesting 'full unadulterated news (like your pasteurized milk).'[72] A listener on Bell Island, who liked the news, concurred:

> But Mr Sponsor, why let it become sour by the infiltration of those two parasites, known as 'Terry Parker' and 'Mother Wilkins.' Do we have to listen nightly to 'Terry Parker's' mispronunciation of Newfoundland and 'Mother (butter wouldn't melt in her mouth) Wilkins,' talk'n about her

bakin' and cookin' etc? 'Terry' tells us to send coin for our book – no stamps please. 'Al' corrects by saying: 'Owing to difficulty – send stamps please.' Sort of silly don't you think. Please Mr Sponsor tell 'Al' Vardy not to ask 'Terry Parker' to come in to-night. If you must have them on, why not after the newscast. I'd suggest about six hours afterwards.[73]

Another listener on Bell Island agreed with these criticisms and urged 'Mr Sponsor' to have the advertising content read before and after the news.[74] These listeners show an awareness that broadcasters' names were often not the names of the real people, but characters created by the sponsor. The first listener objected to the incongruity of advertising content in the midst of the war news and the second disliked the informal diction and fake folksiness of the advertising copy.

While local sponsors influenced the character of the national news, the BCN relied heavily upon the BBC for foreign news, allowing VONF to achieve a level of decorum in its broadcast. VOCM wanted to avail of BBC programming as well, but the BBC rejected Joseph Butler's application since its policy was to deal directly with 'national' broadcasters, not those privately owned, and advised VOCM to ask if the BCN wanted to hand over BBC programs it did not need.[75] Meanwhile, the Newfoundland Butter Company complained to the BCN that while it purchased news from the Trans-Radio News Service and paid for Vardy to read it, VOCM gathered news from other broadcasters without paying for it. Since VOCM provided three broadcasts a day, the Butter Company's 'best efforts look insignificant.'[76] Furthermore, although the Butter Company paid for the content, the BCN sold some of the Trans-Radio copy to the daily newspapers, leaving Vardy with less copy than he needed, given his rapid delivery. Two months after the BCN went on the air, Frazer wrote to Donald Manson of the CBC to ask advice on solving this problem. A station in Newfoundland, Frazer reported, had been collecting news from American and British broadcasters as well as newspapers without paying for it and then selling sponsorship of the news broadcast to one of its own advertisers. He wondered if the BCN should enact regulations prohibiting such acts, and asked if copyright existed in news so that the station could be forced to refrain from broadcasting news it had not purchased.[77] Manson replied that while copyright over news did not generally exist, the CBC thought it undesirable that a station rebroadcast a program without the permission of the station from which the item had originated. He suggested the BCN draft something similar to the CBC regulation, which had effectively suppressed the 'pirating' of news. The CBC's regulations allowed privately owned stations to purchase news from a supplier, such as Trans-Radio, and broadcast that news, provided they had the written permission of the CBC and a licence to receive the news from the Department of Transport.[78] The BCN was to periodically become concerned by VOCM's pirating of the news but, since it enacted no such regulations could do little.

Not all news programming was compiled by private businesses. Rather than relying upon Doyle or Vardy, the BCN provided its own coverage of special events, such as the world's first crash of a civilian jetliner – an aircraft belonging to the Sabina Airlines – near Gander in September 1946. Galgay himself travelled to the airport town to cover what was by the time of his arrival an international news story. The crash site was inaccessible so the difficult rescue took several days, and Galgay had an opportunity to interview at length some of those involved in the rescue as well as one of the survivors. Galgay then returned to St John's by train with the recorded interviews, which were later broadcast with connecting commentary.[79] As he reported, the character of his broadcasts was different from that of other commentators:

> It was the opinion of the airport authorities that our coverage was much more accurate than other news sources. It would have been very easy to flood the station with sensational bulletins on the various incidents surrounding the crash but it was my opinion that this was neither dignified nor desirable ... A number of recordings were made on the spot and in these I believe we have the best coverage of the entire incident. In particular we have a very important recording by Mr T. McGrath operations manager who was responsible for the direction of all work. This is the only authoritative statement so far released. Other recordings include an interview with Roland Pinsent, Newfoundlander who guided Dr Martin to the scene of the wreck and a description by Miss Helen Henderson one of the survivors. I think that we have taken a different angle from most reporters and we have stressed the part played by Newfoundland throughout the series.[80]

Listening to recordings of these interviews reveals that Galgay's coverage lacked the drama of the report filed from Gander by American radio journalist David Brinkley, for example – a characteristic of which Galgay seemed proud.[81] Galgay did not attempt to portray danger or excitement in his voice, or emphasize the fact that he was on the scene of the efforts to coordinate the rescue. Galgay asked questions and let those he interviewed go on at great length in their description of the challenges of rescuing people from the remote crash site. The interviews contained no information upon the cause of the crash itself. Rather, the story was treated very much as a local story of the hardship and challenges overcome by the Newfoundlanders making the rescue attempt, and not exclusively the experiences of the crash survivors. This approach could be contrasted with the radio coverage of another difficult rescue a decade earlier, that of trapped miners at Moose River, Nova Scotia, in which J. Frank Willis used his theatrical training to promote the drama of the rescue for the entertainment of the listeners.[82]

In addition to music and news, listeners had a great deal of interest in information about Newfoundland and in hearing themselves reflected in radio programming. That potential audience was realized by Joseph R. Smallwood's *Barrelman* program. Smallwood had been born to lower-middle-class parents in 1900, and as a boy in St John's developed a love of reading and a boundless ambition. A largely self-educated nationalist intellectual, journalist, political operative, and sometime union organizer, he had dabbled in leftist politics but had distanced himself from radicalism with such things as his 1927 radio broadcast 'Why I Oppose Communism.'[83] He had worked for the Liberal Party, openly admired the populist William Coaker, founder of the Fishermen's Protective Union, and counted among his friends such members of the establishment as the businessman Chesley Crosbie. In the midst of the Great Depression, Smallwood convinced Crosbie to back his edited two-volume collection of essays on Newfoundland history, society, and culture. Upon the completion of the modestly named *Book of Newfoundland* and once more without an income, Smallwood began a regular *Daily News* column in July 1937.[84] The title, 'From the Masthead, by the Barrelman,' was a reference to the man in the barrel attached to the mast of a ship who would be able to see farther than others and warn of obstacles ahead or direct the ship toward seals whelping on the ice during the annual seal harvest. The column consisted of brief items of news, curious bits of information, and comment upon issues of the day. By September Smallwood had taken the column to the air on VONF, and soon had a sponsor in Francis M. O'Leary. Doyle's competitor in the patent medicine business, and his friend, O'Leary now had an advertising niche similar to the *Doyle News*. While the newspaper column's folksy style carried over to the radio program well, as Hiscock pointed out, the *Daily News* column became more of a political dialogue with readers over the weeks it was being published, much as one would expect from newspaper editorials. The radio program was rarely overtly political, but was nearly always implicitly political.[85] As of June 1938 Smallwood had a steady income of thirty-five dollars a week for the radio show, and an additional salary of fifty dollars a month for editing a newspaper also entitled the *Barrelman* (and later renamed the *Newfoundlander*, which recycled items from the radio show and contained advertisements for O'Leary's products). This allowed Smallwood to cease publishing his newspaper column. In a less-than-astute business move, however, Smallwood sold the rights to the trade name *Barrelman* to O'Leary for one dollar.[86] Much of his life to that date had been hand to mouth, and he had a wife and children, so it is not surprising that he accepted O'Leary's offer of a steady income.

The *Barrelman* program had parallels in other Depression-era programming, such as the American newspaper column and radio program *Ripley's Believe It or Not*, but it was an inventive use of radio. Each evening, Monday to Saturday, listeners would hear a ship's bell being struck six times, followed by the announcement 'F.M. O'Leary Ltd, presenting the Barrelman in a programme of making Newfoundland better known to Newfoundlanders.' For the next fifteen minutes they heard brief anecdotes, stories, facts, and tall tales interspersed with descriptions of the benefits of the sponsor's products, all punctuated by Smallwood striking a ship's bell. As Smallwood recalled,

> It was a peculiar blend of Newfoundland history, geography, and economic information, with stories of courage, endurance, hardship, inventiveness, resourcefulness, physical strength and prowess, skill and courage in seamanship, and a hundred other aspects and distinctions of our Newfoundland story – all of them 'making Newfoundland better known to Newfoundlanders' and intended to inspire them with faith in their country and in themselves, and to destroy what I continually denounced as our inferiority complex.[87]

The unobtrusive shift back and forth between content and advertisement, particularly since many of the advertisements relied on the same sort of hyperbole for comic effect, made the program seamless and ensured that listeners would follow the advertising copy as closely as they did the stories of Newfoundlanders' great feats. For content Smallwood relied upon published sources, archival records, and conversations with his extensive network of acquaintances.

He also encouraged listeners to write in their stories of Newfoundlanders, to provide evidence that his program was popular since there
were no surveys of radio listeners in Newfoundland during this period,
and also because it provided inexpensive content. Smallwood told
his listeners to write, saying, 'The only way of telling whether a radio
program is popular or not is by counting the number of letters that
come in.'[88] Listeners wrote the *Barrelman* for a variety of reasons. Some
wanted their names read over the air, thinking that friends and family
would be surprised and pleased to hear it, and asked for their letter to
be read as a specific time so they would be sure to hear it. Others asked
that their story be read but their name be kept confidential. A few did
not sign their names.

Smallwood's extensive use of hyperbole prompted listeners to start
sending him tall tales. Smallwood used these tales since they provided
some humour to lighten the didactic tone, but was careful to insist that
his program was not fiction. Sixty-five years later, Clayton Johnson of
Jacques Fountain, remembered sending a story to Smallwood in which
he had faithfully reported true events but had exaggerated the number
of woodpeckers because that was the form of storytelling that people
expected.[89] In addition to adding tall tales, Smallwood constantly
varied the program's format to keep it fresh. For awhile, he used the
broadcast as a kind of quiz show, offering samples of tea to listeners
who submitted questions he could not answer or those who wrote in
with proof of purchase for the things O'Leary distributed.[90] The quiz
show had been a successful format for American radio during the pro-
ceeding decade. For these segments he invited MacLeod to join him to
ask the questions about Newfoundland that listeners had submitted,
then he would answer, somewhat like the *Answer Man* format used on
American radio. Smallwood also occasionally interviewed people,
such as the oldest living woman in Newfoundland, Ellen Carroll,
whom the *Barrelman* made into a celebrity in a rare remote broadcast
from her home.[91]

Peter Narváez has shown that through the *Barrelman* program Smallwood operated as a folklorist, collecting and preserving stories in oral
culture. Further, Narváez argued that by promoting aspects of Newfoundland folk culture to a larger national audience through radio
broadcasting, which normally brought high culture and modern culture, Smallwood validated these local folk stories.[92] In a similar analysis, Hiscock has shown how folk culture is made of the materials at
hand, some of which was from oral tradition while other material came

from published sources or items heard from the radio. He pointed out that Smallwood encouraged listeners to submit local items about Newfoundlanders, offering samples of O'Leary's products to listeners and encouraging them to write so that he could prove to O'Leary that the program was popular. Smallwood broadcast items from listeners that conformed to his polemical agenda, promoting that vision of Newfoundlanders as the national popular culture.[93]

This chapter opened with Smallwood expressing a hope that a Newfoundland popular culture would encourage patriotism, and the nationalist implications of his program were always evident. At the most basic level, Smallwood also used the program to promote himself as a nationalist leader at a time when elected office did not exist. Several politically ambitious men of his generation who might have had a political career, had elected government not been suspended in 1934, now used radio to achieve a national public profile.

It cannot be forgotten that although listeners submitted much of the content, Smallwood selected which items made it to air. He thus shaped the popular culture his correspondents helped him create, while cultivating the image that he was only the conduit though which listeners expressed a genuine Newfoundland popular culture. As one scholar put it, Smallwood projected the idea that he was 'the voice' of the people.[94] On one occasion a listener caught Smallwood in a minor factual error (given the thousands of pages of script he banged out on the typewriter, often up to the last minute before going on air, it is remarkable that there were so few errors). Smallwood defended himself by saying that the material came from Newfoundlanders. The listener demanded he get his facts right, prompting Smallwood to respond,

> If he thinks that I'm setting myself up to educate the people of Newfoundland, he's making a mistake, because I'm not. It's the other way about – the people of Newfoundland are educating me. Whose programme is this, anyway? Is there anyone so badly informed that he thinks it's my programme? Does anybody really think that all the material and information I've been giving every night for nearly three years past came out of my head? Of course is didn't. It came from my listeners, from the people of Newfoundland.[95]

Smallwood was not content to suggest the material came from just from his listeners; he asserted that his listeners were synonymous with 'the people of Newfoundland.'

Many listeners enjoyed the program and approved of the *Barrelman*'s nationalist polemic, but some resisted his reading of Newfoundland culture and society. A few listeners wrote to the editors of the St John's newspapers, taking issue with things Smallwood had said.[96] A listener in Fogo, an island off the northeast coast of Newfoundland, praised the *Barrelman* but did not like the stories that listeners had submitted because they stretched credibility. 'Give us nothing but facts,' the listener insisted, 'and be sure your facts are true.'[97] Another listener wrote Smallwood directly, arguing that Canadians and Americans listening to the radio would hear the 'nonsense and silliness' on the program and would get a poor idea of the intelligence of the people of the country.[98] Yet another listener commented that he didn't believe the stories but did not blame Smallwood, since he was 'only the medium though which these stories are made known to us.'[99] A few listeners wrote Smallwood to say they disliked the tall tales, but those complaints were far outnumbered by listeners who submitted tall tales for Smallwood to use. Listeners came to the *Barrelman*'s defence as well. Smallwood had given some children the opportunity to perform on air, prompting a listener, who called himself 'Disgusted,' to write the *Evening Telegram* complaining of the amateur quality of the program. 'Solomon' then wrote to the competing *Daily News* suggesting that 'Disgusted' listen to a different station if he or she didn't like what was on. 'The Barrelman's Programme is the only outlet they have to prove their talent,' Solomon continued, and 'where can you find an orchard minus a bad apple.'[100]

Newfoundland radio broadcasters during the 1940s did not have access to listener surveys, which would have allowed them to measure the popularity of their programming in demographic segments. Letters from listeners were one of the few mechanisms that provided feedback to sponsors, allowing them to judge the popularity of the programming for which they were paying. In the 1940s listener surveys conducted by phone had largely replaced surveying letters from listeners as a tool used by American network programmers, which effectively gave listeners the ability to veto programming decisions after the fact by not listening to them. But audience surveys did not provide a mechanism for listeners to make positive suggestions about what they wanted to hear. During the 1930s, writers of soap opera, for example, had been attentive to listeners' views on how plots should progress, but that became more unusual.[101] Newfoundland listeners continued to influence the content on the *Barrelman* both by directly letting Smallwood know what they liked and disliked, and by sending him material to broadcast. They also responded to each other, submitting stories that had been prompted by items they heard on the show.

Of the listeners who wrote Smallwood directly, not all conformed to the conventions of fan mail, providing an example of how people used broadcasting in their own ways. Some people in hardship wrote to the Barrelman hoping he would send them financial aid or used clothing, or help them get a job. A few seem to have had the impression that Smallwood would empathize with their poverty (which he probably did) and that his connections would enable him to help them. As one listener who wanted a berth to the annual seal hunt wrote,

> So far as I can judge you are the one, and only one who is known all over the Island, and I wonder if you could get me a birth [sic] ... Some how I am thinking you can do it, because the whole country know[s] you and is very much interested in your work.[102]

In his subsequent political career Smallwood effectively used such patron–client relations. Not all of his listeners wanted something from him. A few of his correspondents were rural and impoverished, but many more were well-educated, middle-class, and urban.[103] Given the high levels of illiteracy among the poor and rural population, being able to write a letter to the *Barrelman*, even one with spelling mistakes, made the correspondent exceptional in his or her community. Smallwood later made much of his birth in the rural community of Gambo, but his childhood and education were in St John's. Yet he was of outport parentage in a St John's society in which such things were important in setting people's social place. Many listeners would have recognized that his accent was not exactly that of the St John's middleclass, but would have had cadences of 'educated outport.'[104] Rural listeners might have thought that he was one of them, although educated, and that they could write to him without having their writing ability looked down upon. Such an accent served him well during his subsequent political career, and later generations of Newfoundland politicians sometimes affected rural speech patterns so they would not seem to be from St John's. As the Barrelman, Smallwood could claim to be of Newfoundland, neither a St John's man nor a bay man, but someone who could fit into either society. One rural listener commented that men in his community said that Smallwood was 'the plainest speaker they hear of all that speak over the air,' likely reflecting their view that he seemed informal in style compared to other broadcasters.[105]

Any commercial program had to achieve an audience for the advertising content; broadcasters were therefore responsive to what they thought listeners wanted, and a nationalist appeal was effective. Smallwood's and O'Leary's Newfoundland nationalism were genuine, however, although the two men had their ideological differences. Smallwood promoted tales and real-life stories of courage, strength, endurance, and stoicism that responded to the hardship of the Depression with a self-help message to the poor. 'I love to come across stories of Newfoundlanders who have gone out and faced the world and conquered it,' he said. 'These cases prove my contention that Newfoundlanders have got what it takes, whenever they get the chance.'[106] Smallwood's rhetorical style relied heavily upon repetition and hyperbole. In that respect his program was similar to many others throughout North America. He accepted the premise that individual action could ameliorate hardship, rather than the idea that worldwide structures were responsible for economic conditions. Despite his seeing himself as a socialist, his program was conservative in its assurance that there was nothing wrong with capitalism itself, which might encourage collective action, and that each individual could rise above poverty though his or her own effort.[107] To be fair, this kind of self-help rhetoric was the only sort of answer Smallwood could have provided on the radio. The self-help message was one that both the leftist Smallwood and the conservative O'Leary supported. Both also shared a desire for the end of the Commission of Government. Smallwood had become a critic of the Commission, particularly the ways that it had undermined Newfoundland's national identity, such as closing the Newfoundland Museum and allowing its collection to be dispersed as a cost-saving measure. O'Leary was a member of the Newfoundland National Association, which petitioned for constitutional reform, and was later president of the Responsible Government League, which strove to return to the country's former democratic government. Smallwood was careful, however, in his criticism of the Commission on the radio. A listener in St John's had a critique of the Commission itself, which Smallwood included in a scripted interchange between MacLeod, who sometimes read listener letters, and himself:

BOB: The first one tonight is from George Hancock, Topsail Road ... 'If,' says Mr. Hancock, 'the men governing us are merely Imperial Civil Service men, is it possible for them to have the necessary vision, acumen, business ability, and daring required for the rehabilitation of Newfoundland? If they do not have these requirements, and are merely civil servants who retain their positions at the King's pleasure, what chance does Newfoundland have of ever regaining her lost independence – the right of franchise and self-government?' That's the question, Mr Barrelman. What's your answer?

BARRELMAN: I'm afraid, Bob, there's going to be no answer to that question tonight. I'm glad you asked. It gives me the opportunity to say to those listening in that it's useless to send me questions of a political character, as this one is. If the gentleman who sent it in had stopped to think a moment, he would have realized that I simply can't deal with questions of that sort. Political discussions are barred in this particular program.[108]

Smallwood's statement that political discussions were barred was disingenuous. He had provided the opportunity for MacLeod to read the letter on the air without expressing any disagreement with the author's opinion, so listeners could consider Hancock's point of view, while distancing himself from it if there was any backlash.

It is common to observe that Hollywood movies, dance music, and radio comedy provided much-needed escapism during the depth of the Great Depression. The light-hearted comedy of the tall tale provided such relief, and the stories of remarkable feats might remind people, and O'Leary would have agreed, that they could overcome their poverty through strength of will without help from the government. Not all listeners approved of the self-help advice and the Newfoundland boosterism of the *Barrelman*, or the entertainment that they heard on the radio generally. One rural listener commented,

We are sick of listening to the majority of stuff that comes over the radio. I mean the 'dances,' 'balls,' 'excursions,' 'lotteries' and 'sports' and 'dinner lectures'; that are no help or inspiration to the people who must work to live. It is hard for our people in the outports to have patience with a daily feed of such stuff, when they are at grips with the serious problem of how to earn money enough to live. If the folks in St John's want this kind of a programme for heaven's sake don't inflict it on people fighting and striving to keep off the dole and looking and listening for hints to help them in that fight. I would like to hear for instance some items like this: 'John Smith knitted three salmon nets last winter. His wife hooked seven mats and a dozen pair of socks. He was never on the dole and says 'please God he never will be.'[109]

The listener went on to give several other examples of fictional people overcoming hardship in practical ways. Another listener had a similar critique of Smallwood's program, suggesting that fishermen and loggers did not need to be told how hard-working they were, since the hardship of their daily lives was apparent to them. Rather than 'bore' people with 'nonsense,' this critic asked for an explanation of the poor condition of the economy and suggested Smallwood tell people where the wealth of the county had gone.[110] A listener in the lumber town of Bishop's Falls, Thomas Tuck, proposed the Corporation start a program similar to the *Barrelman* but instead of covering history the proposed show would provide a forum for the impoverished to ask questions and listeners could discuss 'ways and means of bettering the living conditions of the people.' 'Why is it that the unfortunate fellow who is today living under such trying conditions,' asked Tuck, 'cannot be heard through the medium of Radio Broadcasting?' Another problem he saw with broadcasting that he saw was that 'so many are advertising how to spend money, but [there is] no-body to tell you how to save money.'[111] Another listener took a different position, writing directly to Smallwood, suggesting that he defeat 'old man fear' by 'preaching optimism.'[112] Smallwood responded on air by saying that his listeners wanted entertainment, not propaganda – a statement that seems more designed to retain his credibility in the face of the negative associations of the word *propaganda* than an accurate assessment of his program. Smallwood continued to write and broadcast stories of Newfoundlanders succeeding in their chosen endeavours, and overcoming hardship, in a way that emphasized the positive qualities of the folk. Smallwood also created cultural symbols of Newfoundland out of folk traditions, rather than symbols created by the state such as a national flag. So Smallwood advocated adopting a national flower and promoted the correct pronunciation of the word *Newfoundland* as the one used by people.[113] At a time in which Newfoundland was no longer self-governing but was governed by the British-appointed Commission, he advanced the notion that a Newfoundland nationalism could be founded upon the positive qualities of the folk rather than political independence or the form of government. The discourse on the past, for example, emphasized the personal pasts of families and individuals over the public pasts of political history.

A show that featured one voice and one format six nights a week, eleven months a year, could become stale without the broadcaster reinventing it. Over the years the *Barrelman* varied in format, trying out many of the innovations of other radio programs. MacLeod asked Smallwood the questions, varying the voice and introducing the opportunity to simulate repartee, in interchanges scripted to simulate a natural conversation.[114] Smallwood also introduced a female voice to read the advertisements, and had a contest in which listeners voted on which of the women who auditioned should become the Palm Olive Girl. Having a female voice reading the advertising copy while Smallwood himself read the polemics could prevent listeners from dismissing the description of the merits of a product as another of the Barrelman's tall tales. But by confining the commercial content to the 'girl,' Smallwood could emphasize the cultural value of the things he said.[115] The more prestigious non-advertising content would be conveyed by his voice.

The Second World War prompted several changes to the *Barrelman*. Smallwood now contrasted the positive patriotism of Newfoundland with the hateful nationalism of Germany, although there were few direct discussions of the war. O'Leary wanted to use the program to support the war effort, prompting Smallwood to add the 'Fish Appeal' to his program. Fishermen who had little access to cash could donate a salted cod, which would then be auctioned to one of the country's fish exporters and the money donated to provide comfort items to Newfoundland servicemen. The revival of the economy also presented many broadcasters, Smallwood included, with more lucrative employment. By November 1943 Smallwood reported that his work had been accomplished now that Newfoundlanders no longer lacked confidence in themselves. The economy had rebounded with wartime spending, and while Newfoundlanders faced occasional insults from foreigners and were perhaps sometimes too quick to be offended, such occurred during the Joan Blondell affair, they responded by expressing indignation in the pages of the local press and letters to the Barrelman.[116] The American actress and singer Joan Blondell had spent several days in Newfoundland in October 1943, as part of a USO tour. She had been warmly received by both American servicemen and Newfoundland civilians alike and had also performed on the BCN's *USO Radio Programme*.[117] While touring the American bases Blondell learned a comic song about the slow speed of the Newfoundland railway, and picked up the jocular phrase 'Stay where you're to, till I comes where you're at.' When home in Los Angeles, Blondell performed the song on the Armed Forces Radio Service program *Command Performance* and made reference to the slowness of the train. Some Newfoundlanders perceived this as an insult.[118] They may have been a little too sensitive in this case, in large measure a result of having heard genuine insults from foreigners, and reacted angrily. Smallwood was not offended by the remarks and urged listeners to not be too sensitive. He must also have been happy to have seen people having the confidence to strike back against a perceived affront.[119]

At about the same time, Smallwood's contemporary, the journalist Ewart Young, reported that Smallwood had received 60,000 pieces of correspondence from listeners – likely an estimate that came from the Barrelman himself, suggesting to Young that the *Barrelman* was likely the second most popular local broadcaster, on the basis of fan mail received (he probably meant second to the *Doyle News*). Young attributed this success to people's desire to hear their names and their stories read on the air.[120] What Young didn't report was that Smallwood was restless. He had a lifelong interest in farming, and had been operating a farm on the outskirts of the city even while doing his nightly broadcast. Having met the commander of the Royal Canadian Air Force contingent stationed at the Gander airbase, Smallwood left his family and his career as a broadcaster behind to move to the base to manage a large piggery. He reported that the letters he received indicated that his program had accomplished its goal, and Newfoundlanders now had faith in themselves and their future. But a survey of hundreds of the letters reveals no significant change in their content. Most continued to be the sort of tall tales that listeners had long submitted. Smallwood appeared as the Barrelman for the last time on 27 November 1943. Years later, conspiracy theorists would claim that Smallwood left so that he could increase his chances of getting elected if Newfoundland returned to responsible government after the war. A more likely explanation is that he had tired of the program and of domestic life and relished the opportunity to prove that, given the chance, a Newfoundlander could create a piggery that would be the envy of the world.[121]

Smallwood later boasted that one result of the program was that 'my voice and personality become part of Newfoundland's very culture,' and yet he was replaced.[122] O'Leary hired the young newspaper journalist and Michael Harrington to be the Barrelman. Harrington had been born in St John's, completed the two years of study available at Memorial University College and in 1936 began a clerical job at the Department of Health. He also hosted a broadcast of phonograph records Tuesday and Thursday nights under the pseudonym 'Ray Alexander' for the then privately owned VONF. This program was sponsored by 'Summers, the Smart Shop for Men,' which he continued after he took an office job at the US Engineer's Department at Fort Pepperell (1941–3). A published poet and aspiring journalist, Harrington had also established his nationalist credentials with a series of newspaper articles and letters to the editor that advocated a return to responsible government.[123] By contrast with Smallwood, the more modest Harrington is not much remembered as the Barrelman, although he wrote and performed the program for more years than Smallwood, leaving to pursue other interests in 1955. After 1943 Stan O'Leary also hosted a *West Coast Barrelman* from the Corner Brook station VOWN, in part from material recycled from the St John's parent program. Smallwood's close identification with the program in people's memories, while the other two men's tenure has been largely forgotten, may have been because Smallwood had created the program, achieved prominence during the key period of the program's influence (during the last years of the Great Depression and the first three years of the war), had a subsequent political career, and was a master of self-promotion.

Recordings of the *Barrelman* during the tenure of its two hosts, Smallwood and Harrington, reveal something of their personality and styles. Smallwood was clearly fully comfortable with himself as broadcaster. On one occasion, for example, he joked that listeners might not share his interest in statistics, and then devoted the full program to the total value of exports of various fish species during the preceding fifty years. While Smallwood's style attempted to convey his infectious enthusiasm for all things related to Newfoundland, Harrington had a more professorial style as Barrelman. Harrington presented, in one example, a biography of eighteenth-century governor William Waldegrave, followed by a discussion of social conditions of working people during his administration and the problems of the shortage of specie. Then came a discussion of the report of a man who rowed 400 miles to his new home because he could not sell his punt and did not want to abandon it – an incident, in Harrington's view, showing that Newfoundlanders in the past knew the value of property. In another episode, after the defeat of Germany but before the defeat of Japan, Harrington discussed Newfoundlanders' contribution during the war and commented that Newfoundland was a 'nation that did not have the vote but fought for democracy.'[124] He later had an opportunity to try to remedy the situation.

Harrington's version of the program contained longer and more factual items and fewer tall tales from listeners than during Smallwood's time at the microphone. He often used a letter from a correspondent to introduce a topic that he expounded upon, rather than presenting a series of seemingly random items from listeners. Shortly after taking over, Harrington invited listeners to tell him what sort of program they wanted.[125] The *Barrelman* continued to represent material submitted by listeners but was now more formal in tone and character. Harrington also convinced O'Leary to sponsor an annual poetry competition, one that awarded significant cash prizes provided by O'Leary's suppliers. 'In other countries,' Harrington told listeners, 'the government ... looks out for that side of the development of the national life and culture,' but in Newfoundland, patronage of national culture was in the hands of businesses.[126] The program consequently had a more literary quality than during Smallwood's years.

Both the *Doyle News* and the *Barrelman* took elements of Newfoundland oral culture out of their local contexts, as well as content and form from outside Newfoundland, and distributed them on the radio to geographically dispersed listeners and across ethnic and class boundaries. Radio could take a story or song from one family or town, or invent a new narrative or song, and make it part of the cultural corpus of all Newfoundland listeners.[127] The popularity of both these 'news' programs lay in both Newfoundlanders' desire for relevant information and a forum for conversation about public issues during a period when no Newfoundland legislature existed. Both programs also consisted in large part of material submitted by the audience, and were thus in part a dialogue among listeners, although mediated by the broadcaster.

When broadcasters created a Newfoundland popular culture, they also formed icons of Newfoundland identity and did so within the dynamic of commercial exchange. Doyle and O'Leary – two of the most important sponsors of programming in pre-Confederation Newfoundland – were not coincidentally two agents for Canadian and American manufacturers. Their employees compiled the content and on-air personnel delivered it, much as broadcasting networks and corporate sponsors in most of North America left the creation of programming to advertising agencies. Not only did such programs try to form a positive Newfoundland popular culture out of genuine nationalist sentiment through broadcasters and sponsors, but creating an imagined community had another purpose. Most retailing in rural Newfoundland continued to be conducted through a local merchant who had not only an economic but also a social relationship with consumers. O'Leary and Doyle were asking people to purchase brand name products from a stranger, and for this reason might have felt that creating the simulation of a relationship with listeners was an effective advertising strategy. By creating a public space in which all listeners were part of the Newfoundland community, people could be encouraged to purchase goods from someone they would never meet. Furthermore the populist political stance and rural cultural content of the programs could encourage listeners to identify O'Leary and Doyle as working-class and of the outports, which would defuse potential resentment of the two as Water Street St John's merchants.

The Commission of Government had created the BCN as a propaganda arm that would aid its reconstruction agenda and unsuccessfully tried to persuade foreign companies to sponsor programming. Newfoundland broadcasters such as Smallwood had access to the air, thanks to the local commercial sponsors, and they were not constrained by the government's limited vision of content that furthered its reconstruction agenda. They used the state-owned station to engage in Newfoundland's cultural life, just as they had used it before 1939. In retrospect, the continuity between private and public ownership is striking, even if there was great fanfare about the 'new' station. Some BBC officials might have felt that there was no talent in Newfoundland, but the requirement for commercial programming to pay the bills ensured that Newfoundland musical and information programming had a prominent place on the state-owned broadcaster.

We also must remember that radio was a gendered medium; some programs appealed to one sex or the other, even if historians are rarely able to measure that popularity. One possible gauge is the letters to the *Barrelman* program, a large portion of which are extant. Those who chose to write letters may not be representative of listeners, of course. Some of the authors wrote because they had read the *Barrelman* newspaper, not because they had heard the radio show, and perhaps some factors that influence the likelihood of writing a letter are not apparent. A review of the letters reveals that the program seems to have been popular with both the very young and the elderly, and both male and female listeners. While listeners from each of these segments of the audience sent letters to Smallwood, male listeners possibly outnumbered female. Certainly men were more likely to write letters to the program than women. About two thirds of the extant letters of which the sex of the author is evident were written by males.[128] One listener told Smallwood, 'I think it is mostly a men's programme, anyway it's mostly men who listen to it here.'[129] His was probably an accurate sense of the audience. Listeners to news programs such as the *Barrelman* and the *Doyle Bulletin* seem to have been disproportionately male.

Each of these news and information programs depended upon the authority and familiarity of a male voice. Galgay's formal delivery and base tones on the *Doyle Bulletin* projected authority, while Smallwood's higher-pitched delivery cut through the ether to simulate the everyman. Listeners didn't hear Gerald S. Doyle himself, but his name and his reputation as a cultural authority were tied to his program. Vardy's confident reading of world news seemed authoritative, and he was sometimes called upon to explain world events to Newfoundland audiences in the lecture hall.

By contrast, few women's voices were heard on Newfoundland radio, except for entertainers such as singers or children's broadcasters such as Kathleen Clift, who used the pseudonym 'Aunt Kate.' An 'aunt' was both the BBC occupational category for women who broadcast children's programming and in popular Newfoundland vernacular a term of respect and affection for older women in the community. The BCN had advertised for a part-time 'lady announcer' in 1939, but does not seem to have hired anyone.[130] Some women's programming had male hosts. 1946 saw the launch of *Wifesaver*, in which comedian Allen Prescott had 'a magic formula' for combining comedy, music, recipes, and household hints – a program 'designed for the tired housewife.'[131] In 1947 the BCN also began broadcasting the CBC program *Happy Gang* – a variety show aimed primarily at women.[132] Local retailer Harvey Brehm created a program to advertise his products much like Doyle's, but specialized in news for women. He provided for a young woman from Newfoundland, Helen Hawkins, to study broadcasting.[133] The BCN launched *Our Woman's World* with some fanfare in the spring of 1947, using 'all the devices of radio and the press to surround her with an atmosphere of superior ability and to impress the public with her complete mastery of household science and home economy.'[134] This effort was unusual; other broadcasters had achieved a distinct radio personality and minor celebrity status through their program, but in this case listeners were being sold on her expertise and popular appeal before her program had even started. Newspaper articles set out that Hawkins had 'lived among Newfoundlanders' so she knew what they liked, and was an authority by virtue of having expertise developed outside the country. She had studied household economy at Mount Allison University, in New Brunswick, before Harvey Brehm sent her for an intensive crash course in broadcasting in New York.[135] The program fell short of these elevated expectations, prompting Galgay to not renew Hawkins's contract the following year and start a new search for a women's broadcaster. As he put it,

> A hiatus would provide time for a more thorough investigation of possible candidates and some exploration of possible improvements in the form of the program. I am satisfied that this program can become an outstanding feature and the individual in charge somewhat of a national figure, if we can only strike the right balance between material and personality.[136]

By the end of this 'hiatus' the Broadcasting Corporation was preoccupied with other things, and it did not hire a women's broadcaster.

Children were also under-represented as voices although some programming was aimed at them as listeners. One program that the BCN arranged was a children's serial adventure with an aviation theme, *Howie Wing*, created by the American advertising firm J. Walter Thompson for the Kellogg Corporation. The local distributor for Kellogg, Charles R. Bell, reported 'thousands of letters from practically all parts of Newfoundland including Labrador.' He went on to claim that the Howie Wing Club membership in Newfoundland was greater per capita than that of Canada.[137] Other dramatic serials were later added. In 1945, for example, VONF began broadcasting the popular American crime/adventure serial, the *Green Hornet*, a 'modern Robin Hood in a metropolitan setting' who each week brought to justice 'criminals and racketeers, crooked politicians and big-time gangsters.'[138]

In his autobiography, Joseph Smallwood reflected upon his time as the Barrelman and described the pattern of listening described the 1930s and 1940s:

> In the outports that had no electricity, and that was the overwhelming majority of them, there were only battery-operated radios. Batteries were expensive to keep up, and so not too many families could afford to have a radio. Those who did not would crowd the homes of those who did, but the owners were careful to always turn their radios only, or mainly, for three programs: mine at a quarter to seven; Al Vardy's at seven o'clock; and the famous Gerald S. Doyle local news bulletin at a quarter to eight each night. In short, my program gave them entertainment and enlightenment about Newfoundland, Vardy's gave them the world news, and Doyle's gave them Newfoundland news.[139]

Aubrey Tizzard's memoir concurred with Smallwood's account. Tizzard reported listening to the *Gerald S. Doyle News Bulletin*, the *Barrelman*, and the foreign news, which he wrote was always referred to as the 'war news' once the war had started. He did sometimes listen to *Superman*, and during the war Margo Davies's program, which is discussed in the next chapter. By restricting his listening to these programs, Tizzard found that his battery would last approximately a year, which was as often as he could afford to replace it.[140] As we have seen, there was much more to the programming of the BCN than these iconic programs, but evidence supports Smallwood's contention that rural listeners looked to radio for news of the world and of themselves more than entertainment.

One characteristic of the Western world's modern era was that authors, publishers, and capitalist entertainment companies appropriated folk culture, whether song or tale, as private property. The cultural commodity could then be sold to consumers, who were sometimes members of the very community that had collectively created the cultural form. Radio broadcasting played a complex and contradictory role in this enterprise. Doyle and O'Leary, for example, sponsored programs that gathered material from the oral tradition, as well as from contemporary authors, then provided it free to listeners in their homes. The cost to listeners was, of course, that they had to listen to advertising for the products that Doyle and O'Leary retailed, but the broadcasters were themselves part of the cultural community. Just as people modified material from the common cultural corpus and exchanged it within communities, so did broadcasters. As Smallwood said, his 'voice became part of the very culture.'[141] Its persuasiveness came not from his position of authority, but from his position as a participant in the culture. Unlike their American contemporary Walt Disney, Newfoundland cultural producers did not take folk culture and transform it into patented commodities, but disseminated it for others within the culture to use and modify.

4 Gibraltar of North America: Wartime Radio

The BCN had signed on the air at a time of building international tensions. It hardly had time to develop its schedule before Galgay and the Board of Directors had to adjust to wartime conditions. As German troops moved into Poland, the Commission introduced censorship and wartime restrictions. As part of the empire, Newfoundland was at war when the United Kingdom declared war, several days before Canada in a symbolic act of independence declared war separately. There was little feeling that Newfoundland might stay out of the conflict, and people's immediate reaction was to steel themselves for the hardship that was to come. No one anticipated it in 1939, but the 1940s were to be a period of significant social change and economic prosperity in Newfoundland. The revival of prices for fish and paper and the economic boom precipitated by the construction of military bases ended the long depression that had affected so many aspects of life in Newfoundland during the 1920s and 1930s. The 'friendly invasion' of thousands of young servicemen and construction workers from other countries also introduced additional avenues though which civilians could consume American popular culture. Radio was also at the centre of many social and cultural changes throughout Newfoundland, not just in the communities near military bases. Canadian and American servicemen took to the air on VONF to provide a range of entertainment programming. The creation of an American military radio station in 1943, VOUS, in particular, created an alternative to the BCN. The economic revival and enhanced access to American entertainment, as well as wartime conditions, distorted the activities of the BCN from what it might have been. Many of its hours on the air were turned over to the war effort, so the station's management were not able to devote their effort to the programming they would have liked. On a more positive note, the revived economy increased people's disposable income and allowed some to purchase radio receivers for the first time. Wartime restrictions upon the manufacture and export of radios for civilian uses limited the number of new receivers that could be purchased, however. Despite the fact that not everyone had regular access to a radio receiver, the Commission's investment in broadcasting was justified by the successful uses of the BCN to support the war effort.

Newspapers had been the public's principal source of information during 1914–18 when radio had been used only for military purposes, but radio broadcasting was a significant participant in the home front during the Second World War. This war was also one in which the home front and the battle front overlapped; civilians in Europe bore the brunt of casualties and civil societies became militarized. North America experienced some of these same effects, but was largely spared the most horrific aspects of war. Radio broadcasting brought reminders of home to the troops and seamen and news of the conflict into the homes of civilians. This made war an experience mediated by broadcasting for many who lived through the period. One historian of radio broadcasting has gone as far as to say that the Second World War was the first 'living room war' in which listeners in their homes heard extensive coverage, on the spot reporting, and eye-witness accounts.[1] The BCN provided just that sort of mediation of events, as well as operating as a coordinating agent for the wartime state. News, entertainment for troops, campaigns selling war bonds, and hundreds of other special wartime broadcasts made it a media war. In Central Europe, radio broadcasting's effectiveness at directing an emotional message from one person to the masses had made it an effective tool in the hands of fascists. Allied governments, including Newfoundland's Commission of Government, also used radio to coordinate the home front and bolster morale. The Commission did not aim any of the programming of its short-wave transmitter VONH at Axis listeners, but did make full use of radio to communicate with Newfoundlanders.

As we have seen, the state-owned broadcaster and the Commission of Government itself were not universally welcome in 1939. There had been some criticism that the Commission was creating a propaganda apparatus in the BCN, but now that the country was at war and Britain was beleaguered, many people felt it was disloyal to question the constitutional status quo or the Broadcasting Corporation's policies. This gave the BCN an opportunity to expand its role without public debate, while allowing it to restrict the expansion of its privately owned competitors. Even in the United States where corporate and ideological resistance to state broadcasting had been successful, the New Deal and the mobilization for the war had provided an opportunity for the American government to move into radio much more than was possible before or after the Roosevelt years.[2] The BCN had a record of public service during the war of which its broadcasters were justifiably proud, but by 1945 they also regretted that wartime conditions prevented the Corporation from fulfilling all of its potential as a cultural force.

This chapter also argues that the BCN's coverage of the war in Europe reinforced the British character of Newfoundland's war effort. By 1939 American, British, and Canadian radio networks had developed news apparatus and were developing actuality broadcasts that allowed listeners to hear distant events while they were comfortably at home. Newfoundland's broadcaster could not afford an overseas correspondent like the Columbia Broadcasting Service's Edward R. Murrow or the CBC's Matthew Halton, but relied heavily upon the BBC for war news.[3] Newfoundland listeners, for example, heard a rebroadcast of the BBC's transmission of Neville Chamberlain's resignation speech, Winston Churchill's first radio address as prime minister, as well as daily BBC news broadcasts throughout the war.[4]

It would be easy to romanticize the quality of the BBC news to which many Newfoundlanders listened; the much-celebrated reputation for objectivity and independence from the government of the BBC news was earned during the war. At first, many Britons had to turn to newspapers or even German propaganda broadcasts such as Radio Hamburg for basic information on how the war was going. During the first weeks, British listeners and public officials widely criticized the BBC for not telling the public the truth about what was happening, but also for hurting morale or giving information to the enemy when it reported the events of the war. Despite the criticism, the BBC broadcasts bridged the home front with the battle front. As one historian put it,

> The British people were only told what their war leaders wanted them to know, were told much that was deliberately false, and were denied knowledge of much more that they may have wished to know ... [but] over the course of the war the BBC News Department went some way in recognizing the needs and demands of its audience and did the best it could to meet them, whether in interpreting military communiqués for the ordinary listener or reporting the Blitz in such a way that recognized the plight

of the blitzed, to connecting the Home Front and the battlefront with eye-witness descriptions of life on the front line. The introduction of 'human-ising' touches lifted the cloud of officialdom before it became too weighty, and made the bulletins come alive at times of good news. War commentar-ies, whether they added much in the way of information, put the fighting into that wider context which listeners sought. War features helped listen-ers to feel, however vicariously, that even in their homes they were part of the struggle.[5]

Each of these observations could have been made of the BCN's cover-age of the war as well.

Although Newfoundlanders were overwhelmingly native born, sev-eral factors reinforced people's sense of themselves as part of the em-pire. The Newfoundland government consisted in part of British civil servants, a large number of Newfoundlanders served in the British Armed Services, and many people thought of Newfoundland as 'Brit-ain's oldest colony.' Newfoundlanders identified strongly with the UK, and hearing the British war news every day reinforced that feeling. In addition to the daily VONF rebroadcast of the BBC news, the BCN also contracted the British-based news service Reuters to be a source of international news. Since the Reuters service, which the BCN pur-chased, had been compiled for distribution in North America, it was designed to inform North Americans of events in Europe. Reuters did not believe it was important to tell North Americans what was happen-ing in their own hemisphere – information that listeners could get from other sources. This left the BCN in the peculiar position of lacking good coverage of American news and having even poorer coverage of Cana-dian news, even though Newfoundland was part of North America. The commander of American forces in Newfoundland, Major General Brooks, for example, later complained that the BCN was 'devoted' to BBC news and failed to give an American perspective.[6] Some interna-tional news was compiled in St John's, but it was written and read by a British-born commentator. The Newfoundland Butter Company, which was owned by the British-based multinational corporation Lever, paid for an international news commentary by Allan Fraser starting in 1939 and running until the end of the war. Fraser was the Scottish-born and University of Edinburgh–educated professor of history at Memorial University College in St John's. Some news content had come from American sources, before the war the BCN had subscribed to Ameri-can-based Trans-Radio News Service, but its alleged 'German connections' led to the service being suspended for a time.[7] As indicated in chapter 3, that news service also consisted in large measure of war news, with some American but little Canadian news. In sum, the news that Newfoundland listeners heard undoubtedly made the war seem immediate and personal, and re-established a feeling that Newfoundlanders had a familial relationship with Britain. The BCN's own wartime commentaries also reinforced the idea that Newfoundland's war was a British war. When Winston Churchill became prime minister, for example, the member of the BCN Board of Governors R.S. Furlong broadcast an address summarizing Churchill's career for Newfoundland listeners.[8]

The BBC created two programs specifically for Newfoundland, as it had for Canada, the United States, and the West Indies. In November 1939 the Empire Service had been renamed the Overseas Service in keeping with the BBC's new emphasis on uniting all those who resisted the Axis powers. In doing so, in the words of one historian, it shed part of its 'peculiar brand of comfortable English parochialism.'[9] The North American Service employed many Canadians and was tailored to North American tastes, even while the content remained British. As the BBC noted, 'The primary audience to this service is accustomed to the American way of putting over radio shows, and that way has been developed for the last twenty years by all the resources that commercial enterprise can command.'[10] These programs generally, and the two specifically created for Newfoundland, did much to bolster morale of Newfoundlanders serving overseas and those on the home front.

The more influential of these programs was variously titled *Calling Newfoundland* or *Hello Newfoundland*, and the other was known as the *Newsletter*. Broadcast at 20:30 GMT on Mondays and Wednesdays respectively, these programs were carried over the BBC short-wave transmitter and were recorded off the air by the BCN and rebroadcast on the AM band over VONF for those who did not have short-wave radio receivers. The first broadcast of the *Newsletter*, on 19 December 1940, began with a talk upon Newfoundlanders' experiences in Britain by D. James Davies, Newfoundland's trade commissioner in the UK. The Welsh-born Davies had earlier lived in Newfoundland and now ran the Newfoundland Office in London. The Newfoundland Office would have been the office of the Newfoundland High Commissioner, but such a position would have been redundant since the Commission answered directly to the secretary of state for dominions affairs. During the war the Newfoundland Office became a coordinating centre for mail and packages destined for Newfoundlanders serving in British forces (whose exact location was secret).

A recording of one of the earliest broadcasts has a group of men singing a few songs, and a British officer speaking about the excellence of the Newfoundlanders under his command. Typically such programs devoted much attention to reassuring Newfoundlanders that their county's contribution was important and valued. Many of the men were then given the opportunity to pass on brief Christmas greetings to loved ones at home.[11] Subsequent episodes of the program followed the same general pattern, with a talk upon Newfoundland's war effort by either Davies or another man, some music, followed by greetings from servicemen. A January 1941 broadcast, for example, included an interview with the Royal Artillery regiment's sergeant major, his description of part of a boxing match between two Newfoundlanders, and a group of men singing a comic song about Hitler.[12] The BBC and the Royal Artillery hoped such programming would give listeners home in Newfoundland the impression that the men of the regiment were in good physical condition and had high morale.

After having several male voices hosting the program during the early weeks, the program settled upon a young woman as announcer and interviewer. This was an unusual step for radio on either side of the Atlantic before the war. In the United States, as in Newfoundland, women generally performed as singers, actresses, and children's entertainers, but rarely as announcers. Although, historians of broadcasting in the US have often under reported the number of women on the air,[13] female announcers were unknown on the BBC until the development of the Forces Programme (as opposed to the Home Service), a service devoted particularly to maintaining the morale of men in uniform but soon popular with civilian listeners as well.[14] Even more remarkably, during the war the program was produced by a succession of women as well. Margot Rhys Davies, daughter of D.J. Davies, took over hosting *Calling Newfoundland* by April 1941. Davies had been born and attended school in Newfoundland while her father had worked for the Newfoundland government.[15] She had finished school in Britain and had acted on the London stage as well as in a couple of British movies. At the start of the war she became involved in the War Comforts Committee run out of the Newfoundland Office in London. She now gave up acting for a career with the BBC. Davies was one of a number of 'girlfriends of the empire' employed by the BBC in London to broadcast to the troops of colonies and dominions.

These girls ... work at night in an underground Theatre in London, broad-casting to the soldiers of the Empire. Each girl 'covers' her own section of the globe, and has a programme built round her voice. Her job is to keep the men thinking of home. One picture [in the *Sunday Despatch*] shows them in the canteen; the other reading fan mail.[16]

The armed services of the period were overwhelmingly male, and mostly young, so a feminine voice provided a little normalcy and reminded soldiers, sailors, and airmen that wives, mothers, and girl-friends were waiting for them at home once their job was done. To her duties broadcasting to servicemen, Davies added the program for the Newfoundland home front.[17] The show's producer during 1943, Miranda Dulley, reported that the Newfoundland 'boys' were brought into the BBC offices 'to fix up the programme that goes to their home, and to settle the details of what they were going to tell their people about their lives and their jobs over here.' This gave the BBC the oppor-tunity to censor any comments as well as ensure that there was enough material prepared for the broadcast. Many of those who spoke on the program seem a little stilted in their speech, likely the result of reading from a script that had been cleared by the censor or perhaps a reflection of their nervousness. As Dulley described the program,

We always end up with a special message to the folks at home. It's so easy to picture those parents in Newfoundland hearing their son telling about what must seem to them his sickeningly breath-taking escapes from death – and then, hearing him come back to normal, asking for some cigarettes and sending his love to them and to the girl friend ... The commentator who looks after the passing of these messages is Margot Davies, herself a Newfoundland girl, who works her never very large self to an even thin-ner shadow in the Comforts Room at the Newfoundland Trade Commis-sioner's Office. She is mother by proxy to every Newfoundlander away from home. She remembers their names and the names of their girls, whom their second cousins married, and what they all used to do back home. In return she has the love and respect of all of them.[18]

It is worth noting, first, that without the particular wartime condi-tions the BBC would not have had such a feminine division. Although women were important consumers of radio during the 1940s there were fewer female producers of radio than male.

Second, as indicated in an earlier chapter, Davies had few female counterparts in Newfoundland radio. In the male world of broadcasting, the principal roles available to women were singers, children's broadcasters, or, as in this case, surrogate mothers (or perhaps more aptly big sisters) to the boys in uniform. Part of the default position of radio as male, the historian Michelle Hilmes suggests, was that the physical appearance of male broadcasters went without comment. Broadcasting was in a medium in which body shape or face should not have mattered, but broadcasting companies frequently described the appearance of women.[19] These things mattered to listeners as well. Three listeners in St John's, for example, argued over the Palmolive Girl's appearance. When requesting Smallwood send them a photograph to settle the dispute, they commented, 'We think it natural to form an opinion of any radio character whom you hear over the air, but have not seen.'[20] Not only did Dulley describe Davies's slender frame, but explicitly set out her role as mother to the boys (not a potential girlfriend, who could be competition to the wives and girlfriends back home). Davies not only reassured listeners that their loved ones were well, but that they were faithful to those at home. A recording of one of her wartime broadcasts includes Davies's comment, 'From the way the boys tell me they miss their wives and girlfriends, the young women of Newfoundland have nothing to worry about in that direction.'[21]

The format of the program varied considerably from one week to the next. A recording of Davies's *Radio Magazine*, as she sometimes called it, has her reading messages from Newfoundland servicemen as well as interviewing two of them about their service and impressions of life in the UK.[22] Davies also frequently read letters from servicemen who were unable to go to the London studio to record their messages.[23] In this respect the format was considerably different from the news, for example, in which an authoritative male voice imparted information. Davies's program consisted in large measure of interviews with servicemen or officers who provided the authority and veracity of the information. She was positioned as an interviewer who did not know military things first-hand and could thus ask the obvious question without looking ill-informed. Women would not be expected to know war from their own experience. She could also stand in for the civilian listener, who could imagine himself or herself asking the same sorts of questions that came to Davies.

While often formulaic and brief (letters generally greeted specific people, said the serviceman was well, and thanked family members for the packages they had sent), the messages could be more elaborate. In

September 1943, for example, Davies read a letter in which a seaman informed his family in Newfoundland that he was now the father of a baby girl and that his wife and daughter were well. The messages in this show were divided into groups – Navy, Royal Artillery, loggers, etc. – each separated from the others by appropriate musical interludes.[24] In one broadcast, which was typical of many, she was joined by Lieutenant Pat Bennett who gave the 'News from Depot' update on the men in hospital, returning home, getting new postings, and getting married.[25] Some indication of the success of her program came in February 1944 when the King gave Davies her decoration as a Member of the Order of the British Empire.

At the end of the war, Warren McAlpine, director of the North American Service of the BBC, appeared on *Calling Newfoundland* to send a Christmas greeting and mark the fact that about four hundred programs had been transmitted to the country. He commented that the BBC saw Davies as one of their own, although she was 'pure Newfoundland,'[26] even though to a Newfoundland ear she had a slightly British accent. Davies continued to interview Newfoundlanders, often asking them for news of other Newfoundlanders they had met, rather than exclusively passing on messages of their own. Davis now expanded the show to allow Newfoundlanders living in Britain, and those visiting on holiday, to speak to their friends and relatives at home over the radio. BBC official H. Rooney Pelletier wrote that he was pleased that *Calling Newfoundland* continued to have a sizeable audience after the war, and asked Galgay for advice on which parts of the program were popular with the Newfoundland audience, since 'we must sometimes feel that we are shooting in the dark.'[27] One recording of the program illustrates its post-war character. It opened with Davies saying, 'Calling from Britain to Newfoundland,' then a band playing a couple of stanzas of Art Scammell's song 'The Squid Jigging Ground.' When the music ended, she greeted the audience with 'Hello Newfoundland, this is your commentator Margot Davies speaking from the BBC with another edition of your Newfoundland corner,' followed by material with no clear Newfoundland connection – a report upon her visit the Welsh industrial exhibit. The show closed with an interview with George Moyles of St John's, who continued to serve in the Royal Navy, who then passed on a personal message to his family and friends in Newfoundland.[28] The BBC short-wave program continued to be hosted by Davies until her death in 1972, when she was mourned by several generations of Newfoundlanders who had found in her a wel-

Robert (Bob) MacLeod playing the VONF studio organ. MacLeod began his career as an announcer and musician on VONF in 1935. He read the Gerald S. Doyle News, provided musical accompaniment to many VONF programs and arranged music for musicians who performed on the air. He also produced programs such as the 'Children's Savings Programme.' Even after leaving the BCN in 1947 he continued as a part-time broadcaster. (CBC Newfoundland and Labrador, NLR0001)

George R. Williams, Chairman of the Board of Governors (left), and William F. Galgay, General Manager, depart Torbay Airport for Ottawa, 19 October 1948. Williams chaired the board during the whole of the BCN's existence. Galgay managed VONF from its inception in 1932, through the years it formed the anchor station of the BCN and then as manager of the Newfoundland region of the CBC until his death in 1966. This photograph shows the two men leaving St John's on their way to Ottawa to negotiate the incorporation of the BCN into the CBC. (CBC Newfoundland and Labrador, NLR0002)

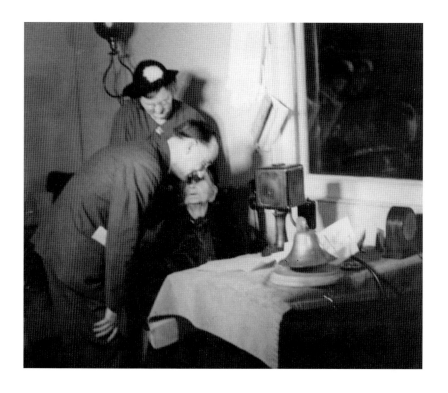

Joseph R. Smallwood speaking with Ellen Carroll (1827-1942) at the VONF studio, likely on the occasion of her 115th birthday in 1942. Behind them is Mrs Carroll's daughter, Nell O'Brien. Smallwood's Barrelman program had made Mrs Carroll into a celebrity through at least two birthday broadcasts. (CBC Newfoundland and Labrador, NLR0003)

VONF announcer Aubrey MacDonald. MacDonald began as a part-time unpaid sports announcer on station VOGY in 1937. When VOGY was incorporated into VONF and purchased by the Commission Government, MacDonald became an announcer with the BCN. MacDonald tried to emulate American sports broadcasters whom he admired. 'Aubrey Mac,' as he was known, later became a popular raconteur and much-loved grand old man of Newfoundland radio. (CBC Newfoundland and Labrador, NLR0004)

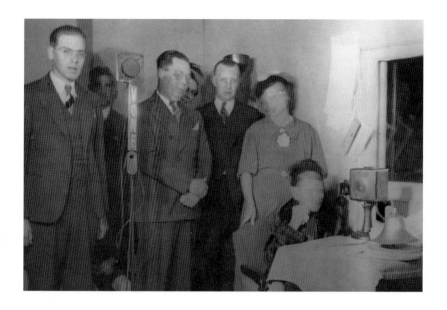

(L-R) Bob MacLeod; Gordon Halley, Accountant for VONF; Oliver L. Vardy, announcer; unidentified woman; William F. Galgay; Nell O'Brien, Mrs. Carroll's daughter, Mrs Ellen Carroll. Halley had been the salesman for VONF when it was owned by Avalon Telephone, and continued to manage the day-to-day finances when it became a public station. Vardy, host of the Newfoundland Butter Company News as well as other programs, was the highest paid broadcaster of his day. His news commentaries made him into a celebrity whose views on world affairs were printed in newspapers and presented in public lectures. (CBC Newfoundland and Labrador, NLR0005)

Michael F. Harrington in 1946. Harrington was one of the early graduates of Memorial University College, a 'disc jockey,' and an aspiring journalist when he was hired to replace Smallwood as the Barrelman in 1943. Harrington was elected to the National Convention in 1946 and was a prominent critic of the way that Smallwood proposed Newfoundland's entry into the Canadian confederation. As the Barrelman, Harrington had a more academic and less populist style than Smallwood, although he was also a nationalist. (*Atlantic Guardian*, 1946, Archives and Manuscript Division, QEII Library Memorial University of Newfoundland)

The 'Premier Pals' (L-R) Mickey Frelich, Reg Ivany, Ralph Ivany, Bob MacLeod. The BCN included a great range of musical styles from 'country' to 'swing,' from 'sacred' to 'popular,' and MacLeod performed or arranged a great portion of all styles. (*Atlantic Guardian*, 1946, Archives and Manuscript Division, QEII Library Memorial University of Newfoundland)

Chief Control Operator, A.N. House, in the VONF Control Room. The studio was located in the Newfoundland Hotel in St John's, while the station's transmitter was located at the former Royal Navy Wireless facility at Mount Pearl. (*Atlantic Guardian*, 1946, Archives and Manuscript Division, QEII Library, Memorial University of Newfoundland)

Joseph R. Smallwood as the Barrelman. The ship's bell on his desk was rung to punctuate each of the items he broadcast. With some justification, Smallwood later claimed his own voice was part of Newfoundland's culture. The Barrelman program and the later broadcasts of the National Convention not only entertained and informed Newfoundlanders but helped launch Smallwood's career in public life. He led the pro-confederation faction during the constitutional debates of the late 1940s and translated his profile and reputation into a political career that saw him serve as Premier of the province from 1949 until 1971. (Archives and Manuscript Division, QEII Library, Memorial University of Newfoundland)

VOGY Studio at Newfoundland Hotel, 1934. This early commercial station had 'home built' transmitters rather than equipment purchased from a manufacturer. As jury rigged as it was, VONF later moved into these studios when it amalgamated with its competitor. It was not until after the BCN became part of the CBC that it acquired its own building. (Archives and Manuscript Division, QEII Library, Memorial University of Newfoundland)

VOGY Studio at Newfoundland Hotel, 1934. VOGY had used several rooms at the government-owned Newfoundland Hotel as its studio, a common practice among radio stations during the 1920s and 1930s since it lent some prestige to the hotel and it was easy to broadcast dances and speeches from the hotel ball room. Carpets and curtains provided a little dampening of the sound to make for more effective broadcasts of music. (Archives and Manuscript Division, QEII Library, Memorial University of Newfoundland)

Reverend James G. Joyce sitting in radio station 8WMC. In 1924 Joyce combined his radio hobby with a desire to transmit church services, and to bring
morally beneficial entertainment to listeners. While he had 'home built' his first
station, this photograph shows the 500-watt commercially built transmitter he
purchased in 1927. Financial donations from each of the Christian denominations supported the station, which was ecumenical and devoted to public
service. The photograph likely dates from between 1927 and 1930. (Radio Station VOWR)

come face in London when they were passing through the city or in the UK studying.[29]

Margo Davies's *Calling Newfoundland* was much like the BBC programs for families of troops in other parts of the empire and its programs for the families of British servicemen who were overseas. It was also similar to the *Doyle Bulletin*. It included some news of general interest on how Newfoundland servicemen were doing with specific messages from one person to his family. The BCN not only rebroadcast *Calling Newfoundland* from Britain, but created its own message program for its allies. A 'Salute to Canada' was broadcast on 3 September 1942. It attempted to reassure Canadians that their sons were welcome and well in their overseas posting to Newfoundland. Held at the Terra Nova Club and hosted by the young part-time broadcaster Donald Jamieson, it opened with 'Oh Canada,' followed by musical entertainment and an address by Lady Walwyn, wife of the governor of Newfoundland, to families in Canada. Canadian servicemen then passed messages to loved ones at home.[30]

While Newfoundlanders were reminded daily of the hardships experienced by their British cousins, the Commission also used radio more directly to create public support for its policies. When the UK government traded the right to build bases on Newfoundland territory for fifty American warships, Leonard Outerbridge, a veteran of the First World War, director of air raid precautions and a prominent Newfoundland businessman, spoke over VONF in an attempt to diffuse potential opposition. Outerbridge countered potential objections by suggesting that Newfoundland's loss of sovereignty over some of its territory was a sacrifice worth making, if it brought the US, which had not yet entered the war, and the UK closer together in the fight for democracy.[31] The Commission did not always hide its policy announcements behind a Newfoundlander who could claim independence from government. It sometimes addressed the public directly. Commissioner of Finance Penson, for example, spoke to the Board of Trade on the government's wartime finance, and had this equivalent of a budget speech broadcast over VONF.[32] In 1941 the economy revived, and the Commission of Government shifted its attention from economic reconstruction to supporting the UK war effort and planning to cope with the effects of a potential economic boom and bust. The Commission sponsored a series of broadcasts encouraging the sale of war bonds to adults and a series for children to encourage the sale of war savings stamps. Such sales not only financed the country's war effort but were part of the

Commission's endeavour to encourage people to accumulate savings they could draw upon during a possible post-war recession.[33]

The BCN soon took upon itself the role of encouraging enlistment. At the start of the war, Galgay joined a committee of Great War veterans and other citizens, formed to discuss recruiting.[34] Starting in December 1939, and running for a couple of years, the weekly *Recruitment Programme* encouraged the enlistment of prospective servicemen and celebrated the accomplishments of Newfoundlanders in uniform. At times the program advertised the benefits of enlistment. In one episode, Colonel W.F. Rendell reported upon program's success in both recruiting and in encouraging recruits to continue to work in productive employment until called up. He also gave addresses for people who wanted to write words of encouragement to servicemen (via the Newfoundland trade office in London).[35] In another broadcast Rendell discussed the British Army's pay scale in considerable detail.[36] The program also cajoled young men into supporting the Newfoundlanders overseas and doing their part for country and empire. During an intensive propaganda blitz aimed at raising 1,000 men – without whom, listeners were told, the two Newfoundland regiments risked being staffed by Englishmen and losing their Newfoundland character – more than twenty speakers were heard during a single week. Commemorating the accomplishments and the sacrifices of the Royal Newfoundland Regiment in the 1914–18 war had been a focal point of Newfoundland nationalism. Recruiters hoped to build upon such pride by challenging young people to maintain the Newfoundland composition of the two artillery regiments during the current war. One of those speakers, newspaper editor C.E.A. Jeffrey commented that perhaps young men did not listen to the *Recruitment Programme*, presumably because they were not interested in the sort of entertainment provided, so their fathers and mothers who were listening should convince them to do their duty by enlisting.[37]

The program used music to entice listeners to listen to the recruitment propaganda and set a suitably patriotic tone.[38] Much of this content was patriotic British music or old standards. As the *Daily News* described one program,

Broadcast from the Ball Room of the Newfoundland Hotel, the regular weekly recruiting programme last night was another in a series of the best patriotic efforts we have had for some time on the radio. Mr H.W. Stirling,

LLCM, and his associates of St Thomas's Choir bore the burden of a varied but most attractive arrangement of solos, part songs, ballads, shanties of the sea, and the ever popular 'There'll Always be an England.'[39]

(That last song had been penned in England during the first weeks of the war in an effort to encourage patriotism.)[40] Another program featured 'Anchors Aweigh,' 'Rule Britannia,' 'Land of Hope and Glory,' and 'J.R. Lench another veteran of the last war sang an original number "The Cream of Newfoundland" which was a distinct novelty.'[41] It was not all martial music, odes to the empire, and the popular music of an earlier generation. The broadcast had been credited with popularizing a swing tune 'Marching Together' written by two Newfoundland servicemen, sales of the sheet music of which raised money for the war effort.[42] By the second year, the *Recruitment Programme* included talks and music by active servicemen who where home on leave, or American and Canadian servicemen stationed in Newfoundland. An example of the latter would be 'a song recital by Leading Signalman J. White of the Royal Canadian Navy, a concert artist of more than ordinary ability.'[43] Besides popular music the *Recruitment Programme* included such things as radio plays related to wartime themes. An English author, Monica Marsden, contributed a play *Contraband Cargo*, written specifically for the Newfoundland station, which a group of amateur actors performed on air.[44] Galgay soon secured the script of a second play from England, *London in Darkness*, which helped listeners empathize with the British home front during the Blitz.[45] Over time the program evolved into a variety show, although it always had a serious and patriotic undertone. A 1942 broadcast consisted of

> opening commentary – the badge of Newfoundland; musical interlude; a true tale of the navy, written by Capt. Taprell Dorling, DSO RN and presented by Mr W.J. Woodford of the Central Recruiting Committee; music interlude; Lewis Waller's Presentation of Henry V at Harfleur from the Shakespearian Play; Impressions of a Newfoundlander in Training with the RCAF, a personal message from Sgt Wireless Operator Clarence Morgan of Bay Roberts; closing commentary, Rule Britannia.[46]

The *Recruitment Programme* was the only program to receive weekly promotion in the local newspapers, for newspaper owners likely saw such promotion as part of their contribution to the war, while advertising commercial programs would have been a boost to a competitor for advertising dollars.

The *Recruiting Programme* also became a message program, somewhat like Davies's:

> Listening into the recruiting programme broadcast on last Tuesday night, Mr J.M. Davis, of Lemarchant Road, was delighted to hear the commentator's extracts from a letter received from Seaman John Farnham of Heart's Content, in which he said he had just met four Newfoundlanders in South Africa, one of whom was an old student at the Prince of Wales College, Arthur Davis of St John's. Mr Davis had not heard from his son for six months and this radio flash was particularly gratifying as indeed were the portions read from the other chaps serving with the Royal Navy and RCAF. The Recruiting broadcast serves as a great means of bringing official news direct to relatives, and this was best demonstrated in the case of Airman James Ledingham Templeton, the message regarding whom was, through the courtesy of Mr Templeton flashed to the country within a half hour of the receipt of the cable. The sponsors of the Recruiting programme are only too happy to have personal letters and experiences from men overseas, and parents who forward these letters may be assured that they are appreciated.[47]

It is apparent that the *Recruitment Programme* used families who had received letters from men overseas as a source of information, which was then presented as 'official' news. Not only was this an effective network for sharing information on the well-being of servicemen, but, like the *Doyle Bulletin*, the news simulated a community among listeners with the details of where men met each other, where they went to school, and a hundred other incidental details.

Wartime is often a period in which the state takes a more overt control over media than is accepted in peacetime, and censorship in Newfoundland was restrictive. Rules prohibited mention on the air, for example, of the name of any ship in conjunction with its location, time of arrival, or departure, or any of the activities of the armed services. Radio was usually a very ephemeral medium, in which broadcasters' comments could be improvised, although announcers in the 1940s did so less than later generations of broadcasters. But in wartime, all talks had to be written and approved by the censor before being broadcast. There was to be no deviation from the written text, and the transmitter operator was instructed to cut the speaker off the air if this rule were broken. This would have made less difference to the tone of the programming than one might think, since announcers often wrote scripts with banter that simulated spontaneity. The chief censor was Frazer's successor as secretary of posts and telegraphs, Major J. Haig-Smith, a First World War veteran who had been seconded from the British Post Office.[48] He delegated the day-to-day censorship duties over radio to people such as Robert Furlong, who would strike out sections with a blue pencil if necessary. On at least one occasion, an intelligence officer with the Canadian Navy examined a specific news broadcast after the fact, presumably to determine if it contained information intended for the enemy, and found it 'quite innocent.'[49]

The tight control over information elicited some criticism from the press. The journalist J.T. Meaney claimed that the Canadian scientist Frederick Banting died unnecessarily because the radio could not notify people who lived near the crash site that Banting's aircraft had gone down.[50] Banting had survived the accident, but later succumbed to his injuries before anyone reached the aircraft. An editorial in the *Daily News* also complained that censorship was more restrictive in Newfoundland than in the UK or the US.[51] It is remarkable how little local news there was of what in retrospect were important events, such as the construction of a military airport in Labrador. The Goose Bay base was first mentioned in the Newfoundland press only after a question had been asked about it in the British House of Commons. Canadian, American, and British newspapers occasionally published items about military activities in Newfoundland that would have been prohibited in a Newfoundland newspaper or on Newfoundland radio. While the newspapers sometimes resented the restrictions, Haig-Smith's role as chief censor and position on the Board of the BCN ensured little conflict between the radio station and the Department of Justice and Defence.

The war prompted operational changes at the BCN as well. F.W. Heakes of the RCAF noted that Allied aircraft benefited from being able to home in on the direction of the VONF transmitter and asked if it were possible for the station to remain on air with programming from 8:00 a.m. to midnight and then broadcast a tone during the remaining hours.[52] As it had during its days under private ownership, the station continued to broadcast during the lunch hour, sign off, and return to the air for the evening. To save electric power and wear on the transmitter, the station did not expand its regular hours. But the station some-times remained on the air for extended hours so that navigators would be able to use the signal as a beacon or signed off early if its signal inter-fered with searchers' efforts to find a lost aircraft.[53] BCN also passed on a coded signal to lighthouse keepers each day: '*A* is for apple, *N* is for nuts.' Had they not received the message they would have extin-guished the lights to make it more difficult for enemy ships to navigate. Such concerns were not abstract. Unlike most of North America, New-foundland was on the front line. Ships in Newfoundland waters were torpedoed, including the ferry that connected the country with Canada, and survivors from German U-boat attacks occasionally arrived in St John's. The country's airfields and ports were part of the war of the Atlantic, and the sense of being a garrison country was enhanced by the arrival of thousands of American troops.

The arrival of the American troopship *Edmund B. Alexander*, carrying the first of thousands of American troops, changed Newfoundland. In this area, too, radio broadcasting transformed people's lives. New-foundland's trade and finances had recovered during 1940, but that was overshadowed the following year by the economic boom prompted by the arrival of the troops and construction workers necessary to build large military bases and smaller outposts. One could have been forgiven for not having realized the significance of the earlier arrival of the Cana-dian servicemen. Not wanting to pass on information that might be of use to the enemy, the Canadians did not publicize their deployment to Newfoundland. Not so the Americans, who were not yet at war. The *Edmund B. Alexander* was the largest vessel to have entered the narrows of St John's harbour, its arrival heralded by the ship's brass band play-ing 'Hail, Hail, the Gang's All Here' as it berthed.[54] Galgay marked the occasion with a broadcast from the pier describing the ship entering the harbour.[55] The construction of military bases soon supported an eco-nomic boom that employed a large portion of the Newfoundland work-force. The servicemen were themselves a cultural force. Over the following decades, contact between civilians and servicemen reinforced the existing taste for American popular culture among Newfound-landers.

The radio remained the only method available to the government to effectively address the public across the island. When the Americans needed 500 labourers, for example, a broadcast announcement over VONF resulted in sufficient applicants for the work.[56] The BCN also provided things such as a series of broadcasts upon air raid precautions to prepare listeners for a possible forthcoming bombing.[57]

The presence of thousands of foreign troops and construction workers revived the economy and, as we have seen, took the wind from the sails of the cooperative movement, but it did not end the need for what was perhaps the longest-standing educational program – public health broadcasts. These had been a feature of VONF since at least the fall of 1935, and had been printed in the newspapers as well.[58] Such broadcasts provided information upon a range of infectious diseases and nutritional deficiencies from tuberculosis to rickets. Radio could be particularly effective in allowing physicians to communicate directly to people at home in an intimate setting. In one undated broadcast, Dr Ray Bennett began his discussion of tuberculosis with the opening, 'I don't want you to think of this as a radio broadcast, but as rather as a friendly chat,' and proceeded to lay out the Health Department's program of vaccination and testing.[59] The Commission's efforts to improve public health are often cited as one of the most progressive and humane areas of its policy, but this was also an area in which the autonomy of the Broadcasting Corporation from the Commission was tested.[60]

Years before the arrival of foreign servicemen, there were occasional public health broadcasts dealing with sexually transmitted diseases. Newfoundland radio was unusual in this regard. Broadcast regulators in most countries banned discussion of such diseases entirely, until the increased risk of transmission during wartime caused them to revise their policies. The public health officials were careful to not offend listeners' sense of propriety during the broadcasts upon VONF, on what was, after all, a technology that brought the outside world into the home where women and children were listening. One such broadcast on VONF, for example, made reference to the fact that one might have syphilis without symptoms in the 'affected area' and transmit it to one's spouse. Such people were advised to seek medical treatment, although the program mentioned nothing about the prevention of the spread of the disease.[61] Presumably a discussion of prophylactics or extramarital relations would have been ruled inappropriate for radio. Newfoundland governments, including the Commission, were fearful of antagonizing the Roman Catholic church.

The Department of Health had a more modern attitude. Infectious diseases were medical problems, not moral ones. Dr Leonard Miller's radio talks on the subject promoted the idea that venereal diseases were germs no different from those that caused polio or diphtheria, and that syphilis and gonorrhoea should be subjects upon which the public was informed. One of the department's broadcasts explicitly argued that the subject should be a matter for open discussion, yet made no reference to sexual contact as the source of transmission. Listeners were directed to Department of Health pamphlets if they wanted information upon the diseases.[62] A later broadcast engaged the subject of transmission only slightly more directly:

> Just as stagnant water usually carries disease germs, so are there in many communities cesspools of infection to trap the unwary. The best way to avoid syphilis is to avoid those likely to be infected – the promiscuous and the depraved. Syphilis is spread by intimate contact ... These special germ diseases tend to appear and spread most rapidly around construction jobs, army camps and in busy ports. Large numbers of men living under conditions somewhat different to their usual mode of life – a few women diseased in body and often in mind.[63]

The only sexual act mentioned by name in the department's publicity was kissing, and no prophylactics were suggested. Discussion on the radio was considerably less explicit than that in newspapers, and was at points oblique enough to almost be in code. While the department argued that sexually transmitted diseases were not different from other germs, the broadcast took the position that the 'special' diseases were as much a moral issue as a medical one.

The arrival in Newfoundland of thousands of young, unmarried Canadian and American servicemen and construction workers during the early years of the war raised the US Army Medical Corp.'s concern about the transmission of sexually transmitted diseases to their troops. This was always a concern to the medical officers of armed forces wherever they were stationed. Even as improved living standards among Newfoundland civilians ameliorated other health issues, such as nutrition, the risks of sexually transmitted diseases rose. In 1943, to prevent such a threat to public health and the fitness for duty of soldiers, the medical divisions of the Armed Forces undertook a publicity campaign on the dangers of 'venereal diseases' in newspapers and in the Capitol movie theatre in St John's. Although the Broadcasting Corporation had not been asked to participate in this campaign, Galgay decided upon his own initiative to head off any such request. Galgay was appalled by the content of the newspaper articles:

It became increasingly apparent that the content of these articles was such that nothing was left to the imagination and if the same so called 'broad-minded' attitude was to be pursued in talks on the air they could not but give offence to a very large number of our audience, and most assuredly could not be listened to in the home by a mixed family circle.[64]

Through 'indirect inquiry' Galgay learned that the BCN might receive a request to take part in the campaign. He then confirmed that some clergy members concurred with his view, objecting to not only the 'plain' wording of the campaign but also to the 'ultra-modern angle from which the problem was being approached.'[65] Galgay sought a ruling by the Board of Governors on the question of whether such broadcasts were to be permitted. At the same time that other national broadcasters were easing restrictions upon such matters because of the threat to military readiness that such diseases posed, Newfoundland moved in the opposite direction. The Board decided that the subject of venereal disease was not a matter for broadcast, but expressed some doubts as to whether the ban should also apply to the Department of Health's regular series of Health Talks.[66] As we have seen, that series had already broached the subject. Galgay told Miller, the medical health officer, of the ruling, and later claimed to have 'intimated' that the Board would consider a representation from the Department of Health for a possible exemption from the regulation. Subsequently, the BCN governors decided that information on venereal disease was not suitable for broadcast, regardless of whether it came from the Department of Health or from the American or Canadian military health officials.[67]

If Galgay intended to exempt the Department of Health from the prohibition on discussions of venereal diseases, as he claimed, Miller seems to have not understood that to be the case. In an angry letter to the secretary of public health and welfare, Dr. H.M. Mosdell, Miller vigorously protested the 'arbitrary decision' that represented a 'setback in modern practice.' He objected to non-medical personnel dictating what the Health Department was able to say over the air, and threatened to cancel the whole series of Health Talks.[68] Mosdell supported Miller and insisted to the Board that venereal disease presented a grave menace to the members of the Armed Forces and to family life. Mosdell wondered why the Department of Health had not been asked to express its opinion before the BCN banned discussions of the subject, upon which the department had frequently broadcast in the past. He also asked why no notice of the impending decision had been given. Lastly, he asked for an explanation of the grounds upon which the decision had been made.[69]

Both sides dug in. Galgay condemned the arrogant tone and wording of the correspondence from Miller and Mosdell, who seemed, in Galgay's view, to put the view of the Department of Health above that of the Broadcasting Corporation. The Department of Health set what was appropriate for health, he wrote, and the BCN set what was appropriate for broadcast. Galgay cited the regulations of both the CBC – which determined that all information broadcast should be appropriate for mixed company of adults and children – and the American National Association of Broadcasters – which suggested applying 'the yardstick of good taste and a decent regard for the social sensibilities.' He felt the Board need not justify its decisions to the Health Department, 'particularly when demanded in such an autocratic manner.'[70] The commissioner for public health and welfare, J.C. Puddester, sided with the doctors in his department, but the Commission did not overrule the Board of Governors. Puddester made good on Mosdell's threat, cancelling all the Department of Public Health and Welfare's broadcasts.[71] Galgay's view of the matter was that

> at that time we were in receipt of a request for time from the Armed Forces for the purpose of discussing this subject and, as the Medical Officers of the various units were conducting a vigorous campaign purely from the preventative viewpoint and without regard to the Moral issues, a general regulation was made that no discussion of Venereal Disease would be permitted. At the same time it was felt that the Health talks of the Department of Public Health on this subject had been handled in a most discreet manner and had been quite inoffensive. It had not been intended that the regulation would apply to the local health talks but some misunderstanding arose and we were forced to take a definite stand.[72]

A major opportunity to use the government broadcaster to disseminate public health information had been missed, out of sensitivity about the potentially explicit content of the broadcasts and Galgay's determination to retain control over what was broadcast. The Newfoundland state was not monolithic, and sometimes, as in this case, branches of government worked at cross purposes to each other. More to the point here, the arms-length relationship between the Commission and the Broadcasting Corporation, which had been designed to shield the Commission from criticism, gave the broadcaster autonomy from its owner. Five years later, in 1948, Miller asked if time would be available for public health broadcasts and if there would be restrictions upon the topics such a program could discuss.[73] Galgay passed Miller's request on to the Board. The general manager now attributed the earlier fracas to a misunderstanding, but insisted that the reaction of the Health Department officials had required the BCN to take a definite stand against broadcasting such material.[74] The Board approved the request for free time for health talks. Chairman Williams expressed the Board's understanding that talks upon VD would be conducted by a medical doctor and 'that the medical profession can be relied upon to give these addresses in good taste without offense.'[75]

The American officers' concern about sexually transmitted diseases was also met by the desire to use broadcasting to give off-duty servicemen wholesome activities. American servicemen were stationed at three major bases – St John's, Argentia, and Stephenville – and small numbers of servicemen worked at numerous outposts. None of these places were able to provide adequate leisure-time activities for their new residents. This deficiency encouraged the American Newfoundland Base Command to turn to radio broadcasting to keep in touch with men and maintain morale among those who had few leisure activities during their off-duty hours.[76] Starting in October 1942, a series of live radio variety shows from the auditorium of the new USO building were carried over VONF. The USO brought in high-profile entertainers from the United States and servicemen stationed in St John's and Newfoundland civilians performed for the troops. The program included a range of popular music and comedy, much like American network variety programs. One included a 'hill billy' trio in costume singing 'Down That Old Texas Trail,' followed by an experienced musician playing 'boogie woogie' on piano. Next came a comedy monologue in which Private First Class Ira Scher imitated the voices of several Hollywood actors. The Musical Commandoes accompanied the guest vocalist, Corporal 'Chick' Cumbo. The program was hosted by Sergeant Bud Rice.[77] Before the war Rice had owned his own radio station in the US, in addition to hosting the USO program, which became known as *Prepare for Action*. He also occasionally wrote dramatic skits for presentation.[78] Master Sergeant Harold Young and his Musical Commandos also performed 'blues.'[79] Something of the flavour of the show was captured by an article in the *Daily News*:

> *Prepare for Action* the radio show of the American soldiers was broadcast again from the USO on Tuesday night over VONF and VONH. The previous two Tuesdays while the troops were quarantined transcriptions of

past broadcasts were aired, but the other night one again the audience were clapping and whistling as nine o'clock came around, while Sargent Bud Rice and Tech. Sargent Harold Young stood ready to begin the programme. In its usual variety form the show featured soldier performers and the Music Commandoes under Sergeant Young. Outstanding was pianist Gene Marshall, a recent arrival at Fort Pepperrell. Sixteen years of professional playing as an accompanist and soloist in many of the larger cities of the United States is what Private Marshall now brings with him to musical circles here and his nimble finger work and deft touch brought a ready response from the studio audience. Another instrumentalist showing fine talent was Corporal Frank Bucco who played with great finesse a six-string electric guitar. A humourous discourse on how to prepare for an attack by mosquitos was given by 'Professor Needlenose' another soldier who preferred to remain anonymous. Private Michael Pasaro sang two popular songs.[80]

The thousands of Americans posted to Newfoundland included some career soldiers, but most came from a variety of civilian occupations. Some, such as Rice, had experience in broadcasting, while many more were professional or skilled amateur musicians and performers. It's not surprising that the men would recreate a version of an American network variety program, complete with a range of musical styles and genres. *Prepare for Action* came to an end after five months, to be replaced by a similar programme of popular and classical music by members of the Canadian armed services, *Comrades on Patrol*.[81] Captain F.R. Davies, the public relations officer with the Canadian troops, produced and directed a later programme, *Stand by for Music*, which also drew upon many skilled musicians.[82]

Not long after the end of the *Prepare for Action* series, the American special service officer who was in charge of morale, Major G.B. Bildergack, arranged with Galgay to have the BCN broadcast the American War Department's transcriptions, popularly known as the Armed Forces Radio Service (AFRS). As of 1 July 1943, VONF carried forty American War Department programmes, for a total of about twenty-five of the total of sixty-three hours per week that it was on air. With the exception of Sunday, on which the only American programme the BCN carried was *Hymns from Home*, at peak the Newfoundland government-owned broadcaster provided as many as nine American programs per day in addition to the commercial American network programming.[83] The broadcast of VONF for Tuesday, 3 August 1943 (see table 4.1) provides an example of that summer's fare.

Table 4.1 BCN Program Schedule, 3 August 1943

Hour	Title
10:00 a.m.	Summary and Devotional Service
10:15 a.m.	String Ensemble
10:30 a.m.	Downbeat (AFRS)
11:00 a.m.	Big Sister (CBS)
11:15 a.m.	Terry Snyder Trio
11:30 a.m.	BBC News
11:45 a.m.	Melody Roundup
12:00 p.m.	Serenade
12:30 p.m.	Jubilee (AFRS)
1:00 p.m.	Romantic Cycles
1:15 p.m.	Reuter's News
1:30 p.m.	Sound Off (AFRS)
1:45 p.m.	Local News
2:00 p.m.	Sign Off
6:00 p.m.	News Summary, Green Hornet (MBS, Blue)
6:30 p.m.	Selections from Operettas
6:45 p.m.	Sound Off (AFRS)
7:00 p.m.	Green Label News
7:15 p.m.	Forbidden Diary
7:30 p.m.	Bargain Hour
7:45 p.m.	Local News
8:15 p.m.	BBC News
8:30 p.m.	Are You a Genius? (AFRS)
8:45 p.m.	Lucy Linton
9:00 p.m.	The Rondoliers
9:15 p.m.	Yarns for Yanks (AFRS)
9:30 p.m.	Betty and Bob (CBS)
9:45 p.m.	Hour of Charm (CBS)
10:15 p.m.	Words and Music – Fred Cooper
10:30 p.m.	Sammy Kaye Record of the Day (NBC, ABC, MBS)
10:35 p.m.	Command Performance (AFRS)
11:00 p.m.	News Summary and Sign Off

As is evident from this list, a large portion of the BCN programming on this day had originated in the United States, whether from the AFRS or direct from an American network or the advertising agency.

This AFRS programming was a great success with military and civilian listeners in Newfoundland, both of whom had a taste for Hollywood motion pictures and American network radio. The shows consisted of two types: entertainment specifically created by the AFRS in Los Angeles and intended to entertain troops, such as *Command Perfor-*

mance, and commercial network programming that was recorded and modified to be suitable for overseas transmission. This modification, which, in an interesting choice of words, the AFRS call 'denaturing,' included removing advertisements and anything that was judged harmful to morale. In effect, commercial content was *natural*, and removing the advertising, or 'denaturing,' made it unnatural.

Despite its popularity, the BCN Board of Governors quickly drew back from turning so much of their station's time over to the American War Department. On 20 August 1943 the governors reduced the AFRS transcriptions to two programs per day on VONF, down from as many as nine. The other BCN station, VOWN in Corner Brook, which had just begun operating, continued to broadcast the full selection, likely for lack of alternative content.[84] American Service personnel protested the curtailment of their programming on the Newfoundland station, especially since some of them saw little merit in the BCN's own programming. Major Harford Powel, who had worked in advertising in civilian life and had taken over as special service officer at Fort Pepperrell in St John's, had a low opinion of the quality of Newfoundland programming. He was frustrated that VONF had 'little or no local talent, music or other features' to fill the afternoon hours but preferred to go off the air rather than accept the American transcriptions.[85] Undoubtedly there were weaknesses in the BCN's programming compared to that of NBC, for example, but one must also account for a certain amount of chauvinism among some Americans who valued only their own programming, which was familiar. Powel believed that the unreasonable governors of the BCN denied Newfoundland listeners what he saw as the best programming in the world. Powel wrote that 'Galgay is an American' and agreed that by using the AFRS programming, 'VONF would have a daily program not excelled anywhere in the world, since the transcriptions include the cream of all programs offered by the National, Columbia, and Mutual Broadcasting Systems of the United States, with advertising matter deleted.'[86] Powel reported to his superiors that the BCN's decision was based on one Board member's opinion that these programs were 'infiltration.'[87] The BCN did not object to American programming on principle; even after turning down the War Department's programs, it purchased new American commercial programming such as the serial mystery *Beyond Reasonable Doubt*.[88] Part of the problem from the BCN perspective was that the station needed advertising revenue, and commercial spots could not be sold on the AFRS programs. That was a condition of the agreement in which the American networks and the American Federation of Musicians allowed their content to be provided to servicemen without charge. Powel many not have realized that the BCN was financed in part through licence fees paid by Newfoundlanders (the fees were waived for American servicemen) and in part by the commercial spots it sold. If the Corporation were to forego advertising during the better part of its schedule, which was a requirement of using the American military programming, Newfoundland listeners would have to pay for a service dedicated to the needs and tastes of American servicemen, since the AFRS programming could not include any commercial announcements (the BCN was not able to raise revenue through the broadcast of the transcriptions).

The American military commanders were unwilling to have local officials stand in their way for very long, and the United States was usually forceful in pressing ahead with its agenda in Newfoundland. The Americans appealed to the Commission and began constructing their own radio broadcasting station. Not only would the Americans no longer be at the whim of local authorities, but on their own station they would be able to broadcast during the hours that servicemen and women were off duty. The BCN had provided some of this programming during working hours.[89] The commanding officer of the Newfoundland Base, Major General J.B. Brooks, asked the Judge Advocate General's Office if they had the legal authority to establish their own station in Newfoundland. Staff judge advocate, Major John H. Doughty, replied that the pertinent clause of the *American Bases Act* read, 'Except with the consent of the Government of the Territory, no wireless station shall be established, or submarine cable landed, in a leased area otherwise that for military purposes.' He rhetorically asked and answered,

Can it be said that the broadcasting of music, drama, news, etc., intended for military personnel is an act having a 'military purpose'? It is believed that such an endeavour would be clearly considered one for military purposes. Sustaining of the morale of all military personnel must be, at all times, a major aim of the military ... Unfortunately, many of the programs broadcast from the United States cannot be received by personnel on duty within this command, by reason of various factors, such as lack of shortwave radios, etc. As a consequence, it is believed that the programs thus denied to the members of the armed forces stationed within this command could be re-broadcast by radio owned, maintained and operated by the military on and within areas acquired by the Bases Agreement and that such operation of a wireless station by the military should be considered as one for a 'military purpose.'[90]

This stretched the definition of *military purposes* pretty far. The Americans habitually interpreted the language of the bases' agreement very liberally when it served their agenda, so it is not surprising that the Newfoundland Base Command pressed ahead with planning its own station without waiting for the Commission to review the Board of Governors' decision.

Brooks favoured creating an American station, even if the BCN relented and resumed broadcasting the full nine programs a day. In addition to the ability to broadcast transcriptions during the off-duty hours, it would be able to create its own programming.[91] Powel recognized that Newfoundland civilians would listen to the station, commenting that it 'will give the local residents an equal or greater amount of radio entertainment than they have enjoyed while our programs were presented by Station VONF.'[92] An American-owned station could also provide news from an American perspective, rather than the British point of view promoted by the BCN. On 9 October an official letter from the Newfoundland Base Command informed the secretary of posts and telegraphs that under the authority of Article 15 of the Bases agreement the Headquarters was constructing a station with 400 watts of power to be operated on 1480 kilocycles.[93] It is by no means assured that the Board of Governors of the BCN would have granted such an application, or that the Commission would have overruled the BCN's board. Neither the Commission nor the BCN had granted any licences for new broadcasting stations. The government favoured a public monopoly of broadcasting, which it believed best protected Newfoundlanders' public interest.[94] The 'international incident' of which Powell had warned didn't develop, since the Commission granted permission for the establishment of a broadcasting station at Fort Pepperrell for the duration of the war and for six months thereafter.[95] (At the end of the war the licence was extended for as long as the American bases lasted.) The Commission seldom successfully resisted the American Armed Services and did not choose to make this an issue upon which to fight. Perhaps to save face, the Commission granted the Americans permission to establish a station, and in what may have been a symbolic act of exercising sovereignty suggested the Americans use a call sign with the initial characters *VO* (as had been assigned to Newfoundland by international agreement). The Americans adopted the Commission's suggestion of the call sign VOUS for their new station.[96] After a series of experimental broadcasts starting 1 November 1943 (nine days before the Commission granted permission), the station at Fort Pepperrell began its regular schedule from 5:30 p.m. to 10:00 p.m.[97] American servicemen could now bask in familiar entertainment programming on their own station, and at times tailored to their work schedule.

These AFRS programs not only made American servicemen more at home in Newfoundland, but reached Newfoundland civilian listeners as well. Powel, for one, thought that the station was the principal agency that represented the American military to civilian Newfoundlanders and was thus vital to how Newfoundlanders perceived the American forces:

> This [station] has absolutely blacked out the local radio stations, except for their BBC news three times a day, and their local news. They have no talent or recordings which can compete with our transcriptions from Los Angeles. We also offer many original Army Band programs, Chapel organ recitals, and the like. VOUS has been a great maker of local good will for us, and we have been careful to ask many residents to appear on its daily orientation programs.[98]

The programming was devoted primarily to maintaining morale among servicemen, but the public relations function Powel attributed to the station presumed the existence of a civilian audience.

VOUS gave Newfoundland civilian listeners another avenue through which they could consume American mass-produced culture, providing more American music, comedy, drama, and information than had been available before. VONF and VOCM also now had a competitor for the attention of Newfoundland listeners, presenting a challenge to the Newfoundland-owned stations. While VONF was not a bastion of elite culture like the BBC, by comparison VOUS seemed less stuffy and more vibrant – containing as it did the cream of the American popular culture industry. VOUS also compared favourably to a privately owned commercial station such as VOCM, which produced Newfoundland popular culture and rebroadcast American popular culture, but had to do so by including advertising content. In 1949 VOUS expanded its schedule so it was on the air during the afternoon when the Newfoundland owned stations were not, adding to its popularity.[99] The programming on VOUS was the best that commercial radio could produce and had the attractive feature of not forcing listeners to listen to the commercials. In the absence of market research, we can only speculate about Newfoundland listeners' habits. Likely many young people listened to the dance music and latest hits from America provided by VOUS. Mature listeners likely continued to avidly follow Newfoundland news and public affairs programming on VONF. At the end of the war, VOWN at Corner Brook still relied heavily upon AFRS programs, broadcasting sixty-six of the American programs per week. When in November 1945 the Americans decided to cease offering AFRS programming to the BCN, the Americans and Newfoundlanders agreed that the US Army would provide the BCN with some records to help the stations wean themselves off the American programming over a period of three months. This step was not too difficult for the St John's station, but VOWN had to reduce its AFRS programming by about six programs per week.[100] Galgay had to scramble to provide replacement programming for the west coast station.

Although it makes intuitive sense to assume American military radio programming had a great effect upon Newfoundland popular culture, we must be cautious. The authors of one of the few studies of the 'roots and sources of Newfoundland popular music' compiled a comprehensive list of music recorded by Newfoundlanders and interviewed a number of musicians active during the 1950s to 1970s, to determine where people learned their music. The authors began with the assumption that the American bases during the Second World War had a 'major influence in introducing popular music, especially Country-Western music' but found little evidence to support that possibility. While their informants were of the view that the American presence was an outlet for popular music, the authors suggested that 'Newfoundlanders influenced American [servicemen's] taste in music rather than vice-versa.'[101] Both Newfoundland musicians and listeners had gathered music from published sources, continental radio stations, phonographs, and travel – never from a single medium. Informants on the west coast of the island, for example, reported learning music from stations in the Canadian maritime provinces as well as the eastern seaboard of the United States. Unfortunately measuring the effect of radio through other sources is difficult. News from Europe and local wartime problems preoccupied the local editors and those who wrote letters to the editor, so while during the 1930s the St John's newspapers contain some discussion of radio programming, once the war started such matters no longer garnered the same level of attention.

Just as many Newfoundlanders had first heard of the war and followed the fortunes of war on their radios, so too the announcement of the end of the war reached some families though the radio. Things were soon able to return to normal, and wartime programming, much of which had good entertainment value, came to an end. Some listeners regretted that the Canadian Army program, for example, would no longer be available.[102] The end of the requirement to submit local news for censorship as of 1 July 1945, however, was likely regretted by no one. The wartime economic boom had created a powerful competitor for listeners' attention in VOUS, and it had also increased the costs of doing business. The Newfoundland Hotel proposed to increase the rent for the studio from $225 to $330 per month, and that for facilities that Galgay judged unsuitable. The studio could not accommodate groups larger than fifteen people, which was compensated by the Corporation's ability to broadcast from the ballroom on the ground floor. It lacked adequate storage space for the transcription library, and rehearsals were often interrupted by complaints from guests of the hotel. Galgay had tolerated the conditions while waiting for the USO building – which would, in his view, be 'an ideal broadcasting house' – to revert to government ownership.[103] But Galgay's proposal failed, because the Department of Education took over the building after the war, leaving the BCN with its inadequate studio until after union with Canada, when the CBC made better arrangements.[104]

On the whole, wartime was a good time for state-owned broadcasters. Even in the United States, where nearly everyone accepted the fact that private ownership of broadcasting and freedom from government influence were in the public interest, the challenges of the war enabled the Roosevelt administration to establish a place for the state in American broadcasting.[105] But, unlike the situation in Canada or the United States, privately owned broadcasters in Newfoundland remained unable to expand their businesses as the economy revived. The rhetorical debate over public vs private broadcasting was quiet, however, because patriotism ensured that no one criticized the expansion of the BCN or the restrictions upon VOCM. The Commission of Government's welcome had worn thin, and in the spring of 1943 changes to tax regulations had prompted the Board of Trade and many members of the public to demand constitutional change with such slogans as 'No taxation without representation.' It was clear that the demands for change would emerge when peace returned. Meanwhile, the revival of trade that accompanied Allied military spending gave advertisers much more money to spend and increased the number of licensed receivers. These

conditions might have allowed for growth of privately owned broadcasters, but the BCN did not approve power increases or new licences to
privately owned stations. The exception was the establishment of three
American military–owned stations: VOUS at Fort Pepperrell, and later
VOHF at Harmon Field and VOUG at the military airfield in Goose
Bay.[106] The Royal Canadian Air Force also established VORG at the
Newfoundland Airport in Gander. The BCN did not see these stations
as precedents for the licensing of commercial stations, but as part of the
war effort. Joseph Butler had accepted the need for VOCM to live with
the existing low-power output of his transmitter as long as hostilities
continued, even if the licences issued to the American stations rankled.
With the defeat of the Axis, Butler resumed his campaign for government permission to increase the power of his transmitter.

The war was an exciting time for Newfoundlanders in St John's and
many communities near bases. After the bleak years of the Depression,
young people found the dances, Coca-Cola, and cash exhilarating. The
Canadian and American servicemen filled many of their leisure hours
with music – live and broadcast by radio – and civilians were part of it.
The lasting impression of wartime swing sessions, barn dances, etc.
encouraged many to believe that the friendly invasion had introduced
American popular music to a land of folk music, but that impression is
exaggerated. Long before the *Edmund B. Alexander* docked in St John's,
phonographs, movies, live concerts by travelling musicians, and radio
had all provided jazz, the early variants of country music, and other
musical forms to Newfoundlanders. The AFRS programming and the
American servicemen themselves had provided more American popular music during wartime than had been available before, of that there
can be no doubt. Just as in the UK, the presence of American servicemen in the country and the desire to serve that new audience encouraged broadcasters to adopt a more popular style. But these musical
styles had been available on the radio in Newfoundland and popular
with younger listeners before the war, and the BCN did not have the
same agenda of cultural uplift.

Galgay and the governors had good reason to feel a sense of accom-
plishment for the contribution the BCN had made to the war effort and
the level of service it had maintained. In its last war-related duty, VONF
now took a role in publicizing the Commission's policies for the repa-
triation of Newfoundland servicemen and the programs to re-establish
them as civilians.[107] But the sense of self-congratulation for a job well
done was tempered with regret that the national emergency had pre-

empted the Corporation from improving its programming. As one internal memorandum put it,

> Within six months of its inception the Empire was at war, all plans had to be postponed or abandoned and the corporation as an important unit in the scheme for defence and active prosecution of the war effort placed all its facilities at the disposal of the armed forces authorities. It must be remembered that Newfoundland became the Gibraltar of North America and one of the most important focal points for the Battle of the Atlantic. It must be remembered too that VONF situated within a few miles of the most easterly point in the hemisphere projected a steady signal over eight hundred miles across the Atlantic not only in the direction of Ireland but to Ireland and the Azores. Within the Island it was the only single medium of communication which could immediately 'alert' the civilian population as well as the military forces. Its immense possibilities were immediately recognized and it was promptly integrated into the Hemispheric Defence Plan.[108]

Radio brought war news, the *Recruitment Programme*, *Calling Newfoundland*, and hundreds of war-related special broadcasts into people's homes. This may have had effects in raising Newfoundlanders' expectations of a North American consumer lifestyle after the war. Broadcasters had also tried to re-forge the ties of King and country, reminding Newfoundlanders that they were fighting a British war. The impact of these movements is unclear. Dissatisfaction with the Commission of Government grew and the people were aware of the irony of Newfoundlanders dying for democracy when they were unable to vote. That is a subject to which we can turn our attention in the next chapter.

5 Most Important Work: Broadcasting the Confederation Debates

The wartime economic revival had raised Newfoundlanders' expectations for a better life and reopened the question of what sort of government they would have. Between October 1946 and January 1948, the BCN embarked on an ambitious project that fulfilled the highest potential of public broadcasting and exemplified the impact broadcasting could have upon political life – the broadcast of the proceedings of the constitutional debates of the National Convention. Joseph Smallwood, who led the campaign to join Canada, later claimed a central place for these broadcasts and his own mastery of the medium:

> I had spent many years broadcasting and I knew the magic of it. The sheer, sheer magic, especially in a place like Newfoundland with so many isolated people. Radio, I've always contended, was invented by God especially for Newfoundland, and having done it for Newfoundland, He graciously allowed for it to be used in other parts of the world. It was *meant* for Newfoundland. It was meant for a remote and isolated people who never met. Who never saw each other. Radio was the great unifying thing. I knew how to use it. I never let my mouth turn away from that microphone. Never. Many of the debaters at the Convention disdained the microphones. They wouldn't go near them with the result that my point of view was heard loud and clear ... My pro-Confederation stand was heard in every home. The anti-Confederationists, distaining radio as they did were not heard. The result was that when the referendum was held, Confederation passed by a narrow margin. I credit that margin to the use of radio.[1]

Setting aside Smallwood's habitual hyperbole, historians agree that these broadcasts played a crucial role in the Confederation debate of 1946 to 1948. Some people have even wondered if the Commission placed microphones in the assembly chamber with the intention of giving the pro-Confederation and experienced broadcaster Smallwood an advantage. Such conspiracy speculation is not supported by the evidence and prevents an understanding of the issues and challenges that the state-owned broadcaster faced. It also diverts attention from the question of the effect the broadcasts of the National Convention had upon the votes cast by listeners.[2] This chapter argues that the BCN played a greater role in Newfoundland's constitutional debate than anyone could have anticipated in 1946.

The Commission of Government had not fully envisioned the role the broadcasts might have. It fell to the initiative of Galgay to make the most of the medium. This was not the world's first broadcast of a legislature, for the New Zealand Parliament started broadcasting its proceedings in 1936, but the BCN's coverage of the convention was a remarkable technical achievement that had a great effect upon the constitutional debate.[3] No public opinion polls were held, so it is difficult to measure the degree of influence the convention broadcasts had among the listeners, but the Commission ordered its rural police force, the Rangers, to report upon public opinion, allowing us to say something about the reception of the broadcasts.

The Commission of Government had worn its welcome thin by the start of the Second World War.[4] The revival of exports and the economic stimulus of Allied wartime spending had given the Newfoundland government a surplus by 1941. Rather than receiving an annual grant in aid, the Commission now lent money to the UK for the war effort. Newfoundlanders enthusiastically contributed to the war effort, but tax increases in 1943 prompted a minor tax revolt. Many objected to a new tax at a time when the government's books were balanced, especially since the money raised was to be lent to Britain rather than being spent locally on the great many areas of need. The Board of Trade and many political commentators now demanded a return to self-government. In the face of this response, the British government realized that once the war ended it would be unable to resist Newfoundlanders' demands. When the British Parliament suspended responsible government in 1934, it had pledged to return self-government once Newfoundland met two conditions: the government had to become financially self-supporting and Newfoundlanders had to ask for the resumption of responsible government. The Newfoundland government was now self-supporting, so people need only request constitutional change.

R.B. Job, a member of the former Legislative Council, suggested a 'national conclave' to discuss a return to responsible government.[5] The Dominions Office feared that these demands would become irresistible if it did not keep control over the political agenda within Newfoundland. It hesitated to have Newfoundland resume democratic government immediately, fearing that once the abnormal wartime conditions ended, the economy would again collapse, and the British Treasury would be forced to reassume responsibility. To meet this possibility, the British turned to a two-pronged policy. They would undertake economic reconstruction while creating a mechanism to allow Newfoundlanders to decide upon their future form of government. The Dominions Office decided to create a citizens council similar to Job's proposed national conclave but called the 'National Convention.' Newfoundlanders were to choose their own course after the war, but the British had no intention of sitting on the sidelines and waiting to see what happened. Britain would frame the terms of reference of the convention to achieve its goals.

While the British officials designed a convention that would achieve their constitutional goals while minimizing the dangers, the other side of their policy – economic reconstruction – was stopped in its tracks by the British Treasury. Britain's own financial situation at the end of the war made expenditures in Newfoundland impossible, particularly since the UK government faced severe shortages of American and Canadian currency and any British investment in Newfoundland would have to be paid for in dollars. The best way of ensuring that the Newfoundland government did not look to Britain for further financial aid was therefore to have Canada take responsibility for the island. With that in mind, a senior Dominions Office official, P.A. Clutterbuck, went to Ottawa to see if the Canadians were willing to help. To his surprise, he found the Canadians willing – but only if Newfoundland became a Canadian province. The Canadian government, for its part, had several economic and strategic interests in Newfoundland. It had decided that bringing Newfoundland into the union would be the best way of protecting these interests and that it should not miss the opportunity to do so while Newfoundland lacked a legislature that would make union into a partisan issue.[6] Both British and Canadian policy now became devoted to encouraging Newfoundlanders to join the Canadian confederation before Newfoundlanders resumed democratic government. This policy had to remain confidential, however, since the British and Canadian officials believed that if it appeared that they were interfering with Newfoundlanders' choice, the backlash would harm the chances of union. The secretary of state for dominions affairs, Lord Addison, prepared a document for British Cabinet approval that outlined the goal, the method, and the limits to British policy. Newfoundlanders would be free to choose their own form of government, and the British would do nothing that made Newfoundlanders less likely to choose confederation with Canada as that form of government.[7] The National Convention was now more than a mechanism for people to consider their political future; it had evolved into a machine to create Newfoundlanders' consent to join Canada. At this stage no one could have foreseen the central role that radio broadcasting was to play.

The British had to act cautiously, but expeditiously, if they were to meet the letter of their pledge to allow Newfoundlanders to ask for a return to responsible government but delay handing authority over to Newfoundland politicians until hints from Britain could make confederation with Canada a popular option. The Dominions Office hoped to postpone the evil day when politicians would again control the agenda until Newfoundlanders had an opportunity to consider union. Ever since the Amulree Report had blamed politicians for Newfoundland problems, the Dominions Office worried that creating democratic government would reawaken graft and corruption. More to the point, once democratic government resumed, the British would lose control over it. The British officials also worried that partisan politics would kill the idea of confederation – so they needed a sort of halfway house to democratic government. This transitional point would, they hoped, satisfy Newfoundlanders that their country was moving toward democracy but still keep enough control in British hands to maintain the momentum toward confederation. The convention delayed Newfoundlanders from making that request until the government could turn Newfoundlander's attention toward Canada and confederation could become a popular option. As was standard policy for the British as they oversaw parts of the empire moving toward independence, the terms of reference of the convention would make sure that the Dominions Office remained in control of the agenda. With some careful management, Newfoundlanders in the convention might conclude that confederation would be best and recommend that to the voters. The British also reserved the right to reject the convention's recommendation of the options to place upon the ballot if partisan politicians in the convention did not reach the conclusion the British favoured.

The British intended the convention to serve another function. It would make the suggestion of confederation appear to come from Newfoundlanders. The Commission had long been sensitive to its non-democratic nature and often tried to generate popular support for its policies and attempted to make it appear that Newfoundlanders were partners in government. As we have seen with the committee that drafted the broadcasting act, when the Commission wanted to enact a potentially sensitive policy, it sometimes appointed a committee of Newfoundlanders that would recommend that policy. If an elected representative group within the convention were to propose confederation, it would not appear that the British-appointed Commission was trying to pass Newfoundland to Canada but that Newfoundlanders were recommending union. Another benefit of having an elected convention was that it could stand in for the suspended Newfoundland Assembly and have the moral authority necessary to negotiate proposed terms of union. Now that the war was over, a few people criticized the Commission for not negotiating a quid pro quo when the United States was given ninety-nine-year leases to military bases in Newfoundland. It would have been difficult for the Commission, which its critics charged was a toady for the government in London, to have negotiated with Ottawa. These negotiations were on the British and Canadian agenda. Even before the delegates to the Convention had been elected, the Canadians decided they were willing to meet with a delegation to discuss confederation, and the cooperation of the convention would prevent the appearance that Britain and Canada had dictated the terms of union.

The British did not risk having the convention ask for a return to responsible government without first making confederation an option. The convention's mandate was to investigate the state of the economy. Then, after taking into account the fact that solvency was the result of wartime spending, it would recommend which 'forms of government' would appear on the ballot in a national referendum. The British hoped that the Newfoundlanders in the convention would take the hint that the financial self-sufficiency of the Newfoundland government would not last. If the Dominions Office and the Commission of Government had developed a script for the convention to follow, it would have been something like this: delegates would be elected representing all classes in Newfoundland, who would then study the economic and financial situation and decide that independence was not feasible, and proceed to Ottawa to ascertain what terms of union with Canada might be possible. The convention would then recommend that confederation with Canada appear on the ballot in a national referendum, and dissolve. But plans such as these rarely run the desired course.

While the government prepared for the National Convention, the Broadcasting Corporation faced challenges in the post-war political climate. The BCN had to allow political discussions if it was to be relevant to Newfoundland's political future, even if that meant allowing the Commission's critics access to the government's station. Furthermore the impending end of wartime censorship made it difficult for the BCN to avoid such critics without being accused of being a mouthpiece for the Commission. Galgay wanted to ensure a balance of opinion on the air, but that approach proved difficult since control over the news and information programming was in the hands of private businesses such as the Newfoundland Butter Company and Gerald S. Doyle. To take one example, F.M. O'Leary wrote to Galgay letting him know that the *Barrelman* program intended to broadcast letters that expressed opinions on the proposed forms of government. Galgay suggested that the program attempt to present a cross section of opinion and asked that such scripts be submitted to the Corporation in advance of broadcast, not to be censored, but 'as an indication of good faith on the part of the compiler of the scripts.'[8] Meanwhile, he assured the Board that since the BCN had the ultimate ability to change the program if didn't meet the Corporation's approval, it had sufficient safeguards to allow O'Leary to proceed without potential embarrassment to the Corporation.[9] Many listeners, with Harrington's cooperation of course, now used the *Barrelman* program to express their views on the forthcoming National Convention and the larger debate about the future. Harrington, perhaps out of a sense of propriety, was careful to not campaign on his program, even after he decided to run for the National Convention.

Concern over embarrassing, if not libellous, partisan debate was not a hypothetical issue. A former member of the Assembly, Peter Cashin, began a fiery campaign against the Commission and in the spring of 1945 requested time upon VONF to address the public. Cashin was no novice; he had regularly broadcast over VONF as early as the spring of 1933.[10] The BCN Board of Governors, which had based its regulations on controversial broadcasts upon those of the CBC, hoped to protect the Corporation from libel charges while allowing debate upon forms of

government. Access to the air was available to those who had a legitimate claims to have their opinion put forward:

> Former Cabinet Members and Members of the Legislative Council wish-
> ing to discuss particular or general public questions may be accorded
> broadcasting facilities free of charge. Such broadcasts are not to contain
> any attack on any person or class as to his or their private or public activi-
> ties. It is also agreed that applications from others to speak on similar mat-
> ters will be considered. Statements that might render the Corporation
> open to an action for damages for libel must not be permitted.[11]

Cashin had been minister of finance between 1928 and 1932 so was
qualified to speak. When Galgay saw the first of the speeches, his reaction was to ask the governors to share responsibility of approving the
material. His memorandum to George Williams is worth quoting at
length, for it reveals both the weakness of the BCN's regulations and the
absence of an adequate administrative structure to handle the situation:

> Further to our conversation of this afternoon with reference to the regula-
> tions regarding speeches on public questions. The regulations contain
> only two provisions: (1) Such broadcasts are not to contain any attack on
> any persons or class as to his or their private or public activities. (2) State-
> ments that might render the Corporation open for damages for libel must
> not be permitted ... The application of regulation (1) depends entirely on
> the definition of the word 'attack' and even the dictionary definition is
> such as to make the interpretation particularly obscure in the sense used
> here. This is the first occasion on which the corporation has had to make a
> serious decision on the context of a broadcast address and, as I stated this
> afternoon, I fell [sic] that the possibilities for repercussions are such as to
> be more than I should be expected to assume responsibility for alone, par-
> ticularly in view of the meagre and loose nature of the regulations. If the
> corporation was constituted as other similar organizations it would be
> within the jurisdiction of the General Manager to handle the matter. How-
> ever he would simply hand it to the legal department who would be
> responsible for interpretation and application. As we do not possess a
> legal department, it is my opinion that the responsibility and application
> of regulation (1) should be shared with at least one Member of the Gover-
> nors. With regard to regulation (2) the interpretation of libel laws are so
> involved as to require the advice of competent legal authority. In the event
> of an action for libel as the result of a statement passed by me or other

officers of the Corporation, the first question to be asked will be whether or not we had legal advice. Should the Corporation lose a libel action without having sought legal advice, it will be regarded as gross carelessness and neglect of the ordinary precautions unvariably taken by similar radio organizations.[12]

Galgay went on to request that one of the governors be appointed to act with the general manager in cases such as Cashin's and that a law firm be contracted to clear such speeches of libellous content.

Williams told Galgay to send Cashin a copy of this regulation and left it to Galgay to review the script to ensure that it conformed to the rules before being broadcast.[13] Galgay submitted the first of Cashin's proposed addresses to the Board for approval, but he remained concerned about the content of the speech, even after Cashin had agreed to a number of Galgay's deletions and changes of wording. Galgay continued to want the Board to approve the address, again suggesting the Board obtain a legal opinion on the script. He also asked if an insurance policy against libel might be purchased.[14] Galgay also sent a copy of Cashin's second and third speeches to W.J. Carew, the secretary of home affairs.[15]

In the absence of elected government, outside of a couple of municipalities, a series of radio broadcasts was one of the few paths to a national public profile available. Cashin relaunched his political career through these broadcasts, while feigning a reluctance to engage in 'politics.' Politicians had somewhat unfairly taken the blame for the fiscal crisis of the 1930s and there was a broad sentiment in favour of men and women who put the needs of the country ahead of partisan advantage. Cashin positioned himself as the Commission's greatest opponent, while playing the part of the reluctant hero who, because no one else had risen to Newfoundland's defence, was compelled to do so himself. He correctly sensed in the ambivalent public statements from the Dominions Office that it was not eager for Newfoundland to resume responsible government. But he did not know, at this point, that it favoured Newfoundland's entry into the Canadian federation. The BCN prefaced and followed Cashin's speech with statements that the Corporation did not endorse the views that were being broadcast. Cashin's initial speech turned to the events in the early 1930s that had led to the Commission of Government. He argued that since the people had not given their consent to the suspension of responsible government, the Commission itself was unconstitutional and every piece of legislation it had enacted since 1934 was illegal.[16]

Galgay took note of an editorial in the *Grand Falls Advertiser* that expressed surprise that the government-controlled station had allowed such a frank criticism of the Commission. The editor wondered if the BCN would allow the subsequent speeches in the series to be broadcast. The paper praised the broadcaster, even while wondering if the Corporation had reviewed the address. If it allowed Cashin's broadcasts to continue, the editorial commented, then that would be proof that freedom of speech still existed in Newfoundland.[17] The BCN's Board and Galgay must have recognized that as bitter a pill as criticism of the Commission over their station may have been, now that the expectation had been raised that Cashin was going to broadcast a series of exposés, they risked criticism if Cashin were to not make the speeches.

Cashin's second broadcast criticized the 'totalitarian' government's record in administering the economy and public finances. Galgay deleted numerous potentially libellous statements in which Cashin accused members of the Alderdice government of having accepted bribes to buy their acquiescence in the creation of the Commission, such as the following:

> Immediately the Commission were sworn into office in February 1934, they at once started the pay-off, in part at least, to members of the corrupt legislature for services rendered to the cause of totalitarianism. In all, eleven members of the Alderdice Government, which included two Newfoundland Commissioners were installed in Civil Service appointments, whilst others received their 'pieces of Silver' in a more indirect manner.[18]

He also continued to hammer at the theme that the Commissioners were men who lacked administrative abilities and were in place to do the bidding of their civil servant masters in London.

Galgay remained concerned about the content of the speeches, even after deleting the most objectionable sections. As he wrote to Williams,

> Whilst the facilities of the Corporation may be made available for discussion of Public Affairs, they should be used only in a dignified and courteous manner. The challenge to Sir John Puddester, Mr Winter and Mr Walsh, in my opinion, is not a subject for broadcast, particularly as Major Cashin is herein voicing a personal challenge as does not represent any recognized Association or Organization. It is my suggestion that in future cases of broadcasts by individuals like Major Cashin, definite limitations

should be laid down as to the scope of the address. Major Cashin was given permission to broadcast on the events which led up to Commission of Government and its operations up to the present. He has wandered far from the scope of this permission. The attached address is filled with purely personal opinions and unsubstantiated observations, and to make it suitable for broadcast requires considerable re-writing.[19]

In the third speech Cashin hinted that he was being muzzled by the Commission, and in a thinly veiled reference to his speech having been censored suggested, 'If the continuity of my remarks tonight may seem somewhat disjointed, I know that you will readily appreciate the peculiar circumstances.' Having argued that the Commission was a colossal failure, he demanded that the governor appoint a Newfoundlander to head an administration and hold an election. The government's policy of holding a plebiscite was, Cashin suggested, a way of confusing the issue and pursuing a technique of divide and rule.[20] Cashin was a fine orator, although prone to sentence fragments that are more obvious when the speech is in text than heard. He called upon people to demand self-government:

All men are born politically free and equal by divine and natural law, that sovereignty resides in the whole people and its object is their common welfare and that Representatives in this Sovereignty are selected by the people and responsible to them. Newfoundland is, I am now sure, fighting for her God-Given Rights, for her Industrial Freedom, Educational Freedom, Social Freedom, and Political Freedom, Freedom of Speech and of the Press and of the AIR. Newfoundlanders with very few exceptions believe that any political, social or economic system which does not recognize the rights and duties flowing from the fundamental dignity of human personality is a vicious system destructive of democratic government ... Our God-given Rights are being endangered by enemies within the country. Our freedoms are abused in the very name of freedom. Shall the people of Newfoundland permit the blow and stabs from without or the Poison and Cancer from within to rob us of our God-Given Rights and destroy our God-blessed Country? The answer must be NO. From our ancestors both political and commercial we have a heritage not surpassed anywhere among the children of men, a heritage for us to cherish, to defend and perpetuate. The Forces of evil materialism have been surging ahead in Newfoundland for the past ten years. This must be stopped. Democratic or

responsible government, believes in Liberty, teaches Liberty. Let us work
and fight, Let us live and die, that Newfoundland and Newfoundland's
God-given Rights shall not perish from the earth.[21]

Such rhetoric could not have soothed the worries of those within the
Dominions Office who hoped that the political elite of Newfoundland
could be eased into union with Canada without first resuming responsible government.

By this point, rumours circulated that a forthcoming elected body of
Newfoundlanders would debate constitutional options. While Newfoundlanders waited for the Dominions Office to announce its policy,
one correspondent to the local press suggested a novel use of broadcasting. In a letter to the *Daily News*, 'Avalon' proposed a weekly 'radio
forum' that would allow democratic input before the delegates from
Newfoundland began to discuss the county's political future. They
could answer questions posed by listeners and ask their own questions
of representatives of the Commission and the Board of Trade. Various
trade unions, war veterans, and representatives of women's societies
could all participate. Then, in the spring, when candidates canvassed
their districts, people would have an informed basis upon which to
vote.[22]

On 11 December 1945 British Prime Minister Attlee announced that a
National Convention would give Newfoundlanders the opportunity to
request a return to responsible government or another form of government. Many Newfoundlanders welcomed the announcement, including Joe Smallwood, who now resolved to run for election upon a pro-
confederation platform, but not Cashin. Perhaps finding the censorship
of the BCN too great, he took his campaign to VOCM. In a broadcast on
12 January 1946 Cashin set out his case against the National Convention
and argued for an immediate return to responsible government. He also
sent a recording of this address to Attlee and had the text printed as a
pamphlet for circulation within Newfoundland. His speech on VOCM
alluded to the censorship of his earlier talks on VONF. The BCN, upon
the initiative of Commissioner Wild, purchased an expensive portable
recorder with the aim of recording addresses that were broadcast over
VOCM, presumably to gather evidence that might be used against the
station if it were to decide to suspend the station's licence or in libel
suits.[23]

In the VOCM speech, Cashin repeated his earlier accusations and
argued that the *Newfoundland Act* of 1933 had specified that the Com-

mission would continue until such time as the government finances were balanced. Cashin pointed out that this condition had been met. Upon this basis, Cashin concluded that the governor was obligated to immediately call upon someone to form an administration and call an election. The National Convention would therefore be illegal, in his view. He accused Attlee of creating the convention for the purpose of extending the rule of the Commission, and thus giving the Commission time to appropriate the surplus of the Newfoundland government for the benefit of the United Kingdom. He closed with an appeal to Newfoundlanders to organize local committees and contact him to coordinate an 'all-Newfoundland Movement' to end the British rule.

> Reverting for a moment to the original plot to deprive Newfoundland of responsible government in 1933–34 ... Lord Amulree was consulting with the then Prime Minister regarding the future of Newfoundland, and I have read communications between Prime Minister Alderdice and another Minister of the Crown definitely indicating that, in order to get members of the House of Assembly to vote for Commission Government, permanent positions in the Civil Service would have to be arranged for many of these gentlemen. I state definitely now, that Sir John Puddester, Present Commissioner for Public Health and Welfare and Deputy Chairman of the Commission, would not have voted for the abolition of Responsible Government unless he was definitely assured of being one of Newfoundland's Commissioners. Everyone knows that the present Commissioner for Justice [Harry Anderson Winter], who was a member of the Alderdice Government and who voted for the abolition of responsible government, who was not at first appointed a Commissioner, openly criticised the actions of the Commission in the public press and was later appointed a Commissioner; that his brother [James Alexander Winter] who had been Commissioner for Home Affairs and Education was placed in a permanent Civil Service position to make room for the present Commissioner, who later became Commissioner for Justice after Sir Edward Emerson's appointment as Chief Justice of the Supreme Court of Newfoundland.[24]

This was the sort of potentially libellous statement that Galgay had so carefully edited on VONF, but Butler of VOCM took no such precautions. While his reawakened political career had been founded upon such attacks upon the Commission and the convention, Cashin announced that despite the fact that the convention was a trick, he would stand for election.

Newfoundland had not had an election since 1932, and the Commission quickly pressed VONF into service to help create the mechanism to elicit public consent to constitutional change. Two weeks after arriving in Newfoundland, the newly appointed governor, Gordon McDonald, took to VONF to announce forthcoming election to the National Convention and to discuss its terms of reference. He dismissed charges that the convention was going to be a waste of time and encouraged public-spirited citizens to stand for election.[25] The chief electoral officer directed the organization of the election through broadcasts aimed at the district electoral officers, since so many areas did not have telephone service and a long period of time had elapsed since there had been an election.[26] On polling day itself, the BCN stayed on the air the whole day, on the chance that the electoral office would need to communicate additional instructions to returning officers. The returns of the election were then broadcast, enabling listeners to follow the returns from each district throughout the country as they were received.

Broadcasting was used for more than organization and reporting of results, for the BCN had also allowed campaigning. Many candidates canvassed through the BCN and VOCM in the weeks before the election, and more than fifty addresses by candidates were broadcast on VONF. The small set of these speeches extant show candidates putting themselves forward as advocating a return to self-government. Without parties or platforms, candidates had little to distinguish themselves from each other, making broadcasting a good way of introducing themselves. One candidate went farther. W.E. Mercer, who ran unsuccessfully in Bay Roberts, suggested that some candidates secretly favoured continued Commission and argued that those who recommended keeping an 'open mind' were hiding their pro-Commission convictions.[27] Radio had an indirect effect as well; two of the elected delegates, Smallwood and Harrington, owed their public profile in part to the years each of them had spent as the Barrelman. Whitefield Laite, who had broadcast the cooperative program, unsuccessfully ran in Trinity North.

The editor of the *Daily News* commented that broadcasting had allowed candidates to appeal to widely dispersed voters by radio, saving them a great deal of travel and expense, but that campaigning by broadcast had weaknesses and some dangers:

> Of course, broadcasting cannot fully replace the personal canvass and the public meeting. Talking to an unseen audience is often a chilling experi-

ence and the warmth and excitement of a public meeting are often needed to put the speaker on his mettle. But the radio reaches into the home and gathers into the audience thousands of voters who never attended meetings and must be used with discretion. Recalling some of the things said on political platforms in the past, it may well appear desirable that a policy should be framed to prevent the abuse of the privilege of broadcasting. The printed word cannot be obliterated and what a newspaper says in print it must also accept responsibility for in the courts. Broadcasting is not under the same restriction. There is another difference between the press and radio. Newspaper articles cannot have the same inflammatory effect as the human voice used to raise human passions. The printed word is cold and unargumentative. The spoken word by mere inflection of voice may appear to say something far more than the ordinary meaning of the words used. This suggests the need of considering not censorship or control so much as wise supervision.[28]

This view reflects more than competition between the two media; it shows an anxiety that irresponsible politicians might use the power of radio to sway listeners' emotions. On another occasion he warned that broadcasting the proceedings of the convention would be a mistake. Few people would listen to the routine work of the convention. 'Nor would any useful purpose be served in making it too easy for members to talk to the country for the purpose of advocating their own special ideas,' the editor went on, 'instead of concentrating as members of a responsible committee on the achievement of the best results from this national conference.'[29] Instead of live broadcasts, he advocated having a reporter compile a fifteen- to thirty-minute daily summary to keep the public informed.

Governor MacDonald reported to the Dominions Office that retired judge F.J. Morris proposed that radio broadcasting be used to inform the public of the implications of each form of government – a suggestion that he said had met support from the editorial writers.[30] MacDonald took up the question of whether the BCN would cover the nation's deliberations within the forthcoming National Convention. In a broadcast over VONF he appealed for all possible publicity to be given to the convention's work and expressed the hope that the convention would have its deliberations broadcast. Members of the public concurred that radio could be used to inform people of the possible forms of government. A committee of citizens telegraphed the *Doyle Bulletin* to say they had passed a resolution supporting a weekly radio report on the deliberations.[31] One person went farther: union activist E.D.C. Hiscock suggested broadcasting the convention proceedings.[32]

These discussions spurred Galgay to consider the matter of how the BCN would cover the deliberations. He acknowledged that arrangements had to await the approval of the convention, but wanted to begin technical preparations, for the Corporation needed to prepare if a significant portion of the deliberations were suitable for broadcast, and in any case intended to broadcast the opening ceremony. Galgay thought that sending a single parliamentary reporter to the gallery was inadequate and responded with an elaborate plan to give full coverage. He believed it was neither possible nor desirable to broadcast the whole of the convention proceedings, so proposed that permanent recording equipment be installed in the Assembly chamber. The reporter covering the deliberations could choose, at short notice, to record a portion of the debate for later broadcast or for reference when compiling reports. Routine deliberations would be summarized by the BCN reporter and highlights could later be broadcast.[33] The Board instructed Galgay to advertise for a reporter, male or female, who would attend the convention and prepare for broadcast a daily synopsis of the discussions.[34]

VONF broadcast the official opening of the convention on 11 September 1946, a special event that Galgay believed had achieved a wide audience, and then settled into broadcasting summaries of the proceedings. During the regular sessions, in the afternoons, the BCN had a reporter and a stenographer in the gallery, as did the newspapers. At the end of each day, the reporter wrote a summary, which was read by an announcer that evening on VONF and repeated on VOWN. Early in its deliberations the convention formed into seven committees to investigate the economic state of the country, prompting Smallwood to worry that their work would no longer receive publicity. He suggested they meet in general assembly at least once a week, so that people would continue to follow their important work. It would be a pity, he thought, after the period of political death during the Commission, if the 'informative and even brilliant broadcasts' that had aroused public interest in national affairs during the preceding seven or eight nights were suspended entirely while the committees conducted their investigations.[35] Through the life of the convention Smallwood was consistently devoted to the effect the debates had upon the public, even while other members thought such things should take second place to the work of the convention's investigations.

Broadcasting summaries of parliamentary sessions was fairly standard procedure, but Galgay found it unsatisfactory. An example of the BCN reporter's summary of Smallwood's comments upon the importance of continued publicity through broadcasting remains among Galgay's papers.[36] Galgay attended the early sessions to evaluate the accuracy of the reports as broadcast and assess their 'value.' He reported to the Board of Governors,

> It was soon apparent that while the reports were accurate to a certain degree, many statements were subject to the interpretation of the individual reporting, many significant statements were missed, and as it was impossible to transcribe the proceedings in full, the reports were generally incomplete and left a false picture of the particular discussion or debate. Even more noticeable was the fact that the reports failed to reproduce the atmosphere of the Convention, and as the announcer who read the report had no knowledge of the background, he frequently emphasized or dramatized the insignificant while parts of greater significance were merely read in a monotone.[37]

As an experiment, Galgay sought and received permission from the convention chairman, Chief Justice Cyril Fox, to record a session for broadcast. This proved to be a pivotal broadcast in Newfoundland history, because, in Galgay's words, 'fortunately or unfortunately the day upon which the experimental recording was made coincided with the introduction of the now historic debate on the motion to send a delegation to Ottawa.'[38]

Smallwood had campaigned on a pro-confederation platform during the election to the convention. During the train ride to St John's he had attempted to put together a pro-confederation coalition among his fellow delegates and now had a sense of how much support for union with Canada there was among members. He must have realized that confederation lacked sufficient support at this early stage. At the beginning of October the Steering Committee of the convention had discussed seeking possible terms of union from Ottawa and decided to finish the convention's investigations before sending a delegation. Many felt that to negotiate union with Canada before finishing work on the convention's terms of reference would abandon the task that had been set out for them and prejudge Newfoundland as unfit for responsible government. An observer might have concluded that confederation was a dead issue until the committees had reported upon the Newfoundland economy.

Smallwood, therefore, caught the nation by surprise when, during the first broadcast of a regular session of the convention, he proposed sending a delegation to Ottawa to negotiate confederation with Canada. Members of the convention had not been told that the microphones were being installed, but delegate Michael Harrington later reported[39] that Smallwood knew ahead of time that the proceedings were to be broadcast. Smallwood may indeed have had advance notice of the BCN's plans, since as a former broadcaster he may have learned of the technical preparations from someone other than Galgay. Learning that the BCN would soon broadcast the proceedings may have encouraged Smallwood, on 25 October, to give notice to the convention's Steering Committee that in three days he intended to propose sending a delegation to Canada to determine if suitable terms of union between Newfoundland and Canada could be reached. Despite the earlier decision that such a delegation should wait, the committee allowed Smallwood's motion, but under the parliamentary rules he had to give one day's notice. With the committee's approval and the microphones turned on, the chairman solved this problem by asking for unanimous consent from the convention to allow Smallwood's motion to be heard that day, the 28th. Smallwood scribbled onto a scrap of paper his motion to ascertain possible terms of union and rose to make his move.[40] In a tactical manoeuvre made over the heads of the anti-confederates in the chamber to the listeners at home, Smallwood made the motion on what might have been the only day the proceedings were to be broadcast.

Galgay's surprise that Smallwood made the confederation motion on the day of the experimental broadcast seems genuine, but he may have been wrong about it being a coincidence. Smallwood's desire to take advantage of the broadcast is a more likely explanation for the timing of the motion than either coincidence or the suggestion that the Commission or its Broadcasting Corporation chose to place microphones in the chamber when it got wind of Smallwood's plans. Since three of governors of the BCN – Furlong, J. S. Currie, and Charles Hunt – were to become active members of the Responsible Government League, it's unlikely that they were striving to give confederation any kind of advantage. Smallwood chose to make the motion when its public impact would be greatest and might have been the only day on which he could appeal to the electorate directly without the mediation of the press. His precipitous move also made the experimental broadcast a success, and Galgay reported to the Board of Governors that it 'aroused

such heated interest that we had no alternative but to continue recording the sessions.'[41]

This broadcast of the daily sessions soon posed challenges. As Galgay reported,

> The National Convention Reports, Recordings and Broadcasts have been
> the most important work since last meeting. The broadcasts of recordings
> of the debate on the confederation motion necessitated cancellation of a
> considerable number of our sponsored programs as well as a number of
> regular features such as the agricultural talks and the Co-operative Pro-
> gram. The recording and subsequent broadcast of the Convention requires
> the full time services of practically all the studio operating staff and the
> shortwave transmissions of the same material to Corner Brook further
> complicates matters.[42]

The Board was not committed to broadcasting the entire proceedings –
a task it felt was impossible – and wanted only the important debates to
be broadcast. It struck a committee to consider the subject.[43] In the
meantime, Galgay continued broadcasting the sessions.[44]

Smallwood's motion established him as the leading pro-confederate,
ensured that the rest of the proceedings were broadcast, and changed
the nature of the deliberations themselves. The majority of members
believed that the timing of the motion made no sense within the time-
table of the convention's investigations into the state of the nation. In
fact, the motion prejudged the viability of the Newfoundland state and
ensured that moderate delegates who might have been won over to
confederation through the study of the financial situation now committed themselves to a resumption of responsible government. While the
convention had been designed to follow parliamentary procedure and
was analogous to the former House of Assembly in many respects, it
had not been organized into parties, nor was there a 'government' and
'opposition' to give shape to its deliberations. The delegations to London and Ottawa, the investigations of the committees, and the months
of debate all earned confederation few new advocates within the convention members. Smallwood's motion divided the convention into
pro- and anti-confederate 'parties,' which lasted until the convention
dissolved. Most delegates who rose to their feet to oppose the motion in
October 1946 also voted against placing confederation upon the ballot
in January 1948. The responsible government 'party' had its own cau-
cus meetings, and now that the division had occurred, it was clear that

it had the majority of delegates on its side. This gave the advocates of responsible government a false confidence that they would prevail, since they had a majority of votes in the chamber and believed the convention would not recommend that confederation be placed upon the ballot. But their logic was flawed, since the convention's mandate was to advise on the options, not set the options on the ballot, and the British government reserved the right to select the options on the ballot itself. After the motion had been defeated, Smallwood used the daily broadcasts of the convention as a platform from which to address voters. He and other members of the convention were aware of the microphones and often spoke to the radio audience more than their fellow delegates. At one point, he explicitly admitted to the chairman of the convention that he addressed himself not to his fellow convention members, but to the prospective voters listening on the radio.[45] His ally Harold Horwood later claimed Smallwood would visit friends at the BCN to find out what time the convention debates would be broadcast so he could time his remarks to when they would have the maximum number of listeners during the evening.[46] The radio broadcasts encouraged uncommitted Newfoundlanders listening to the debates to consider union with Canada as an option.

The broadcasts of the proceedings stand as a remarkable example of radio broadcasting allowing the people to follow the debates upon their political future in their national assembly, but the broadcasts posed some difficulties for the BCN. The broadcasts required that the BCN cancel all programs after 9:15 p.m. The Corporation not only forwent revenue but had extraordinary expenses, prompting Galgay to comment that such a public service 'could not possibly be undertaken by any broadcasting company other than a nonprofit organization such as the corporation.'[47]

On 28 February 1947, Cashin placed the BCN in a position where its broadcasts became potentially libellous. The chairman, Gordon Bradley, who was appointed after Fox's death, warned Cashin not to make personal references and that such charges were outside the mandate of the convention. Cashin repeated on the convention floor his earlier accusation that many members of the Alderdice government, including A.J. Walsh, H.A. Winter, and James Winter had solicited bribes in the form of promises of government appointments in exchange for their support for the bill suspending responsible government.[48] These accusations had been made on earlier occasions, both over VOCM and in print, but this time the three justices sued him for libel. Despite Galgay's concerns, the

BCN was not named as a co-defendant, even though the claimants suggested that the fact that the accusations had been broadcast made the libel worse. Adding to the farcical character of the proceedings, the claimants were represented by Furlong, the secretary of the BCN, and the case was heard by Justice Brian Dunfield, the judicial colleague of the claimants. In the celebrated case, Cashin defended himself, perhaps because lawyers were wary of questioning the ethics of three justices of the Supreme Court before the court, or perhaps because Cashin's defence was based upon convincing jurors that he was a little guy like them and was being ganged up upon by professional lawyers.[49] Since VONF had been the medium though which the allegedly libellous statements had been delivered, in theory it could have been named as a co-defendant, and the plaintiff's lawyer might have been called as a witness. As indicated in chapter 3, in the case of *Jones v. The Great Eastern and Import Oil Co. Ltd*, one year earlier, Dunfield believed that broadcasting a libellous statement made the damages worse, since millions of people might hear it. But at that time he had thought there could be no finding of damages for libel, since the words had not been published and no statute extended libel provisions relating items in print to items broadcast. He was now not so cautious and instructed the jury in the Cashin trial differently. Dunfield suggested that since the words were recorded in a permanent form on a Broadcasting Corporation disc and could be reproduced, they were therefore potentially libellous.[50] He also dismissed Cashin's defence of parliamentary immunity, arguing that the convention was not a legislature. Despite Dunfield's charge to the jury favouring the plaintiffs, the case resulted in a hung jury and Cashin claimed to have been vindicated.[51]

Cashin's comments in court had also raised the question of whether members of the convention wanted the broadcasts of their proceedings to continue. The convention had not requested the broadcast of its proceedings, but Galgay, who felt the dramatic first broadcast demonstrated the importance of continuing, reported that the delegates and the general public favoured its continuation. He now asked Bradley for reassurance that the convention approved of the broadcasts.[52] Many members of the convention expressed the view that they would not have approved of the broadcasts had they been asked before they began, but now that they were underway it was important that the public continue to be able to follow deliberations on the radio. A couple of members felt that the presence of the microphones encouraged speakers to be long-winded, but they agreed that the benefits of the public being able to follow the debates outweighed that annoyance.[53] The convention voted unanimously in favour of continuing to have its proceedings broadcast,[54] and the BCN governors agreed to broadcast debates of the convention in their entirety.[55]

Having completed most of its investigations by the spring of 1947, the convention sent fact-finding delegations to London and Ottawa. Members of the London delegation hoped to have the British promise aid to Newfoundland if it resumed responsible government, and the Ottawa delegation negotiated draft terms of union into the Canadian federation. The delegation to London returned empty handed, since the British government was determined to offer nothing that would make responsible government attractive. Only the Ottawa delegation was welcomed by people who wanted to offer something to Newfoundland. Through the summer of 1947, the Canadians and Newfoundlanders tried to reach an agreement generous enough to Newfoundland to be accepted by the Newfoundland public but not so generous that existing provinces would demand that they be given the same deal.

While the convention delegation was in Ottawa, a group outside the Convention, the Responsible Government League (RGL), prepared to campaign. The RGL had felt constrained by the principle that the convention should impartially investigate forms of government, but was angered that the delegation to Ottawa had taken it upon itself to negotiate proposed terms of union. The RGL now belatedly engaged in the fray in a series of ten broadcasts, starting in August. Galgay pointed out to the Board that such broadcasts would raise precedents for all such campaigning. He suggested that the Corporation had to establish a policy for editing programs and decide to what extent it would allow 'speakers to criticise, attack or ridicule individuals, groups or parties.'[56] He recommended that a lawyer be appointed for the duration of the campaign to oversee the content in the talks. Such regulations were all the more urgent, since he believed 'that the expected "campaign"' preceding the referendum would not be conducted on the 'highest ethical level.'[57]

Upon the return of the Ottawa delegation, the convention settled into the last two tasks: the debates upon the Economic Report of the Finance Committee, which set out the case for an independent Newfoundland, and upon the Ottawa delegation's report. Smallwood used the latter debate to explain to the listening public the material benefits they could expect if union with Canada became a reality. The other side of his argument has received less attention but is as noteworthy. Smallwood attempted to connect in people's minds the hard times of the Great Depression and the exploitation of the truck system with the responsible form of government and to make a vote for confederation a vote against Water Street merchants. Confederation was an opportunity to get the tangible benefits of the Canadian welfare state, and Smallwood also presented it as a vote for a North American consumer lifestyle. He remained devoted to making the best use of these broadcasts; when the convention began night sessions, Smallwood proposed limiting these sessions to the hours upon which the Broadcasting Corporation was on the air. He expressed concern that the public was hearing half the debate – the discussion of the Finance Committee's report – but might not hear the other half – the explanation of the terms of union with Canada. The convention's night sessions ended before VONF's 11:00 p.m. sign-off.[58] The BCN committed itself to record and broadcast these evening sessions.[59]

Smallwood's exposition of the benefits of union might have had some effect, but it is not possible to prove that people were convinced by the broadcasts to favour confederation. Not all listeners were interested in the convention's proceedings or even thought that broadcasting was the best way to keep the public informed. A letter to the editor from a reader in rural Newfoundland argued that the summary published in the paper was sufficient to keep the public informed and suggested that the broadcasts were a waste of money. 'I've listened to one record broadcast,' wrote Malcolm Pelley of Smith's Sound. 'I don't intend to listen to another.'[60] Listeners can hardly have found the procedural debates and committee reports entertaining, although the debate on the terms of union provoked more interest.

Reports on public opinion of the Newfoundland Rangers are one of the few measures of the reception of the convention broadcasts. Rangers in Belleoram and Bonne Bay reported that most people in their districts had been paying close attention to the broadcasts during the debates on the confederation terms.[61] Ranger C. Parsons in Port Saunders thought that Smallwood's speeches had swung public opinion in favour of confederation.[62] The Ranger in Englee wrote that there had been considerable interest in listening to debates upon family allowances and old age pensions, but then it had been lost in the proceedings and people viewed them with 'utter contempt.' He believed that many people listened only for the 'enjoyment of listening to the humorous arguments.'[63] In Gambo the Ranger also remarked that people attended to the debate for entertainment rather than information,[64] while the

Ranger in Burgeo suggested listeners were dissatisfied with the slow pace of the convention's deliberations.[65] Rancour might have hurt the cause of responsible government, for the Ranger in Deer Lake commented that a few listeners expressed their disgust for the proceedings and thought the partisan disputes within the convention might be a harbinger of what they would get under responsible government.[66] The report from Marystown similarly claimed that people were irritated that the convention had become 'little more than a debating society with political ambitions.'[67] On the other hand, the report from Meadow's Point suggested that the broadcasts of the RGL had made some headway in changing opinions.[68] The Ranger is St Anthony believed that radio propaganda could not take the place of campaigning in person, as he put it: 'It seems that unless men are put in the field, propaganda for any form of government being broadcast from St John's will have little or no effect.'[69] While these reports are not objective readings of public opinion, on balance the Rangers seem to have thought there was much more support for the Commission (their employer) than existed. Furthermore, the reports remind us that voters were not necessarily swayed by radio propaganda.

At the end of the convention's deliberations the majority of members recommended that the ballot read 'responsible government as it existed in 1933' (this wording was approved, since they did not want Britain to grant some lesser degree of constitutional autonomy than the colony had earlier enjoyed) and continued Commission. Now advocates for responsible government believed that the matter was settled, but Smallwood immediately launched a petition asking for confederation to be placed upon the ballot as well. Here Smallwood was pushing on an open door, since the British had always hoped Newfoundlanders would choose confederation and had originally set out to have the convention play only an advisory role. Despite the protests of the RGL about the lack of fair play, they learned with the rest of the country that confederation was to be placed upon the ballot, through a prepared statement from the governor read over VONF.

The responsible government forces had a more difficult task than did Smallwood. The RGL started from behind in articulating a clear vision of a future for Newfoundland. They had to convince people to forgo the personal benefits of Canadian citizenship and, as Smallwood had reminded his audiences, risk a return to fishocracy – economic and political domination by a fish-exporting elite. His critics were not too far off the mark when they accused Smallwood of fomenting class warfare. The RGL's appeal was primarily nationalistic; its slogan was a simple 'Don't sell your country.' The confederates countered that rhetoric by tying confederation to renewing the connection to the empire, with placards that proclaimed 'Confederation – British Union.'

Once more, radio became a tool of election campaigning. To provide a level playing field the BCN gave both the newly formed Confederate Association and RGL equal time upon the public station. This approach had worked fairly well during the campaign up to the first referendum, in which responsible government won a plurality, confederation came second, and continued Commission of Government placed a poor third. The RGL declared victory, and its members were angered when the British announced that the third option would be dropped and another referendum held. The second campaign brought out the worst in both sides. Smallwood and his confederates took advantage of an editorial in the Roman Catholic *Monitor* recommending that Catholics vote for responsible government, by appealing to the members of the Orange Lodge to vote for confederation rather than be dominated by the church. The first referendum also prompted newspaper owner Geoff Stirling and broadcaster Donald Jamieson to form the Economic Union Association (EUA), a new political party that tried to make responsible government more attractive by advocating free trade with the United States. This stance posed a potential difficulty for the BCN, which decided in fairness to divide the time so that advocates for each form of government would get a total of one hour per week. The Confederate Association received one hour, and a second hour had to be shared between the two organizations that favoured responsible government.[70] Between 5 and 17 July, advocates of the two ballot options would be allowed twenty-minute addresses at times set by Galgay.[71] This decision pleased neither side. Smallwood protested to Commissioner R.L.M. James that three members of the Board of the BCN were active members of the RGL, and they unfairly limited the Confederate Association's access to the air.[72] While James thought that the Board's handling of the situation had an 'arbitrary flavour' and that it had unduly restricted access to the air in this important national matter, he worried about the lack of precedent for overruling the Board.[73] This restriction on the hours raises the question of whether the anti-confederate members of the Board thought they were giving responsible government an advantage by limited access to the more skilled broadcaster, Smallwood. In any case, the responsible government advocates also felt aggrieved by BCN policy. To limit the demands upon the resources of the Corporation, the BCN allowed air time only for representatives of the three recognized political organization. Thus when the lawyer and convention chairman J.B. McEvoy, who was secretly a confederate, requested air time to warn of the potential dangers to the fishery posed by economic union, his request was denied. Galgay suggested that he would be welcome to express his views if the Confederate Association assigned him their time. Galgay was not swayed by McEvoy's argument that he was not going to discuss forms of government, but only discuss the danger of retaliation toward the fishery.[74] McEvoy published his correspondence with Galgay in the *Evening Telegram*.[75] In another example, the BCN blocked the EUA's attempt to breathe new life into a floundering campaign when it solicited a statement by the American senator Weyland C. Brooks. Brooks had stated that there was support for economic union within the US Senate. Stirling judged that hearing the words would be more compelling than reading them, so he had an actor record Brooks's words. The BCN decided that having an actor read Brooks's statement constituted a 'dramatized political broadcast,' which was prohibited under the *CBC Act* of 1936, which the Commission had used to draft its own act.[76] This decision prevented the EUA from broadcasting the recording and limited Jamieson to summarizing Brooks's words.

Confederation carried the second referendum by a narrow margin of the popular vote. Commentators often point to the 'poor majority' and credit the victory of confederation to Smallwood's skill as a radio propagandist. Such an interpretation must be tempered with recognition that the districts that voted most heavily in favour of responsible government were those on the Avalon Peninsula. That was also the area with the highest level of radio ownership and most reliable reception of VONF. Rural areas, with fewer listeners and those more poorly served by the national broadcaster, were those that voted overwhelmingly in favour of union with Canada. While radio did much to publicize the terms of union, other factors must explain why people voted the way that they did.

With the referenda campaign over, most anti-confederates, such as RGL president F.M. O'Leary, reconciled themselves to having lost. A few continued to struggle to have the referendum results overturned, on the grounds that under the *British North America Act* only an elected legislature had the authority to request Newfoundland be admitted to the federal union. The RGL's secretary successfully requested time to publicize the league's efforts to circulate a petition.[77] Two fifteen-minute broadcasts set out the league's opinion that the process had been illegal.[78] Having satisfied the minimum level of coverage of this point of view, the BCN banned continued political debate. Cashin tried to evade the prohibition by maintaining that he was not representing any political party and cited the regulation that entitled former members of the Assembly to address the nation upon matters of public interest. The Board rejected the request, since 'all Political Broadcasts and Broadcasts on Political Matters have been suspended for the present.'[79] Not surprisingly, the RGL protested the Commission's 'highly dictatorial ... muzzling of this means of communication.'[80] The RGL perceived the prohibition on political broadcasts as an attempt to interfere in its efforts to prepare a petition requesting that the referendum results be set aside.[81] Despite RGL President Marshall's protest that the *Broadcasting Act* of 1939 had not been intended to prevent people from being informed about matters of national interest, Commissioner James maintained the ban on political broadcasting.[82] On 24 November 1948, the RGL made another application for air time, this time to broadcast the report of their members who were about to return from London, where they had presented their petition.[83] The Board of the BCN rejected the request, pointing out that as of 9 October the commissioner of finance had directed the Corporation 'to refrain, until further notice, from broadcasting matter sponsored by the Responsible Government League or other political organizations.'[84]

Now that the Dominions Office had its desired outcome, the BCN shut down political debate just as it detractors had warned it would. Suspicion lingered among those who questioned the wisdom of confederation that broadcasting the proceedings of the convention had been part of a concerted effort to give Smallwood an advantage. The New Zealand Parliament, for example, began broadcasting its proceedings because the Labour Government did not trust the conservative newspaper owners to communicate the government's message to voters.[85] Similarly, the Dominions Office officials did not trust the Newfoundland political elite to give voters a fair chance to choose to join Canada. But, as we have seen, the government did not direct the BCN to broadcast the debates; Galgay took the initiative when the summaries of the debates fell short of giving the people a full sense of the deliberations. The British and Canadian officials were undoubtedly pleased that the public broadcaster chose to broadcast the proceedings, and once they had the outcome they favoured, they were happy that the BCN shut down access to the air to those who sought to overturn the referendum outcome.

Except for the first month's proceedings, the BCN had broadcast nearly the whole of the debates of the National Convention over VONF for listeners on the east coast. The BCN continued to have a reporter in the gallery, who compiled reports that were transmitted via its short-wave transmitter. The Corner Brook station, VOWN, recorded these reports, which were transmitted that evening to west coast listeners. An *Evening Telegram* columnist complimented the excellent job the BCN had done in giving people in faraway places the opportunity to follow the debates, although the columnist questioned if the 'presence of the microphone in the Convention aided or impeded the deliberations.'[86] There is little doubt that broadcasting had a great effect upon the work of the convention as well as the lessons people drew from it. One listener compared the convention members to 'small children playing and throwing snowballs at each other' and likely had his reservations about politics under responsible government reconfirmed.[87]

Galgay's post-mortem of the first referendum campaign suggested that there had been too much political broadcasting and that the campaigning had started too early. He also revealed the extent that the debate had polarized the politically active. Galgay complained that it had not been possible to get a legal opinion in cases where scripts were questionable, since all the country's lawyers were taking part in the campaign.[88] He reported that 256 hours and forty-five minutes of the convention's debates were broadcast, and it is doubtful that any commercial broadcaster could have undertaken such a large-scale public service.[89] This mammoth undertaking strained the financial and staff resources of the BCN and slowed its planned expansion into Gander and Grand Falls, and the construction of new facilities in Corner Brook and St John's. Not only did the BCN have to pay for blank recording discs and needles, extra salary for a recording technician and a reporter, and the depreciation of the Corporation's equipment, but the nightly broadcasts meant the cancellation of all commercial programs after 9:15 p.m. and the consequent loss of income.[90] The broadcasts of the convention were followed by referenda campaigning, during which the corporation provided free political broadcasts – serving a vital public service but again passing over the opportunity for revenue that might have allowed VONF to improve its programming. Focusing upon the missed opportunities to do other things, however, is to take too narrow a view of the BCN's mission. The convention broadcasts allowed Newfoundlanders throughout the country to participate in the constitutional debate only a few hours after the discussions took part among their elected representatives. Years later, many people remembered listening to the debates in their nation's legislative chamber and having those debates on the future of their country spill over into arguments in their homes. The size of the listening audience likely varied, depending upon the nature of the report being presented or the topic being debated, but during crucial debates on proposed terms of union there is little doubt that a large number of listeners tuned into the dramatic debates.[91] As many commentators at the time and subsequently noted, these debates did much to inform listeners of the specific benefits of union with Canada. Smallwood might have been right that, given the closeness of the referendum results, the broadcasts were decisive in determining the outcome, but his view of every household in the country tuned into his every word is an exaggeration. Judging by the reports on public opinion of the Rangers, people were sceptical of much of the propaganda they heard and sometimes viewed it as a source of entertainment rather than information they would use to inform their decisions. We have to look to factors other than the supposed persuasive power of radio broadcasting to explain voting behaviour.

The unique features of this case underline some of the democratic potential for radio broadcasting. When the colonies of British North American united in 1867 it was primarily though accommodations made by elites, for voters in most colonies did not have the opportunity to accept or reject confederation. In Newfoundland in 1948 not only did voters have the opportunity to vote in a national referendum, but they were fully informed of the specific implications of the terms of union though the broadcasts of the debates. In this instance, radio broadcasting provided a national forum for the articulation of views of the future of the country and allowed geographically dispersed citizens to participate in those arguments through their listening and ultimately their ballots.

6 Personal and Intimate Character: The Transitions of Post-war Radio, 1945–1949

We have examined the BCN's role in the confederation debate, but not many of the other questions faced by the Corporation after the war. In reflecting upon the BCN operations during 1945, Galgay emphasized the public service of the 'national institution.'

> A review of the operations disclose that a large volume of public service was rendered. Apart from the features of entertainment the Corporation has become a National Institution for the dissemination of News, Public Announcements, Educational Addresses to isolated Folk as well as to the larger centres of population, to the men in the lumber woods, in the mines, and to those who go down to the sea in ships. Our programmes reach out to the lonely men in the lighthouses, to the people of Labrador and to the folk on the various islands off our coast. These broadcasts keep our citizens where ever so dispensed in touch with the local and foreign news of the day.[1]

Victory in Europe allowed the Corporation to return its attention to improving programming and service, but as we have seen, it soon had its resources taken up by the demands of broadcasting the country's constitutional debate. Despite these challenges, the BCN reviewed its programming in ways that it had not since the Corporation had been first established. This chapter examines the other uses of radio broadcasting between 1945 and 1949. That period, like the war years, saw remarkable social and economic changes. At one level, the confederation question was whether to embrace Newfoundland's place as part of North America or maintain the country's identity as 'Britain's oldest colony.' This chapter argues that parallel to the confederation debate ran a debate among broadcasters and listeners between those who wanted American popular culture and those who wanted greater 'British' character to their broadcasting. The reopening of political debate and question of whether Newfoundland was to follow the British model of administration or the Canadian one also reopened the question of how much government control there was to be over the privately owned broadcaster. This chapter also points out ways that the negotiations with the government of Canada affected broadcasting in the year leading up to union. Confederation had won the day, but the tensions between public and private and entertainment and educational all remained unresolved as the Corporation moved toward its ultimate absorption into the CBC. Through all of this, Galgay remained committed to Newfoundland radio. In the end, he convinced the CBC, which in 1949 became the new owner of VONF, to maintain the personal and intimate character of Newfoundland radio.

Despite the pressures of the Second World War, the BCN had expanded its role as the national broadcaster. In 1943 it established the 1000-watt VOWN in Corner Brook to provide coverage to listeners on the west coast, who frequently had difficulty receiving VONF or its short-wave transmitter. The original plan had been for VOWN to operate on a limited schedule 'to re-broadcast the announcements, functions, and statements, etc., of National interest which are broadcast through VONF and to give a limited entertainment service to the west coast.' VOWN soon expanded to operate a schedule with nearly as many hours as its St John's counterpart.[2] The small staff at the 'Voice of Western Newfoundland' – manager Clifford Hierlihy, a stenographer, and three 'studio operator/announcers' – created their own programming and rebroadcast programs from St John's and other networks, and did so at a profit. They also replicated some of VONF's programming. F.M. O'Leary, for example, sent out copies of the *Barrelman* scripts to be read over VOWN by the West Coast Barrelman – his brother, Stan O'Leary. By 1946 had Galgay set aside money for the construction of a Corner Brook Broadcasting House, when the hotel hosting the VOWN studios wanted the space back. In all, VOWN was a great success. In 1947, Galgay, who remained committed to a public service broadcast model, observed, 'Although VOWN presents many more commercial programs than VONF, its popularity and appreciation by the public is very much higher.'[3]

More by chance than design, the BCN acquired a third station in 1946. During the war the Royal Canadian Air Force had operated a low-power broadcasting station at the Gander airport, not only for the entertainment of personnel, but also because the transmitter could guide lost aircraft trying to find the airfield. With the peacetime transfer of the airport to the Newfoundland government, VORG went off the air on 1 April 1946. When Galgay visited Gander, he found about $4000 worth of valuable equipment was now in the possession of the government. The airport authorities reported that the average listener in Gander lacked a receiver able to receive VONF, and that the existing VORG was necessary not only as a medium of communication but also for its use in emergencies. The Civil Aviation Division was willing to transfer VORG assets to the BCN free of charge if the Corporation would operate the station; otherwise the station would be handed over to a former member of the RCAF who wanted to operate it. Galgay felt that all broadcasting stations should be in the hands of the Corporation and recommended to the Board that it take over the station immediately. Not only would this serve the two or three thousand people in Gander, but residents of Grand Falls, Windsor, Bishop Falls, Botwood, and many other communities, for a total population of more than 10,000 potential listeners. He believed that some of the VORG's expenses could be covered by local advertisers, but recommended that the BCN carry the station without counting upon revenue. The Corporation had to move swiftly before VORG's equipment was scattered, some of which could be transferred to St John's, where it could be used. Since there was now a telephone line between St John's and Grand Falls and the Corporation hoped to use such a line to support a station in Grand Falls in the future, Galgay believed the time was right to negotiate use of the line to the station at Gander.[4] The proposal was accepted, but bringing VORG back into operation was delayed until 1947 because of demands on the staff created by the broadcasts of the National Convention.[5]

Despite the improvements at VONF, the short-wave transmitter VONH, the construction of VOWN, and later the acquisition of VORG, many listeners continued to complain about the same things they had before the war. People still resented paying the licence fee for their sets and continued to find reception was sometimes impossible because of static. While in the 1920s listeners welcomed any local broadcasting, regardless of its quality or character, by the 1940s people had become more discriminating. The expanded access to American radio broadcasting, through Newfoundland-based stations such as VOUS as well as high-powered stations in the United States itself, had made Newfoundland listeners and Newfoundland broadcasters familiar with a style of radio announcers very different from Galgay's preferred delivery. It would be an exaggeration to say that he emulated the BBC's formal style, but Galgay endeavoured to have VONF conform to a high standard of respectable public service and authoritative delivery. Some younger broadcasters, however, such as Vardy and Jamieson, the latter of whom did occasional work on both VONF and VOCM, used more colloquial language and more rapid speaking styles than the older generation of announcers, more like the American commercial broadcasters they heard. MacDonald, for example, consciously emulated the American sports broadcaster Lowell Thomas, whom he admired and with whom he corresponded.[6]

Not everyone liked the American style of radio announcers. Even while public service continued to be the dominant motive for the programming and the BBC news continued to be heard regularly, some Newfoundlanders were concerned that the Voice of Newfoundland was losing its local character and becoming like North American commercial radio. In 1946, the editor of the *Daily News* looked back with nostalgia upon the radio broadcasting before the war:

> The average radio programme may continue its raucous course unheeded: it is so much noise, and some people must have noise to be happy. But the church service gets close attention from its listeners. Grandmother gets out her hymn-book or her bible and follows the service as reverently as though she were seated in her pew. On beds of sickness where weakness prevents any such active participation, the weary or pain-wracked patient forgets for the moment the discomfort. In this country it is not forgotten that the earliest efforts at regular broadcasting came from such services, and that interest has never been lost. Perhaps it is partly because there is less reiteration of the church service. It comes only once in the week, instead of being cheapened by the daily monotony which commercial programmes produce. But it is more likely that it appeals with a dignity and sympathy which the average programme misses.[7]

Similarly, in January 1946 the *Evening Telegram* columnist 'Terranovan' argued that a privately owned radio station could give the same service as the BCN, without the subsidy of the licence fees. The column went on to criticize both the BCN and VOCM for the American character of their programming:

> As to local radio fare, both stations are using too much 'canned' music and

are not, as they should be, fostering local talent. In fact it seems the stations are going all out to Americanize their programs regardless of the feelings of the listeners. There are too many so-called dramatic recordings, some of which have a weird and sinister message, not altogether fit for children who, nevertheless, glue their ears to the speakers in order not to miss anything and then spend a restless night in bed. Even in local broadcasts persons seem to think they must use American pronunciation and even tone of voice to be effective.[8]

A Bonavista Bay listener wrote to Harrington, suggesting that he create a series of programs of music, poetry, and prose that could 'correct' Newfoundlanders' enunciation and eliminate Americanisms such as OK.[9] Terranovan did not hold up VOCM as an ideal: if VONF's programming was 95 per cent imported recordings, the columnist claimed, then its privately owned competitor broadcast 96 per cent. The columnist accused the BCN's Board of Governors of being 'inactive' and suggested it create a broadcasting code that would range from restricting programming that emphasized 'underworld activity' to setting the correct pronunciation among its broadcasters.[10] A letter from a listener concurred that 'our radio and reading matter today is conspicuously American' and suggested the BCN rebroadcast more British programming to lessen the 'misunderstanding that now exists between Newfoundland and Britain,' although the author did not specify the nature of that supposed misunderstanding he or she believed existed.[11]

Not only did the daily newspapers occasionally comment upon the BCN's shortcomings. Furlong also evaluated the programming in a confidential report to the Board. His conclusions were based upon his own listening, rather than any systematic research upon listeners' opinions. He heard little he liked. He began by critically assessing the station's fare and ended with eleven recommendations. Furlong found that the Doyle News, 'probably one of the most important programmes,' had declined from an excellent news service to a state of being uninteresting and badly written. The Barrelman, 'a very important contribution to our national culture,' had become dull and flat because Harrington's style of delivery lacked 'the conversational touch.' The Green Label News contained more advertising content than news. Furthermore, these advertisements were 'in the Canadian mode and in a voice and manner entirely foreign to Newfoundland.' (Furlong would later join the RGL and campaign against confederation with Canada, so his view of Canada as 'foreign' is consistent with his broader politics.) The entertainment programs aimed at women and children were no better, in his view. The commercial sponsors had, he thought, selected personnel poorly for the *Coca-Cola Children's Programme*. The announcer of the commercials 'has succeeded in imitating to a high degree of perfection the slick and artificially insincere manner of the worst type of American and Canadian announcers.' The young woman who read the children's stories was, in Furlong's view, 'uninspired' and had bypassed the wide field of children's literature to read nothing but 'the modern type of story' that was a product of commercial programming. He suggested that 'the elimination of this entire program would be a contribution to child education in Newfoundland.' He admitted that a balanced program schedule had to have some 'soap operas' but argued that the existing five such 'cheap and trivial' programs were an 'over-dose' and were 'indigestible.'

> The worst to be said of the 'soap operas' however is their commercial announcements. The amount of time that is occupied, say in 'Lucy Linton's Stories from Life' in the boosting of the manufacturers' soap is not only out of all proportion to the worth of the product, but what interests us more is out of all proportion to the amount of time the programme has on the air.[12]

As a lawyer, he also worried that if a product did not live up to promises made in the advertisements, consumers might sue the BCN.

As for music programming, Furlong again found that the BCN relied too heavily upon transcribed programs provided by commercial sponsors, and the result 'reflects very badly upon all those concerned.' He believed 'better' music was readily available, but VONF had not used it. He suggested that greater use of the Corporation's music library could provide excellent broadcasts, 'ranging from the best symphonic music to programmes of the most modern swing music.' Furlong also wanted regular use of the BBC's London Transcription Service, which could provide the 'products of the English studios' and counterbalance the 'American and Canadian propaganda' that 'besieged' the listener from all sides. While the station made poor use of its disproportionately British record library and depended upon the largely American commercial transcriptions to fill the broadcast day, it had not made good use of the locally available musical talent. The lack of 'any definite policy and many preconceived programme plans' had defeated attempts to enlist local musicians for broadcasts. The BCN's use of live talent had dwindled to a couple of 'mediocre' programmes, which were popular only by virtue of the fact that they were the only live talent on the air.[13] Furlong was not only unhappy with the American and Canadian style of the programming. He also wanted to purge the station of colloquial speech patterns. All announcers, both staff and commercial announcers, should, he proposed, be allowed upon the air only if they were reasonably well-educated and 'that their voices and their announcing manners are devoid of any local accent, mannerism or other idiosyncrasy.'[14]

Had Furlong solicited listeners' views, he would have found a range of opinion. One listener complained that children's minds were being disturbed by American crime dramas such as *Superman*, the *Green Hornet*, and the *Shadow*, when they should have been listening to beautiful plays, stories, and music.[15] Another listener, 'Critic,' disagreed, suggesting that it was only natural that children were interested in such shows, and argued that the moral of these stories did no harm.[16] The American producers of such programs as the *Green Hornet* provided violence for its entertainment value, and then ensured that criminals in the stories were punished so that broadcasters could assure critics that the stories had positive messages for children. 'Critic' pointed to the generational difference among listeners as well: 'One cannot expect a child to listen attentively to cultural music such as operas like Faust,' he or she argued. 'The limited entertainment our fathers and grandfathers received certainly isn't enough for our generation.'[17] 'Critic' had also put a finger on an important question about radio listening. Did listeners listen 'attentively' to programming that would have a beneficial effect upon them, as Reith of the BBC had advocated, or did listeners relax and enjoy entertainment as American commercial entertainment exemplified?[18] 'K.W.' complained that Newfoundland radio was 'only an advertising medium.' 'In between the ads we get a burst of Jazz and people moaning their life out, love sick and everything else' he or she commented.[19] 'Another Listener' enjoyed the opera carried by the local stations, and although he or she reported not liking hillbilly music, accepted the fact that there were many people who did.[20]

As we can see, some listeners recommended reducing the commercial content and enhancing the BBC sort of programming, which aimed to improve listeners' education and taste in entertainment; others wanted more radio in the North American style. Furlong favoured the former. He advised a reduction in the number of transcribed dramatic programs, the elimination of commercials during the programming itself, the restriction of commercials to the beginning and end of the program, and limiting of the total amount of time commercial announcements could take up. That would have effectively restricted the BCN from purchasing many of the most popular of American serialized women's and children's dramas. He recommended replacing some of the existing commercial programs with programs produced by the station's staff as well as the regular use of the London Transcription Service. The locally produced programming should, in his view, include 'serious, light, popular and dance music.' Furlong wanted to actively recruit musicians, and perhaps go a step further:

> The general standard of music appreciation in Newfoundland is not high, but the average Newfoundland listener is essentially fond of music. Consideration should be given to the establishment of a permanent choir and a permanent orchestra, under the auspices of the Corporation. The object of these musical groups would be to hold a series of concerts and broadcast regularly. The Corporation should endeavour to secure from abroad the services of the necessary conductors and choir masters, so that over a period of years a substantial musical group can be set up within Newfoundland.[21]

Had this proposal been taken up by the BCN, it would have been a significant attempt to foster a change in taste among Newfoundlanders.

During the preceding six years, Furlong reported, the Corporation had 'made no real headway' in recruiting a qualified program director. He thought some existing members of the BCN staff could be lent to the BBC or the CBC for a period of training in programming that would prepare them for the job of programming director.[22] His recommendation that the BCN loan staff to one of these two 'public broadcasters' underlines his view that entertainment on the Newfoundland station should be didactic and not merely popular, as was some American network programming. To be accurate, though, American networks such as NBC provided serious music with high-profile musicians to enhance the prestige of their networks. So any characterization of American culture as lowbrow should be seen as a rhetorical generalization, not an accurate observation.

Furlong had a few practical suggestions about scheduling as well. He proposed having a set program schedule with which listeners could become familiar and using advertising in newspapers to make the public aware of when particular programs were being broadcast. This would have helped to build an audience that might have found the programming to be hit and miss. Meanwhile, listener research undertaken by station staff could elicit listeners' views upon the programming.[23] The BBC had not embarked upon any listener research until the mid-1930s, since knowing what listeners liked might tempt programmers into giving the public what it wanted rather than what was good for them. It was not until the Second World War that the BBC began collecting data on listeners' preferences to aid management in making programming decisions.[24] The British broadcaster had also been slower to adopt fixed programming schedules than American commercial broadcasters, who built loyalty to specific programs by making it easy for listeners to predict when a show would air. Furlong wanted to make the BCN programming more like the BBC, and he, too, accepted that it would be beneficial to have a picture of what listeners liked and disliked. Advertising a regular programming schedule was more an American form than British.

The Board of Governors unanimously accepted Furlong's report and tasked him with implementing his recommendations. But the complete reorganization that was envisaged did not happen, despite some encouragement from the BBC's Michael Barkway, who visited the BCN in 1947. In a speech to the Rotary Club, which was broadcast, Barkway claimed the *BBC World News* had provided people in occupied Europe with their only source of accurate information and expressed the belief that radio was too important to be allowed to degenerate into a jukebox. He also assured the BCN that the BBC would lend any assistance necessary, within its power.[25] The Board instructed Galgay to reduce the number of transcribed dramatic programs, eliminate commercials in the middle of programs, and increase the number and length of sustaining programs. The new schedule was to be advertised and a program department established. Yet a year after the Board adopted Furlong's recommendations, he complained that the Corporation continued to consider signing contracts for commercially sponsored transcription programs.[26]

The tension between Newfoundland's North American and British orientation also emerged when the BCN re-evaluated its foreign news. As of 1945 the BCN was buying twenty-two hours of news per week from Reuters, which it not only sold to the local businesses that sponsored the broadcast of news but to the St John's newspapers as well.[27] At the end of the war the BCN found that Reuters was too Eurocentric for post-war Newfoundland. News of events in North America was notably lacking in Reuters, and British news was increasingly out of step with life on the island, once the soldiers, sailors, and airmen had returned home. At the same time, the BBC decided that with the end of the war the BCN should assume the transportation costs for its copies of the Empire Transcription Service and make a 'modest' payment toward the costs of production.[28] BBC content would no longer be free to the BCN, thus encouraging the re-evaluation that had already been undertaken.

The BCN was prompted to reconsider its programming policy when MacLeod, the only staff musician and one of only two full-time announcers, resigned in 1947 to work in the insurance business. The Corporation did not have a director of music, but if it had such a job title, the talented MacLeod would have held it. Galgay reported that it would be difficult to replace him with a staff pianist 'who has the necessary flexibility of performance to fulfil the requirements of the Corporation.'[29] Earlier, Galgay had given MacLeod permission to charge commercial sponsors a professional fee above his salary, since his value to the Corporation was 'out of all proportion to that of another member under the same classification and whose salary is in the same brackets.'[30] Eventually, Richard G. O'Brien replaced MacLeod as an announcer, but it found no director of music.[31] MacLeod continued to occasionally perform on VONF as a part-time professional musician. George Williams, Galgay, and Furlong struck a committee to reorganize programs, now that MacLeod was gone.[32] The three produced a summary of the Corporation's history that highlighted its goals and the constraints under which it had worked. From the beginning, they commented, the governors felt an obligation to do more than provide entertainment. The Corporation aspired to provide instructional and educational programs that served the fishery, agriculture, cooperative, forestry, adult education, etc. The governors had also hoped to establish a system of school broadcasts. In addition to occasional broadcasts by local specialists, the BCN arranged the purchase of school broadcasts from the CBC, BBC, and the United States. Since the population was scattered along a lengthy coastline, religious broadcasts, local and foreign news, and weather forecasts were all viewed as necessary programming. In what would have been a fundamental change to the way the BCN worked, the Board had also considered establishing both a national service and a local service for St John's on a lower-power transmitter. Programming on the two 'services' could thus have been tailored to the needs of urban and rural listeners. The governors believed that the existing VONF, because it was a St John's station, devoted much of its attention to broadcasting things that were not of interest to rural Newfoundlanders. As Galgay noted,

> Plans were also made for expansion on the program side but it must be born in mind that public service is of paramount importance with the corporation and, whereas the small local station can arrange its programs to appeal particularly to the St John's audience, the corporation has to meet the demands of a multitude of tastes throughout the outports as well. It must also serve as the only medium of instruction and information for the great majority of listeners who have no access to the newspapers and who are barely aware that they exist. This type of service invariably brings no monetary returns and would not be provided by privately operated stations, the owners of which are concerned only with programs which produce revenue for the station.[33]

The Corporation had never been able to develop separate services for urban and rural listeners, or make many of the other improvements to programming, because its plans were pre-empted by wartime needs and the demands of the constitutional debate. Nevertheless, Galgay argued that its primary public service role had been fulfilled and that lighter entertainment programming had not been neglected. Sustaining musical and dramatic programs had earned large listening audiences. VONF and VOWN had presented 22,872 programs between them during 1946, only 37 per cent of which were commercial programs. The Corporation also intended in November of that year to increase on-air time by five and a half hours (9:00 a.m. to midnight). On balance, the BCN saw its programming as a success. As the internal review concluded,

> The corporation does not contend that its programs are ideal. It is realized that there is always room for improvement. The program staff of the corporation has had many years experience in attempting to deal with the likes and dislikes of the listener. Those who are actually engaged in programming not only in Newfoundland but elsewhere, soon realize that there are no set standards which may be used as guides, trial and error are the only guides to what the public wants. The broadcaster may present what he thinks is the finest program in the world, but he has no control over who will listen to it. The fact that it is a worthwhile program means absolutely nothing, researchers have found that no one can set himself up as an authority on what programs are good and what programs are not

good. The individual or individuals of like education and intelligence can only decide what they like best themselves. The old proverb 'what is one man's meat is another man's poison' – is truest when applied to radio programs. Perusal of the log sheets of the corporation will demonstrate that the corporation had followed the policy, within its limitations, of providing a variety of programs in which each type of listener has received a fair proportion of his particular preference in entertainment. I do not say that the listener has received as much of his particular preference as he may desire but I reiterate that he has received a fair proportion of his preference, which, amidst the multiplicity of tastes to be satisfied, is all to which he is entitled.[34]

This document reveals more than Galgay's self-congratulation for a job well done. It also shows that he had accepted the North American goal of attempting to serve the variety of tastes in music, rather than attempting to shape public taste, as Furlong seems to have favoured.

While in practice the Corporation had come down on the side of appealing to listeners' musical taste rather than changing it, at the end of the war the BCN also revisited the question of whether or not to allow the expansion of privately owned broadcasters.[35] Partly in response to a rumour that Butler was about to reapply for an increase of power for VOCM and then sell the station to a 'foreign interest,'[36] Galgay suggested the Board of Governors establish regulations governing privately owned stations. His concern may also have been prompted by an application for a broadcasting licence from the *Evening Telegram*, which promised to not only develop Newfoundland broadcasting talent but also to rebroadcast American and Canadian programming to fill what it perceived to be a forthcoming void, once VOUS went off the air.[37] A note in the BCN's correspondence, in Galgay's hand, suggests he believed that this proposal was really being made by the Canadian-based Thomson group of newspapers.[38] While the BCN issued no new broadcasting licences, another business hoped to enter the broadcasting field by entering into a partnership with the BCN. At the beginning of 1947 the *Sunday Herald*, owned by the young entrepreneur Geoff Stirling, proposed purchasing time between 7:00 a.m. and 10:00 a.m., when VONF was normally off the air. Although the arrangement would be profitable for the BCN, Galgay thought that the idea of 'time block buying' was likely to lead to disputes that would reflect badly upon the Corporation. He thought it unlikely that the *Sunday Herald* would use all of the time itself. Stirling would, therefore, want to sell some of its allotted time to other sponsors and expect a profit for his trouble. Galgay believed this proposal was not feasible since it would require selling time in the early morning at higher price than the rate for the more attractive period later in the day. He also believed that there was little demand for broadcasting during the early morning. Last, he warned the Board of Governors against the BCN forming an affiliation with a private interest that might 'be highly biassed or even diametrically opposed to those of the national system.' Those who opposed the corporation, Galgay worried, would welcome the opportunity to imply that the BCN was biased in favour of the *Sunday Herald*.[39] Galgay recommended disallowing power increases, and regulating privately owned broadcasting stations more closely. In March 1946, Galgay proposed that privately owned stations be required to provide proof that they had permission from originating stations to rebroadcast the content of their news reports. He also reiterated his view that regulations were needed to govern the establishment of new stations, the method of renewing licences (to make it clear the licencee must be the actual operator), and that licences were not transferable.[40]

Butler had his lawyer, Leslie R. Curtis, prepare a detailed response to these proposed regulations. Curtis objected to the potential restrictions and argued regulation was unnecessary:

> Now that the war is over, and the need for censorship in any form no
> . longer exists the Corporation proposes to adopt regulations which will
> have the effect of empowering it to censor and completely muzzle public
> opinion in Newfoundland, and this station insists that, at such critical time
> above all others in the history of Newfoundland, such dictatorship should
> not be seriously considered ... We unhesitatingly say such a proposal is
> 'ultra vires' the corporation.[41]

Curtis suggested that the BCN had no more right to tell VOCM what it could broadcast than it had to tell newspapers what they could publish. The proposed regulation requiring the station to submit programming to the BCN before broadcast was 'dictatorship at its worst.'[42] Government commissions had a role, he conceded, 'but as for these commissions starting in business in opposition to and partially capitalized by the private organizations they are appointed to regulate, even an apathetic public should shiver in its shoes, for under such a state of affairs, democracy becomes a myth and freedom of speech a fading memory.'[43] Considered in its context, this reveals a conception of the word *democ-*

racy that was different from the usual and more narrow meaning of elected government. Newfoundland had not had an election since 1932, and despite fighting a war in the name of democracy was still governed by a committee of civil servants appointed by the Dominions Office. Condemning commissioners as 'petty dictators' and comparing them to Goebbels, as Curtis did, could be used to condemn the policy as one imposed by outsiders rather than one that came from legitimate sources within the community. But Curtis was not talking of elections; he was using the word *democracy* to connote the freedom of business to operate without government restriction or competition from state-owned enterprises. The reference to 'freedom of speech' becoming a 'fading memory' might seem incongruous, but American broadcasters had successfully argued that only commercial broadcasters ensured freedom of the air, since they depended on serving the public if they were to survive. State broadcasters, or broadcasters owned by other institutions such as trade unions, for example, were a threat to freedom because they would serve their own interests rather than the public's.[44] The Canadian situation had been slightly different from either the American or the Newfoundland case. Canadians, too, accepted the fact that a competitive market system in broadcasting was analogous to democracy in government, but privately owned Canadian broadcasters welcomed the creation of a mixed private and public system. What they disliked was being regulated by what was in effect a competitor, the CBC, and theoretically restricted in their ability to form a privately owned network.[45] Curtis condemned the Newfoundland regulations; which went farther than the Canadian regulations had:

This section constitutes the corporation a 'star chamber' and enables it to meet in secret, and, presumably by a majority vote, pass judgement and enforce same by suspending the licence of a private station for any period not exceeding three months. This is a very heavy penalty that cannot be assessed in dollars; yet power of imposition is taken by the corporation from the courts. The corporation thus constitutes itself a judge in its own cause – a most dangerous and iniquitous precedent, not contemplated by the act. It is submitted that the clear intention of the act was that the corporation should define the offense and prescribe the penalty ... but the whole question as to the guilt and, if so, the penalty should be determined by a court of law after a fair and public trial ... It may be noted that the government station is *not* liable to any penalties for infringement of any of these regulations, and it can with impunity completely disregard the same ...

Regulations should be equally binding on all stations and enforceable only by independent courts. Such discrimination places the government station *above* the law, which the broadcasting act never contemplated.[46]

Galgay maintained that rather than being restricted by the BCN, VOCM benefited from the BCN protecting it from any competition, since it was the only commercial station that had a licence.[47] He was annoyed that while he perceived his dealings with VOCM as fair, his old colleague Butler used 'the banner of "free speech" as a cloak' to libel the Corporation.[48] Based toward Galgay's recommendation, the BCN's Board denied Butler's requested power increase for his AM transmitter, and for a licence for a short-wave transmitter.[49] Butler then appealed to Commissioner of Finance James, and added a request for permission to experiment with frequency modulation (FM). Butler may have hoped that, by adapting FM technology – which had several advantages over AM – before his state-owned competitor, he could gain some commercial advantage. Butler complained that his applications to the BCN had never been 'honestly considered' and that the BCN's real motive had been 'curtailing the operation of an independent station.'[50] He claimed that VOCM provided all the same public services provided by the BCN, but, unlike VONF, VOCM did so without censorship. He went on to suggest that his station would be best able to provide impartial information to the public during the constitutional debate. Since three of the governors of the BCN – Currie, Furlong, and Hunt – had endorsed the platform of the RGL, Butler argued the Corporation might be biased during the coming referendum. 'A powerful and free and independent station, which VOCM has demonstrated itself to be since its inception,' he wrote, 'may be considered a "must" if a full and intelligent educational campaign is to be permitted.' Butler further suggested that the BCN was subsidized by the government, lost money on its operations, and charged advertisers such a low rate as to subsidize advertisers.[51]

Galgay reminded the Commission that the question of state or private ownership had more at stake for the BCN than competition with Butler's VOCM. VONF's 640 kc was the only frequency available that could provide coverage to both coastal Labrador and the fishing fleets on the Grand Banks. Broadcast frequencies were assigned by international treaty, and the little country had little influence or power to force other nations to not use 640 kc and thus ensure it would be available for Newfoundland exclusively. If Cuba, for example, allowed a station to build a high-powered transmitter using that frequency, then many listeners in

Newfoundland would be unable to hear the St John's station. New-foundland had successfully asked other North American countries for greater protection for 640 kcs than it was entitled to, by virtue of the size of the country's population, by arguing that radio in Newfoundland served a vital role in protecting life. Galgay had argued that marine weather forecasts, for example, prevented disaster, and that in New-foundland radio was not primarily used for entertainment as it was in most countries. If VOCM, a privately owned for-profit corporation, which primarily provided entertainment to listeners, were to expand, Galgay worried, other countries might no longer accept his argument that broadcasting in Newfoundland was special. As he warned,

The entire position with regard to frequency allocation at the next [inter-national frequency allocation] conference is extremely unpredictable, and any change in the present situation is bound to have an adverse effect in Newfoundland. If for some reason Newfoundland should lose its rights on 640kc then the whole picture of Broadcasting in Newfoundland may be changed and the value of the ten-kilowatt station VONF may be reduced to such an extent that many regional stations may have to be established within the Island to give the same coverage as now provided by VONF. In addition to these technical reasons, it is the opinion of the Governors of the Corporation, that the Act from which they receive that authority has placed in their hands the responsibility for the direction of a valuable National Asset in such a manner that the greatest benefit to the public will be assured. But for the outbreak of the war broadcasting in Newfoundland would have developed in an orderly manner and the objects for which the corporation was instituted and would now have been within reach. Instead the corporation is only commencing the development of this national asset, and until such time as the responsibility to ensure the great-est benefit to the public has been discharged, the corporation is unable to consider the exploitation of any part of this National Trust for the primary purpose of personal gain to an individual or individuals.[52]

The Board of Governors agreed with Galgay that it was 'only reason-able' that the BCN have the opportunity to expand to provide full ser-vice to the entire country by having a monopoly on high-powered transmitters. Only at that point would it consider applications for power increases or new transmitters from privately owned stations, which were motivated by financial gain. After the national interest was achieved, the Board agreed, low-powered privately owned stations would be permitted, and then only if necessary to maintain adequate local service.[53] The governors concurred with Galgay's view that the needs of public service outweighed anyone's private interest in making a profit, and suggested that this public service included providing retailers with an opportunity to advertise:

> It is not considered that the present policy of the Broadcasting Corporation is oppressive toward VOCM; if it be restrictive in any sense it is restrictive as to all present operators of broadcasting stations. It should be emphasized that this Corporation regards broadcasting as being a vital and necessary public service, and it adheres strongly to the principle that no private or commercial interests should be permitted to obtain any rights or any monopoly for broadcasting. It is recognized that commercial enterprise has a right to avail itself of the purely commercial side of broadcasting for the purpose of advertising their products. For this reason, and in recognition of this principle the Broadcasting Corporation accepts for transmission programmes commercially sponsored and containing advertising matter.[54]

Each of Butler's arguments had been dismissed, and the BCN remained committed to maintaining its dominance of radio broadcasting while allowing Newfoundland advertisers access to the public airwaves.[55] Newfoundland radio, as was the case with Canadian radio as well, was a compromise between commercial radio, like that in United States, and administrative control by the state, like that in Britain.

One might question how the Newfoundland debate would have gone differently if the country had an elected government. In Canada a forceful industry was able to lobby federal politicians and had influence in shaping federal policy. In the fall of 1946 Butler took his case to members of the National Convention when he was interviewed by the Convention's Transportation and Communications Committee. The elected members of the Convention sympathized with Butler but ultimately accepted Galgay's argument that if it granted a power increase to VOCM, then other applications would have to be approved. Smallwood, who chaired the committee, reported that the committee felt unqualified to argue with Galgay's contention that private stations could jeopardize the BCN's position in international negotiations on frequency allocations.[56] When Smallwood reported as much to the Convention on 12 December 1946, several members objected. Cashin stated that Galgay had lied to the committee during his testimony, when he had claimed there was no censorship upon the BCN, making reference to his own broadcasts being restricted. Trinity North delegate Reuban Vardy also reported he had not been permitted to make a broadcast, on the grounds that it was too critical of the government. Then the debate turned to the question of privately owned stations. The member for Bell Island, Nish Jackman, disputed the BCN's justification for restricting VOCM, maintaining that it was 'an excuse for dictatorship' and suggesting that 90 per cent of people listened to VOCM rather than VONF. He also credited VOCM with the existence of the National Convention itself, without explaining that cryptic remark, and suggested the Convention should protest the limits upon VOCM's expansion. Grand Falls representative Malcolm Hollett concurred with Jackman's scepticism about the BCN's reason for restricting VOCM, and asked Smallwood if he had enquired into the claim. Thomas Ashbourne of Twillingate, Charles Ballam of Humber, and Leonard Miller of Placentia East agreed that VOCM should be given a power increase. Smallwood, himself a former broadcaster upon VONF and a man who rarely failed to express an opinion, reiterated that he was not competent to question the BCN's argument.[57] Chesley Crosbie, the member for St John's City West, argued that since VOUS had been given a frequency, VOCM should have been permitted to expand as well.[58] Months later, during the debate upon the proposed Terms of Union between Canada and Newfoundland, Edgar Hickman asked if VOCM would be permitted to continue to operate if Newfoundland were to join Confederation. Smallwood assured him that privately owned stations operated in Canada.[59] All this was, of course, outside the mandate of the Convention, and nothing came of these statements of support for Butler, yet it reveals that private ownership could have had a more sympathetic hearing in Newfoundland through a democratic political process than it received from the bureaucratic apparatus.

In the rhetorical struggle between state and private ownership, Butler did not suggest that state ownership of business was socialism. That argument might have some resonance during the opening salvos of the Cold War. Instead, he relied upon the argument that American broadcasters had successfully employed against a public broadcasting alternative – that state ownership of broadcasting led to dictatorship of the air, since the government chose what was and what was not to be broadcast. Only the 'free-market' of listeners choosing what to listen to, the argument ran, ensured that the public chose what stations broadcast.[60] In the Newfoundland context, such rhetoric might have been

even more compelling than in the American case, since the Commis-
·sion was unelected and it could easily have been argued that it was
using its station as a propaganda tool. By portraying his station as
'independent,' Butler implied that only VOCM allowed free expression
of opinion and suggested that the BCN's motive for denying his station
a power increase was to muzzle political opposition.

The BCN dismissed the claims that it unfairly benefited from licence
fees, that it undercut commercial advertising fees, or that VOCM served
the public in the same fashion that VONF did. Galgay argued that any
public service programming provided by VOCM was only incidental to
its commercial activities, and thus not a legitimate justification for being
placed on a level playing field with the public station. Galgay was cutting in his assessment of VOCM. Butler argued that his station broadcast local and foreign news, but in Galgay's view,

> The local news is frequently confined to Magistrates Court news and St
> John's gossip. It is often time highly inaccurate and definitely political in
> character. By the use of 'Quotes' it is a subtle form of editorializing. The
> foreign news broadcasts by VOCM is 'pirated' off the foreign news broad-
> casts of American and Canadian Stations.[61]

Butler reported that his station provided religious programming – a
claim that Galgay rejected. He thought VOCM's Bible talks, which Butler delivered himself, did not qualify as religious broadcasting, since
they were not broadcasts of church services. Galgay reported that the
station's broadcasts on behalf of the Jehovah's Witnesses, whom he said
were opposed to all forms of organized religion, were 'very close to
being offensive.'[62] Recordings of two of Butler's broadcasts are extant.
Perhaps Galgay recorded them as evidence of the character of Butler's
program. Butler's talks contained millennial rhetoric, references to the
corruption of all earthly institutions, and the suggestion that many of
those in high positions in churches, government, and business had been
created by Satan rather than God. Butler also invited listeners to attend
an upcoming Bible students' meeting.[63] Galgay was a Roman Catholic
and the larger institutional churches felt threatened by the evangelical
rhetoric of the Jehovah's Witnesses, prompting the government and
police to attempt to suppress them by doing such things as confiscating
their literature and deporting some of their missionaries. The government's initial hostility toward the group had been prompted by its
'broadcasting' its criticism of 'earthly institutions' through the use of

loudspeakers and its pamphlet campaign.[64] Perhaps the medium provoked the reaction as much as the message. Certainly controversy about the group's proselytizing over the radio had prompted the Canadian government to assume greater control over broadcasting and restrict religious groups from owning stations.[65] By contrast, the United Church's VOWR continued to operate in Newfoundland without controversy, because it broadcast church services rather than lecturing listeners upon biblical interpretation. In June 1947, although the government had by then relented in its efforts to rid Newfoundland of the Jehovah's Witnesses, Galgay rejected an application from that group to make a one-hour broadcast, despite having frequently granted similar requests to many other Christian denominations.[66]

Galgay went on to say that, despite Butler's assertions to the contrary, the BCN had received an insignificant amount of public criticism in proportion to the criticism of other public broadcasters such as the CBC and the BBC. He reported that Penson and Frazer had often expressed gratification at how little criticism had been levelled at the Corporation. Successive Commission representatives on the Board had reaffirmed the policy of having a publicly owned station similar to the BBC, but accepting limited advertising.[67] The BCN agreed with none of Butler's accusations and maintained that restricting VOCM was necessary to maintain the privileged position of the BCN in the international allocation of frequencies. As long as Galgay endeavoured to protect the national interest as embodied in VONF, the private interests of VOCM would be sacrificed. If the BCN were to grant permission for a five-kilowatt station to VOCM, in Galgay's view, it would ruin Newfoundland's chance to retain rights to 640 kc.[68] As late as August 1948, when it was clear that Newfoundland would become a Canadian province and discussions were underway to incorporate the BCN into the CBC, Galgay and the Justice Department continued to discuss new broadcasting regulations.[69] In the end, nothing came of these discussions, because after 1 April 1949 the Newfoundland stations fell under the regulatory authority of the Government of Canada.

As the last chapter discussed, the Broadcasting Corporation had brought the pro-confederate message into the homes of Newfoundlanders, thus helping create the conditions whereby Newfoundlanders chose to join Canada. The BCN thus contributed to its own demise as a separate national broadcaster and its incorporation into the CBC, but not all questions had been resolved. Smallwood led in negotiating terms of union with Canada, so he was in a position to influence debate on the implications of union upon broadcasting. The debate upon the Convention's Transportation and Communications Committee's report provided an opportunity for members to consider the role broadcasting would have in the province of Canada if union occurred. Broadcasting was a matter of federal not provincial jurisdiction, and Smallwood assured the other delegates that within Confederation the BCN employees would become federal employees and it would carry the CBC news. Otherwise it

> would remain in many ways what it is today; and in so far as being a Newfoundland station, it would remain entirely what it is today ... our station would go right on as though confederation had never come at all. There is no intention of trying to Canadianise us. They [the Canadians] are quite happy for us to remain Newfoundlanders. We will have our own programmes, our own local news, our own Newfoundland broadcasting.[70]

Charles Bailey questioned if the Newfoundland delegation had enquired whether the Newfoundland government would be able to retain control over the station if the country joined Canada. Smallwood reported that the delegation had asked, but the possibility had been categorically rejected by the federal government. Ottawa, he said, had rejected the Quebec government's earlier proposal to establish its own station, so Newfoundland could not be permitted to own its station.[71]

Two of the Convention members who opposed confederation, Alfred Watton and Albert Butt, asked if the federal government would appropriate the $100,000 cash that the BCN held in reserve for the construction of a new studio in St John's and a station in Grand Falls. They worried that the Canadian government might spend the money elsewhere in Canada. Smallwood assured them that Canada did not want Newfoundland to join so that Ottawa could 'fleece us left and right.'[72] He went on to say that Canada had committed itself to improving and expanding the broadcasting service and would spend much more than $100,000 when it did so. Smallwood also suggested a potential benefit to CBC ownership of the station: no elected Newfoundland government had ever had a government-owned broadcasting network at its disposal. Ownership by the Government of Canada would prevent the provincial government from using it as a political tool; as he quipped, 'I would love to have that Broadcasting Corporation as a sort of private toy of my own.'[73] Generally, the Newfoundland negotiators that the Commission had appointed were enthusiastic about passing potentially costly services to the federal taxpayers, and since Newfoundlanders would no longer be paying licence fees upon their receivers after 1949 it made sense that the CBC take over the responsibility of public broadcasting. A later generation of Newfoundlanders would speculate upon how Newfoundland's negotiators might have demanded a better deal, but the reality was that Newfoundland's terms of union could be little different from the powers outlined in the *British North America Act*.

Not long after the 22 July referendum, the Canadian government established an Interdepartmental Committee on Newfoundland to discuss preparations. On 19 August 1948 this committee of senior civil servants stressed the need for tact when dealing with Newfoundlanders, in light of the fact that nearly half the voters had rejected confederation. It decided that a minimum number of government officials would visit Newfoundland until after the Newfoundland delegation began its negotiations, in order to avoid the impression that Canada was beginning an 'invasion.'[74] In the meantime, the assistant general manager of the CBC, Donald Manson, wrote Galgay, 'It seems that the die is cast and that we are to have the great privilege and pleasure of welcoming you one of these days as Canadian.'[75] He went on to ask for specific information upon information on 'laws and regulations, treaties or arrangements with other countries (eg regarding use of frequencies), and arrangements made for Newfoundland representative at forthcoming Radio Conferences, ... assets, liabilities, contractual obligations, revenues, staff, organization of BCN, wire lines or radio links, last year's balance sheet, any other information.'[76] Manson then asked the Canadian Department of External Affairs to arrange for Galgay to come to Ottawa for discussions.[77] Just as Galgay had shaped VONF from its inception as a commercial station and steered it though a decade of public broadcasting, he now influenced the CBC's view of the mission that broadcasting had in Newfoundland. In the meantime, like many government departments in the wake of the second referenda, the attention of the BCN's staff became focused upon their forthcoming integration into the federal bureaucracy.

Tact and quiet preparations behind the scenes were likely the best policies for the Canadian government, in light of the continued hostility toward confederation in some quarters, especially in the capital. Most of those who had voted against confederation accepted their loss, but the RGL itself continued to try to block union through appeals to the court, claiming the process was illegal. Galgay wisely judged that 'in view of the fact that the Legislation which provided for the Referendum was not questioned and it proceeded according to Democratic Process, there appears to be little hope of success in this direction.'[78] The RGL also arranged for a private member to introduce a 'Newfoundland Liberation Bill' in the British House of Commons, without success. Galgay might have added that since the British government wanted union, it was determined to press ahead, once it had the approval of the majority of the public, and no legal manoeuvres on the part of the RGL would succeed. Galgay thought it was therefore not too early to begin discussions on the incorporation of the BCN into the CBC.

On 24 September 1948 the CBC Board of Governors began discussions with the Canadian government and the Newfoundland authorities on the proposed inclusion of the BCN in the CBC. The CBC governors instructed its officials to 'point out [to the Canadian government] that the Canadian Broadcasting Corporation is not in a position itself to assume extra financial obligations involving commitment above related revenues in taking over the Broadcasting Corporation of Newfoundland and extending service of the national system of broadcasting to Newfoundland.'[79] The chairman of the CBC, Augustin Frigon, later outlined that the Dominion government must be appraised of the fact that the extension of the CBC's broadcasting service to include Newfoundland could not be achieved within the current budget. The treasurer of the CBC, Frigon ordered, should make clear that the Corporation would need a subsidy to take over broadcasting in Newfoundland.[80]

Discussions with Newfoundland officials also had to be handled carefully. Manson represented the CBC on the Canadian government's Transportation and Communications Steering Committee, which coordinated 'sending officials to Newfoundland in order that Newfoundlanders should not be given the impression that they were being invaded or annexed.'[81] The Newfoundland delegation that negotiated union hoped to hand over the financial responsibility for broadcasting to the Canadian government, while ensuring the continuation of some aspects of the BCN. As a member of that delegation, and the presumptive leader of the post-confederation Newfoundland government, Smallwood took a large role in shaping the relationship between Canada and Newfoundland. He, in particular, appreciated the importance of the medium. He was careful to outline to the federal negotiators that, while the Newfoundland and Canadian broadcasting regulations and the natures of the systems were compatible, broadcasting had a unique role in Newfoundland. The BCN, he explained, had provided vital information and services to the widely dispersed population of the island and Labrador, as well as vessels offshore. Smallwood hoped that the CBC would continue to serve the provincial government in ways similar to those services the BCN had provided the Commission. The Newfoundland delegation also hoped that the CBC would continue to use broadcasting to provide listeners with services that broadcasting did not provide in other jurisdictions. As Smallwood put it,

> Broadcasting in Newfoundland has acquired a peculiarly personal and intimate character not ordinarily found elsewhere on a large scale in North America. It has also become a very important medium of expression of Newfoundland culture and atmosphere. It would, therefore, be extremely hazardous to interfere drastically with this situation and fatal if premature means were taken to 'Canadianise' the Island.[82]

In this light, the delegation proposed that the current frequencies be retained and that the provincial government be allowed the same free use of the station for 'educational, informational and propaganda programs' that the Commission had enjoyed from the BCN. The delegation suggested that free time continue to be provided to churches and that political parties be given free radio time as well. It also wanted the local management to be granted 'considerable latitude' in the day-to-day operation of the station.[83] One of the Newfoundland delegates, the young St John's businessman Gordon Winter, privately observed that many Newfoundlanders saw the CBC as 'possibly the strongest agency for the promotion of unity and understanding between Canada and Newfoundland.'[84] Given the anti-confederate sentiment, he also warned that it would not be a good idea to replace the *Ode to Newfoundland* with *The Maple Leaf Forever* or *O Canada* as the opening music of the broadcast day during the first few weeks of Newfoundland being a province.[85] Only days after the referendum in which confederation received a majority, a 'Loyal Confederate' had suggested immediately discontinuing playing the *Ode* on the radio stations and substituting *O Canada*.[86] The next day, 'Loyal Newfoundlander' suggested that the *Ode to Newfoundland* meant more to the people of Newfoundland than the Canadian anthem ever would, even to many of those who had voted for confederation. He added that it was not the time to make 'stupid suggestions.'[87] Another correspondent suggested that 'Loyal Confederate' was the nom-de-plume of an advocate for responsible government who was trying to stir up a nationalistic reaction so as to convince London and Ottawa that the majority of Newfoundlanders did not favour confederation after all.[88] Winter's warning was passed on to E.L. Bushnell, director of programs for the CBC, who agreed it would be foolish to make such a change in the national anthems.[89] Yet these were minor matters when the principal goal of the federal authorities was to bring Newfoundland into a relationship with the Government of Canada that was as close to that of the other provinces as was possible, given Newfoundland's particular situation. And the principal goal of Smallwood was to maximize the immediate benefits to Newfoundland that would come from Ottawa so he could solidify his popularity before facing his first election.

The CBC assured the Newfoundland delegation that it saw no problem in meeting each of the Newfoundlanders' concerns within its existing policies.[90] It normally made no charges for educational programming it conducted on behalf of the provincial governments, and allowed free time for religious broadcasts. The Department of Transport promised to make 'its best efforts to obtain and retain for Newfoundland whatever frequencies are necessary, including the 640 kc channel.' In short, the CBC said that it was 'anxious to ensure that, taking account of special conditions and circumstances, the wishes of listeners in Newfoundland will be adequately met' and promised to allow 'substantial discretionary powers to the management of Broadcasting Stations to meet particular regional needs and conditions.'[91] Term 31(k) of the Terms of Union, which became law with an amendment to the *British North America Act*, provided for Canada to take over the responsibilities and costs of providing a public broadcasting system. And Smallwood, who had done more than anyone to bring Newfoundland into Confederation, had been given promises by the CBC that it would leave the special role of Newfoundland radio intact.

Even as the confederation debate had taken over everyone's attention, and later as the details of the union were being worked out, Galgay worked to complete his vision of a national broadcasting system by ensuring that a station would be built in Grand Falls. Galgay encouraged the Board to proceed with the erection of masts for the antenna, the construction of a building, and installation of a one-kilowatt transmitter in Grand Falls. It had become apparent in 1944 that while it was theoretically possible that a directional antenna system for VONF might give satisfactory service to the Grand Falls area, that was by no means assured and would entail considerable expense. Since the installation of a station at Corner Brook had committed the Corporation to having regional stations, it seemed better to build a station at Grand Falls and then improve the transmitter of that station or of VOWN, rather than try to get additional power out of VONF.[92] Unfortunately, the commissioner of finance, Ira Wild, did not approve the $25,000 necessary to construct the station.[93]

The work of the National Convention and the need to secure an available frequency had prevented much from being done. Before the first referendum Galgay had warned that the Corporation would lose its rights to the frequency if it did not proceed quickly. He also pointed out that electrical interference meant that listeners in the Grand Falls area did not receive the existing stations adequately.[94] The pressures of the political broadcasts during the spring of 1948 delayed much progress. There was no money to build a studio in the central Newfoundland town right away, but the frequency could be lost unless it was used and the new station could be used as a relay for St John's programming until a local studio could be built. Unless construction on the antenna and transmitter building started soon, Galgay warned, weather would delay the project until after union with the CBC, and the new management might choose to not proceed with the station.[95] Galgay pointed out to the governors of the BCN that, under the terms of union, the BCN's cash assets would be transferred to the provincial government, and that since the CBC's existing budget would be strained by the completion of a circuit from the mainland to Newfoundland, the money might not exist to construct a station for the Grand Falls area for a considerable time. The BCN had made no secret of its plans to open a Grand Falls station, and delays would have to be explained to the public.

The Corporation had also made a case for the necessity of a station at Grand Falls to the Engineering Conference in Havana in 1947, and the American Federal Communications Commission officials had gone through considerable trouble to ascertain that 1350 kcs would suit Newfoundland's needs.[96] Galgay warned that at the forthcoming conference in September 1949, Newfoundland would forfeit its rights to the frequency by not having made use of it. He argued that such a delay would cause problems for the whole of the BCN system, since

the whole picture of broadcasting in North America will be reviewed [at the conference]. The requirements of Newfoundland will also be analysed and our position will certainly be weakened when it is found that we secured the frequency 1350 and then neglected to use it. The obvious impression will be that the needs of Newfoundland are not as pressing as we had represented and, if this impression is extended to the 640 kcs channel, the entire structure which we have built up around 640 kcs may collapse. The case for Newfoundland is established almost entirely on necessity and sympathy and any action which depreciates either necessity or sympathy should be avoided if at all possible. As I stated before on the same subject, I do not wish to be unduly pessimistic, but it has to be recalled that Broadcasting in Newfoundland is much more than a medium of entertainment and, if the service is reduced or interfered with to any extent, it has a direct and personal impact upon the way of living of thousands of our people.[97]

VORG might have been near enough to Grand Falls for the CBC to claim that the area was being served and avoid operating a new station. Planning to build the station, Galgay had been careful to not sell advertising time to Grand Falls businesses on the Gander station. He always represented VORG as serving only the airport and Bonavista Bay, to avoid 'the embarrassing situation of trying to sell two stations in the same market.'[98] Despite the BCN's best efforts and the urgency Galgay felt, the closure of a bridge on the railway prevented the delivery of the console, amplifiers, and transmitter in time to have the station operating by 31 March 1949 – the last day before union came into effect. Galgay proposed a statement be made that set out how the station would have been operating had the railway not been closed.[99] All was not lost. The CBC opened the Grand Falls station as CBT on 1 July 1949, two months before the international convention re-examined frequency allotment.[100]

With the impending takeover of the BCN seemingly assured, Galgay had Richard O'Brien prepare a memorandum on the future relationship between the Newfoundland stations and the CBC. O'Brien highlighted a number of areas of concern. To start, he asked if programming decisions would be made by officials outside of Newfoundland. He also wondered if any effort would be made to develop Newfoundland programs for broadcast to other provinces or if the Newfoundland stations would be restricted to producing their own essential programs and otherwise just transmit network programming from Canada. He thought the Newfoundland broadcasters would be unsatisfied with such a relationship and recommended the establishment of a Newfoundland program department, which could one day originate scheduled programs for the network. That would require the CBC invest in a full-time Newfoundland-based program director, who could raise the quality of Newfoundland programming and seek opportunities to present such programming upon the trans-Canada network. O'Brien felt the BCN had proven its abilities with such special broadcasts as the Cabot Anniversary and it could produce documentaries without the investment that entertainment programming might require. He suggested such programming might familiarize Canadians with the new province.[101] For O'Brien, becoming part of the CBC would enable VONF to present Newfoundlanders' voices to the other Canadian provinces, but would require that the CBC make some investment in Newfoundland. It also posed questions of how much local control the Newfoundland stations would have. He asked if the CBC intended to set up Newfoundland as a region itself or make the BCN into part of the Maritimes region based in Halifax. As 'a region' of the network, he understood, Newfoundland would have greater autonomy and potential to create its own programming. He also wondered if the St John's station would act as program director for the other Newfoundland stations and if those stations might have any discretion in selecting which network programs to broadcast.

Working within the CBC regulations would also be a challenge for the local stations. The BCN had relied heavily upon recorded music and transcriptions, such as soap operas, both of which would be restricted under the CBC regulations. If such programming were reduced without greater locally produced programming put in its place, he feared Newfoundland businesses would be unable to advertise on the radio because they would not be able to purchase advertising upon network programming. He concluded,

> For myself, I feel sure you agree, that given the opportunity we can do more than simply exist as a somewhat small part of a great organization. We look forward to presenting programmes of a high calibre, and would have the CBC feel that, with your continued assistance and guidance, we will be in a position to offer something worthwhile in return for what we receive.[102]

The CBC management had provided little guidance on the role of the Newfoundland broadcasting stations after confederation, beyond the general statement that they would continue to serve the special role they had developed. The BCN was a state-owned system that served urban and rural listeners with education and entertainment and provided Newfoundland businesses with opportunities to advertise their products. The new CBC stations would provide Canadian news and entertainment from Canada and the United States, but it was not yet clear if radio was to be a one-way transmission from Canada to Newfoundland or would also allow the Newfoundland station to send programming to other Canadian provinces.

It's difficult to discern listeners' hopes and fears for the new service. A few listeners were optimistic that the CBC would improve the quality of radio programming once it took ownership of the Newfoundland stations. One listener who wrote to the *Evening Telegram* complained of the repetitive 'canned stuff' and poor pronunciation upon VONF and hoped that there would be a 'big shake-up' at the BCN once confederation happened.[103] A columnist in the same newspaper accused the BCN's Board of Governors of 'not having given too much brain work toward improving the Newfoundland broadcasting system' and predicted that the CBC, with greater experience, could introduce improvements to local radio. 'Terranovan' praised many of the accomplishments of the BCN, but underlined the lack of daytime programming and the poor fare on Sundays.[104] During the last months of the BCN's existence as a separate organization, public dissatisfaction remained evident, even as people hoped that joining the CBC would allow VONF to provide music of better quality. 'Many of the recordings which are played over the Newfoundland radio are of poor quality,' one musician who had recently moved to Newfoundland argued. 'As music they exhibit a depraved taste.' The problem, he suggested, was that many local musicians were of 'equally low standard.'[105] A listener in Topsail agreed:

> What has happened to all our lovely music? For example, 'After the Ball,' 'The Blue Danube,' etc. etc. Please Mr Broadcaster, give us some nice English music to soothe our poor torn nerves, and let up for a while on the cheap American stuff, that is so distracting and makes one wish one never had a radio in the home.[106]

Not surprisingly, such questions of taste were never resolved.

In a later column, Terranovan reported that some Newfoundland programs would continue under CBC management but would now be supplemented by radio from other provinces. Local musicians would benefit from the fees that the Canadian broadcaster paid, and, he predicted, 'There will be keen interest in Canada over Newfoundland literature – drama, poetry prose and our familiar songs.'[107] Neither the BCN nor listeners imagined that confederation would be a one-way process in which Canadian programming would be available to Newfoundlanders. They hoped VONF would continue to be the Voice of Newfoundland to both the people of the new province and through the CBC network to Canadians.

While Newfoundlanders worried about what their place in Canada would be, the CBC undertook technical preparations behind the scenes. The CBC decided to not incorporate the Newfoundland broadcaster into the Maritime Region, but to have it report directly to Ottawa for the first year after union, thus allowing the measure of autonomy that Newfoundlanders wanted. In November 1948 W.E.S. Briggs, the Maritime regional representative, and N.R. Olding, the operations engineer, visited Newfoundland to make a survey on behalf of the CBC.[108] Frigon directed that the visit be kept as quiet as possible.[109] Bushnell warned Briggs to

> not give the impression that we have any definite plan in mind for 'taking over' the BCN but that the purpose of your visit is purely to familiarize yourself with their operation. You must be extremely careful to make this plain to those with whom you will come in contact outside the staff of BCN, particularly if you are challenged at all by anyone who gives any indication of being unsympathetic to confederation.[110]

Not surprisingly, the prospect of being taken over provoked some trepidation among the staff. As late as 1949, Galgay had to squelch rumours, remind staff to not gossip, and inform them that no decisions had yet been made regarding the hiring of BCN staff by the CBC.[111] While CBC management had left the BCN employees uncertain if they would have a job, the network purchased new equipment and sent technicians to install it.[112] This promised an improvement in the tone and quality of the station, but more importantly it was necessary for the St John's station to be able to receive and transmit the network programming from Canada. The CBC's first priority was to ensure that Newfoundlanders would be able to listen to the CBC national network on the date of union.

While the CBC took administrative and technical preparations before April 1949, it also took on the political role of informing the public of political changes and of shaping public attitudes. In September 1948 the CBC began planning a series of broadcasting commentaries about Newfoundland to make the new province known to Canadians. The network

decided to produce a series of programs about the Canadian government that could help Newfoundlanders adjust to the new regime, but
wanted the government to bear the $25,000 cost of the programming.[113]
Beginning on 6 June 1949 the Canadian government sponsored the first
of three weeks of nightly broadcasts titled *Know Your Federal Government*. Hosted by expatriate Newfoundlander Ewart Young, the editor of
the Montreal-based magazine *Atlantic Guardian*, it explained the structure of the federal government, its regulations, and its programs of
which Newfoundlanders could avail themselves.[114] The CBC also hired
a Newfoundland teacher then doing postgraduate work at the University of Toronto, Frederick W. Rowe, to give a series of talks to Canadians
to 'promote understanding' of the soon-to-be province. Rowe's first
broadcast, 'You're Wrong about Newfoundland!' argued that many
Canadians had unfair negative impressions of their eastern neighbour.
He laid the blame upon the media, suggesting that 'false impressions
have been fostered consistently by feature writers who emphasize the
primitive and the ancient when they go to Newfoundland on assign-
ment from their newspapers or magazines.' Rowe pointed out that the
reporters who had negative things to say about Newfoundland missed
the fact that parts of their own country were no better off.[115]

   Another area to which broadcasters in both St John's and Ottawa paid
particular attention was news. Newfoundland listeners valued news
broadcasting more than other areas of radio, and this was an area in
which the CBC could provide improvements. It was also an area in
which people cared about the local character. The BCN had left local and
international news to the *Doyle Bulletin* and other local sponsors, while
during the war the CBC had developed its own news division. News
broadcasting was the first area in which the CBC proposed changing the
way that the Newfoundland broadcasters did business. D.C. McArthur
of the CBC proposed establishing a St John's newsroom, which would
operate along the same lines at the Halifax division, with a senior editor,
two assistants, and a junior editor. He informed Galgay,

> The editors in each regional newsroom are expected to use their own
> judgement in presenting news that will have the greatest regional interest
> (including a proportion of the day's international developments, and
> some Canadian news of general importance). But as far as policy is con-
> cerned, the way news is handled and written, and our general newsroom
> operations, we try to maintain a reasonable degree of uniformity through-
> out the whole service. With that in mind I believe that it might be of defi-

nite advantage to have a senior editor with a background of experience in handling and writing news for radio, who would be in a position to give training and direction to the other members of the staff.[116]

McArthur suggested appointing an assistant editor from the Halifax newsroom to head the St John's staff, and recruiting some reporters from the St John's newspapers. To ease the process of taking responsibility for compiling the news, he recommended establishing the newsroom one week before Confederation so that it could get some practice writing news before having to go on the air and continuing the contract with Reuters for a month after union if the St John's staff were not ready or the Canadian Press (CP) service were not available in Newfoundland by 1 April.[117] After a decade of international news from British sources, the Newfoundland broadcaster was about to be integrated into the CBC news and get much of its content from CP. There were greater changes pending in Newfoundlanders' viewpoint of the world: a decade of following world events from the perspective of the BBC and London-based Reuters would in time be replaced with a Toronto perspective.

The CBC was committed to retain both the BCN's public services and its most popular sponsored programs. Local news, which was so important to listeners, would continue to be provided by the *Gerald S. Doyle News Bulletin*. That provided continuity with the past, and Doyle's program evolved into a sort of public service bulletin board as the St John's newsroom developed its own news-gathering ability. Galgay reported that the CBC intended 'that the Newfoundland services should not be materially changed but should be supplemented.'[118] CBC technicians in St John's helped install new control equipment to handle the incoming network programming, sent the old VONF console to VOWN, and VOWN's equipment to VORG. Meanwhile, Canadian National Telegraphs staff worked to open network and press lines across the Cabot Strait. A.D. Dunton, chairman of the CBC Board of Governors, issued a press release reassuring Newfoundlanders that many of the qualities of the BCN's programming would remain:

The geographical distribution of the Newfoundland population, many of whom live in small settlements, without other regular communication, gives broadcasting a special importance. It provides services especially of information, often in detailed forms which are not needed in other areas. The Broadcasting Corporation of Newfoundland has developed some broadcasting services which are of a kind to be especially valuable to Newfoundlanders. It will be the policy of the Canadian Broadcasting Corporation to disturb as little as possible existing programs which are especially useful to Newfoundlanders and particularly appreciated by them. The Newfoundland Region of the system will have considerable latitude in meeting special needs and tastes of Newfoundlanders in broadcasting. At the same time, after union with the Canadian Broadcasting Corporation hopes to be able to add considerably to the broadcasting service available particularly by network programs from the rest of the country. Merging of the two systems will also mean that some programs from Newfoundland will be heard by listeners all across Canada. In this way it is hoped that broadcasting will help the mutual understanding between the people of Newfoundland and those of the other regions.[119]

O'Brien had earlier questioned the relationship that Newfoundland stations would have with the parent corporation; Galgay now appeared to have been satisfied that the CBC would enhance rather than erode the role broadcasting played in the lives of listeners. As Newfoundland's last few days as a separate country passed, the BCN prepared for its incorporation into the CBC. Chairman Williams directed that accounts be brought up to date, so that the Commission Government could present the CBC with a bill for unused consumables when it took over the BCN.[120] Arrangements were made to pay all outstanding accounts that had been undertaken by the existing Board prior to its retirement on 31 March, including the fees due to the outgoing governors.[121] Yet ten days before union Galgay had still not been given any instructions on the nature of the 1 April ceremony nor any information on the transfer of the assets of the BCN to the province of Newfoundland or to the CBC, whichever the case would be.[122]

In the July 1948 referendum voters on the Avalon Peninsula had voted 67.2 per cent in favour of returning to responsible government, against 32.7 per cent for union with Canada. In some quarters, particularly the capital city, anti-confederate feeling still ran high, leading to concern among Canadian officials that any ceremony marking the entry of Newfoundland into Canada might be the site of protests. Amendment to the *British North America Act* had taken place earlier in London, fulfilling all the constitutional requirements. This left the Canadian and Newfoundland governments to undertake some housekeeping to put the new constitution into practice. Representatives of Canada and Newfoundland signed the terms of union at the Parliament Buildings in Ottawa, safely secure from any unwanted protest. It would occur at half-past one, Newfoundland time, when people would be securely at home having lunch. The Canadian high commissioner in Newfoundland advised that it would be best to 'avoid any ceremony here which would attract any crowd of people' and suggested swearing in the new lieutenant governor in a private ceremony at Government House (the official residence of the Governor).[123] Governor Gordon MacDonald, whom anti-confederates resented for having favoured confederation rather than the neutral role they believed was appropriate for the King's representative, had left the country. This left Sir Edward Emerson as the acting administrator of Newfoundland, and he concurred with the high commissioner's view that there should not be any symbolic ceremony in the city and that 'the quieter the day is here and the less opportunity for the gathering of any crowd, the better.'[124] It thus fell to radio broadcasting to provide the virtual ceremony to mark the transformation in Newfoundland's status. Listeners in their homes could hear the Newfoundland broadcaster sign on in the morning, and then symbolically transform itself into the CBC at 12:12 eastern standard time with the cue 'This is CBN, St John's, Newfoundland, transferring you to Parliament Hill in Ottawa.'[125] Minutes later, Newfoundlanders heard the scratch of a pen on paper as they were made Canadian citizens. Union itself took place one moment before midnight on 31 March. This odd choice was a compromise between the Canadian desire for union to occur at the beginning of the new fiscal year, 1 April, and Smallwood's objection to the symbolism of starting Newfoundland's life as a Canadian province on April Fool's Day.

On the eve of being taken over by the CBC, the long-serving William Galgay looked back upon the last year of the BCN's operations. He reported to the outgoing BCN Board of Governors,

> The year 1948 was undoubtedly one of the most difficult in the history of the corporation. It saw the conclusion of the National Convention, the campaigns preceding referenda and the broadcasts of the election returns. The referenda campaigns were periods of many problems and difficulties but an analysis of the entire handling of these situations will reveal to any fair minded individual that the Corporation rendered great public service with impartiality and generosity.[126]

There is little doubt that the Corporation had rendered service to both the government and civil society; a list of regular, occasional, and

one-time special public service broadcasts from government departments and non-governmental charities would run to several pages. But
as we have seen, not all of this programming was synonymous with
public service as conceived by the Commission's critics.

Between 1945 and 1949, Newfoundlanders not only debated the
question of whether to join the Canadian Confederation, but the question of what sort of broadcasting system the country would have. This
debate between privately owned commercial stations and a state-
owned network had not been permanently settled in the 1939. VOCM
renewed its campaign against regulation when politics re-emerged
after the war. The country was changing as well. Newfoundlanders had
long liked American popular culture but liked British popular culture
and British styles of radio as a counterweight to American styles of
music and speaking. Listeners were not advocating the creation of a
public service broadcaster devoted to cultural uplift and education
when they expressed their hostility to American-style radio. They
wanted British music, British popular culture, and British-style radio
voices. We should not uncritically accept their distinction as our own,
however. British popular culture and American popular culture had
long influenced each other, and the BBC had learned much from North
American radio. It is not clear what listeners were imagining when they
expressed a preference for British culture over American. The presence
of members of the American and Canadian services and the constitutional debate had given a new dimension to the question of whether
Newfoundlanders were to be North Americans or Britain's oldest colony. The constitutional debate resolved some of these questions, and
Newfoundlanders ensured that the BCN could continue to be the Voice
of Newfoundland. No one objected to the BCN becoming part of the
CBC network, both because of the prospect of enhanced programming
and the promise that the personal and intimate role that radio had in
the lives of Newfoundlanders would continue.

Epilogue

The CBC operations in Newfoundland after 1949 had a significance that warrants its own study, but we can offer a few words about the continuity and discontinuity with VONF. Galgay's continued presence at the helm of what became the Newfoundland division of the CBC, until his death in 1966, gave CBN a measure of continuity with its past that stretched back into its days as the privately owned commercial radio station that he and Butler had started. The iconic Newfoundland programs – the *Barrelman* and the *Doyle News Bulletin*, for example – both continued into the 1950s, although there were changes. Shortly after Newfoundland joined Canada, O'Leary took the *Barrelman* off the CBC, and for its last five years it was broadcast on VOCM. Harrington continued as the Barrelman as well as working for the CBC on several other programs. Gerald S. Doyle's program lasted until his death. Changes in Newfoundland and Labrador had made both of these programs somewhat anachronistic by the time they ended. Although the station's studios and transmitter have changed location several times, CBN continues to broadcast at 10 kw – the power it had in 1939 – and on 640 kcs – the frequency that Galgay had once worried would be lost to Newfoundland.

Besides Galgay, many of the other broadcasters continued with the station after 1949. The CBC's plans to incorporate the existing BCN staff into the new corporation conformed to the general pattern of absorbing Newfoundland government employees into the federal civil service.[1] The CBC hired the BCN's employees at significant improvement in salaries in some cases, although the new payroll deductions for income tax, pension, and insurance meant that net pay was about the same.

Several months after being incorporated into the CBC, the on-air staff had to submit recorded auditions if they were to remain with the Corporation. O'Brien, MacDonald, and others went on to have long careers with the CBC. 'Aubrey Mac,' who late in his life joked about how often he had come close to being fired, became the much-loved old man of radio into the 1970s, when he hosted a nostalgic program of 'nice and easy' music. Although Robert MacLeod worked in the insurance business, he continued to occasionally perform on the air as a musician. Robert Furlong's association with radio broadcasting ended with Confederation, but he went to an appointment on the bench, eventually becoming chief justice of the Supreme Court of Newfoundland.

With Confederation, the restrictions upon expansion of commercial broadcasting were lifted. Joseph Butler was able to increase the power of VOCM's transmitter and, over time, built a large and successful series of stations. Butler, who was an amateur pilot, died in an aircraft crash in 1956 when helping search for a missing child. His son, Joseph V. Butler, transformed his father's single station into a group of radio stations that long dominated commercial radio in the province, once the CBC got out of the business of selling advertising. Canadian regulatory authorities allowed the expansion of the family business his father had long sought. The change in regulatory emphasis was particularly apparent in the case of the new technology of television. Galgay and the Board of Governors had considered expanding into television in 1946, but decided to wait for the technology to improve and for the debates of the National Convention to end. Canadian policy had been for the CBC to be granted the first television broadcast licence in each market. Partisan considerations intervened, and the regulatory authority granted the first television licence in St John's to a company owned by Geoff Stirling and Donald Jamieson, rather than the public broadcaster. Private interests were now paramount.

VOWR, Newfoundland's first public broadcasting station, celebrated its eightieth anniversary in 2004. The volunteer-administered station continues to serve the public in its own way. The station plays the sort of easy-listening, country, and semi-classical music of an earlier era that people cannot find on commercial radio. The lack of concern for ratings gives amateur broadcasters on VOWR free rein to program as they like. The station also continues to provide public service announcements and interviews, and overcomes the limits of its transmitter by broadcasting over the Internet. Its Seventh Day Adventist counterpart, VOAR, continues to broadcast self-described Christian music.

Several of the people who worked in broadcasting during the 1940s turned their public profile into political careers. Indeed, during the Commission of Government years, 1934–49, there was no forum in which one could have a political career, only administrative appointments, so it is not surprising that some people turned their broadcasting name recognition into political capital. The radio broadcaster and subsequently television newsreader Don Jamieson was elected to the House of Commons, eventually serving as a minister in the federal Cabinet during the 1970s. Allan Fraser left the faculty at Memorial University and his broadcast commentaries when he was elected to the House of Commons during the 1950s. O.L. Vardy served in the provincial Cabinet and later fled the jurisdiction to avoid serving time in prison on charges of bribery and fraud. Peter Cashin, who had reawakened his political career through the radio, was elected to the House of Assembly, first as an independent and later as a Progressive Conservative.

Smallwood had translated his popularity as the Barrelman and his leadership of the pro-confederation forces in the National Convention into being appointed premier of the new province. His mastery of radio and patronage, and his political acumen enabled him to win a series of elections and serve as premier from 1949 to 1972. The radio station was not the personal plaything he had mused about during the negotiations of the terms of union, but Premier Smallwood never lacked access to radio or television. During these years he made effective use of his broadcasting skills to enhance his hegemony over the province's politics.[2] Many of the skills he needed to be premier he had learned as the Barrelman and honed into a political weapon during the broadcasts of the National Convention. During the 1950s and 1960s, the people of Newfoundland sent their individual aspirations to him by letter or personal contact, Smallwood selected which the government would support, and broadcast the benefits of the welfare state to the people. He had a less than graceful retirement (leaders who in their own minds personally embody the future of their nation can never hand over the reins of power easily). In retirement Smallwood returned to his role as the Barrelman. He began a massive editorial project, producing the comprehensive *Encyclopedia of Newfoundland and Labrador*, once more making Newfoundland better known to Newfoundlanders. The other Barrelman, Michael Harrington, ran unsuccessfully in the new province's first provincial election and went on to a long career as a broadcaster and newspaper editor. In addition to twelve years as the Barrelman, Harrington wrote and hosted many radio and television

programs from the 1950s to the 1980s.[3] In his retirement from the
Evening Telegram he wrote a regular newspaper column of 'Offbeat History,' which contained some of the same sorts of stories of feats of sea-
manship and trivia that had once been staples of the *Barrelman*
program.

Richard O'Brien had warned that when the BCN was incorporated
into the CBC it might lose local decision making, and programming
decisions might be made by officials outside Newfoundland. He had
hoped that the CBC would invest in the St John's station, as well, to
enable it to produce Newfoundland programs for broadcast to other
provinces. Smallwood and the team of Newfoundlanders negotiating
terms of union had convinced the Canadian government that the
unique role of radio broadcasting that had developed during the preceding decade should continue. Galgay consolidated these gains when
he convinced the CBC to create a Newfoundland division and allow
that division to continue to serve the specific Newfoundland needs
with their programs. But CBN lost when it came to being the radio
voice of Newfoundland that communicated to Canada. While the CBC
invested in the technical aspects of broadcasting and improved service
in many areas, O'Brien's concern about losing local decision making
was prophetic. His worry that radio would be a one-way transmission,
with Newfoundland unable to regularly transmit Newfoundland radio
productions on the national network to listeners in other provinces,
also came to be. Newfoundland listeners now heard international and
Canadian news written to the standards established in Toronto and listened to 'national' programming. Rarely were Newfoundland radio
productions carried on the national network to Canada. One of the very
few exceptions, a satirical program called *The Great Eastern* (1994–9),
played with this idea. The show's premise was that Newfoundland had
not joined Canada in 1949 and that the program originated from the
still-operating BCN and was being carried on its sister network, the
CBC. This counterfactual history not only provided a venue for comedy
that made fun of the conventions of radio broadcasting, but can be read
as a subtle critique of the place accorded to Newfoundland on the very
network that carried the program. Despite the *Great Eastern*'s brilliance
and popularity, the network withdrew its support.[4] On the whole, the
CBC stations in the province came to have the same relationship with
head office in Toronto that Newfoundland and Labrador had with
Canada. CBN and the other Newfoundland stations became peripheral
to the CBC's metropolis; content, information, and ideology flowed

almost exclusively in one direction. Today, a few mostly inconvenient hours are set aside for local programming, and at the end of those periods a computer in Toronto automatically turns off the microphones in Newfoundland and starts the transmission of network programming.

Radio broadcasting had contributed to each of Newfoundland's political, social, and cultural changes between 1934 and 1949, so not surprisingly the Newfoundland division of the CBC continued to do so, well into the second half of the twentieth century. As an afterthought to the *Farm Broadcast* – a well-established CBC program that was added to the CBN line-up, it created *Fishermen's Broadcast* (1951–).[5] Later renamed the *Fisheries Broadcast*, it not only provided news and weather reports specifically geared to those engaged in the industry, but, in the next logical step beyond the *Doyle Bulletin* and the *Barrelman*, allowed men and women in the fisheries to hear each other's point of view. Advances in technology, particularly tape recording and telephone interviews, enabled listeners to hear each other's voices. Many of the more recent open-line radio shows on stations such as VOCM, with their populist hosts and callers, also continue the democratic conversation that had been so characteristic of radio in the 1930s and 1940s. During the 1950s, CBN also became the site of a nostalgic critique of the changes it had helped to bring about as VONF, such as Confederation and the 'modernization' of the province. When the Smallwood provincial government embarked upon an aggressive yet ultimately disappointing policy of industrialization, it was to radio, the medium at which Smallwood excelled, that the disillusioned so often turned.

During the 1970s Newfoundland experienced a cultural movement in which creative people returned to oral culture to forge a new identity. Theatrical groups such as the Mummers Troupe and folk-rock bands such as Figgy Duff, for example, also benefited from the resources and personnel of CBN. This period of cultural fluorescence is commonly interpreted as a reaction to modernity and the changes provoked by Confederation. The extent to which it was a modernist intellectual movement and shared a continuity with earlier nationalist projects such as the *Barrelman* is not frequently recognized. In both the 1930s and 1970s intellectuals turned to folk culture to provide a basis to invent an authentic Newfoundland popular culture. Perhaps one of the subtle differences is that participants in the movement of the 1970s had a greater sense of the folk culture as threatened and thus they had a more explicit preservationist agenda. In the 1980s, radio broadcasting, and subsequently television, also played a significant role in transforming 'The Mummers Song' into a nostalgic and nativist phenomenon.[6]

'The Broadcast,' as the *Fisheries Broadcast* is known to its many loyal listeners, also gave an opportunity for Ted Russell to create a charming series of monologues known as the 'Chronicles of Uncle Mose' (1953–61).[7] Russell had hosted the cooperative broadcasts during the late 1940s. After Confederation he was elected to the House of Assembly and briefly served in the provincial Cabinet, before leaving because he dissented from Smallwood's policies. While paying the bills by selling insurance, Russell found an outlet for his creative urge when he began broadcasting a weekly story under the persona of 'Uncle Mose.' (*Uncle* was an informal and common Newfoundland title for a usually older man and was generally a term of respect.) These approximately five hundred stories departed from the common genres of radio drama; the monologues were similar to the recitations of Newfoundland oral culture. Set in a fictional outport of the sort that Smallwood hoped to replace with 'growth centres,' Pigeon Inlet, Russell's nostalgic and gentle comedy also included occasional commentary upon political and economic events of the day such as the over-fishing of foreign trawlers. While the more comedic of the chronicles are occasionally replayed on Newfoundland radio forty-five years after he ceased doing them, many of the broadcasts attempted to give helpful information to listeners, much like Russell had done when he had been in charge of the *Cooperative Programme*.[8]

By the time Russell gave up broadcasting to return to teaching school, the self-contained outport culture of which he had written had been inundated by American popular culture. During the quarter century after Newfoundland entered Confederation, radio spread American popular music as it did everywhere else. But there were ironic exceptions. At a point when a commentator might have argued that radio served exclusively to homogenize North American popular culture, it played an unexpected role in another of the periodic revivals of traditional music. Omar Blondahl, a Winnipeg-born folk musician of Icelandic heritage, arrived in St John's and successfully applied for work at VOCM.[9] Upon being given a copy of the *Gerald S. Doyle Song Book* and being asked if he could sing that sort of music, he embarked upon performing the songs on the radio and recording them on phonograph albums. This was the first time either had been done on a large scale. Over subsequent decades many musicians followed in Blondahl's wake; a vibrant and varied Newfoundland popular music existed alongside its American cousins. Perhaps a bohemian-looking Western Canadian using commercial radio to revive Newfoundland traditional music should not come as a surprise. As we have seen, broadcasting had always brought the outside world into people's homes but it had also been the voice of Newfoundland.

Conclusion

Historians of the broadcasting systems in other parts of the British commonwealth have emphasized the administrative history of their respective national broadcasting corporations. They often examine how policy makers tried to reconcile the commercial impulse of American popular radio with their notions of the cultural uplift exemplified by John Reith's BBC. Other scholars have attempted to use content analysis of particular programs to capture the ideological and gender messages imbedded in broadcasts.[1] This book has attempted to integrate an analysis of state policies and the material factors involved in the production of radio programming with the social context in which listeners consumed the content. A social history of a broadcasting station, such as this one, can illuminate the role of radio in the key social and political changes of the period and provide a starting point for a cultural history of the 1930s and 1940s. I suggest it is not possible to separate interpretation of the text from an analysis of the 'conditions of its creation, distribution and reception.'[2]

There had been dangers for Newfoundland in adopting something close to either the American or the British model of broadcasting during the 1930s. Commercial radio, like that in the United States, could allow a private company to wield tremendous power in setting the public agenda, even across national boundaries. The commissioners had not worried about American broadcasting undermining the Newfoundland nation through its dominance of broadcasting, as had many Canadian nationalists during the 1930s and 1940s. Furlong and Galgay did, however, worry that foreign businesses would purchase control over Newfoundland's broadcasting stations or that privately owned radio would expand. Either could threaten the use of radio for national purposes. Some listeners also shared Furlong's dislike for American pronunciation and radio style. On the other hand, they believed that state-owned radio, such as that in Britain, could protect the national interest.

Some public broadcasting advocates in Britain and Canada saw it as a progressive tool that would advance 'democracy.' They meant this in the sense of giving people of all classes access to 'good' culture, rather than the more usual meaning of elected government.[3] The British civil servants administering Newfoundland had a social-reform agenda and wanted to improve the life of average Newfoundlanders. Doing so required preventing them from voting or choosing their radio programming. That educational agenda was consistent with bureaucratic administration; it did not, in their view, require elected government or the choice of alternative programming, which would be provided by privately owned radio. When Newfoundlanders mobilized during the Second World War, they were fighting for 'democracy' but not elections. Newfoundland radio programs, from the *Irene B. Mellon* to the *Barrelman*, all contrasted German beastliness with British decency (and the widespread belief in British fair play helps to explain why those who favoured responsible government felt so betrayed by the Dominions Office in 1948). So choice in programming was a consideration secondary to the Reithian concern to give people the programming that was good for them. But following the model of the BBC also embodied an implicit danger – it could concentrate power over programming decisions and access to the air in the hands of a paternalistic and bureaucratic elite.[4] The private broadcasters and the critics of the Commission both argued as much.

The Commission of Government was itself paternalistic, bureaucratic, and elitist, and wanted to change the culture of Newfoundlanders to make them more independent of government aid. It, in turn, created the BCN as an arms-length corporation so it could avoid the accusation that the Dominions Office was operating a propaganda apparatus. While the government kept an eye on spending, it left the programming and policy decisions in the hands of the Newfoundlanders who managed the BCN. It may be significant that the Corporation finished its decade-long life with all the original members of the board governors, save the secretary of posts and telegraphs, each of whom was seconded from the British civil service for a limited term. Once the BCN had been launched, the Commission had little reason to change its direction. When the BCN first signed on the air, the Commission implicitly claimed that VONF was not a tool of the British-appointed commissioners, but that it grew organically out of the nation. By establishing an arms-length committee of Newfoundlanders to draft the broadcasting act and then establishing an arms-length board of governors, the Dominions Office and the Commission could claim to have achieved national public service. Having failed to buy out all the private interests, and since listeners continued to hear American and Canadian broadcasters, the alternative of private broadcasting remained available to many listeners. Joseph Butler demanded freedom for VOCM to expand so that an alternative voice to the state would flourish by using the analogy of freedom of the press. The tradition of a newspaper and pamphlet publishers owned by private businesses free of government control (a free press) had been a key argument for religious and political freedom in the British world. During the 1920s, 1930s, and 1940s, however, most people saw radio broadcasting as different from publishing. The Commission wanted to establish a monopoly over national broadcasting (even if it tolerated the pre-existing local privately owned stations), so again its rhetorical argument was that independence from the government itself was enough to ensure 'freedom.' This day-to-day autonomy from government control meant that individual broadcasters had considerable latitude to use the station for their own purposes, as long as they did not openly conflict with government policy.

The importance of Newfoundland's broadcasting corporation as a cultural institution transcended the narrow use of the station to promote the government agenda. It produced entertainment and information that released listeners from the daily routine of their lives and informed them of events beyond their horizon. It was also one of the few institutions during the 1940s that created a national Newfoundland popular culture. Yet to a significant degree it was not an institution that created culture itself, or one that had a consistent ideological message; it was a medium through which businesses and individuals provided their creative products to listeners. The Dominion Broadcasting Company had few employees of its own, and businesses such as O'Leary's and Doyle's directly employed those who created much of the programming. That pattern continued when the BCN took over VONF, and even under state ownership much of the content of the programming came from outside the Corporation itself. And, as we have seen, listeners had a role in shaping the programming that broadcasters created and then made sense of that programming in ways that the broadcaster might have not anticipated, let alone intended. The most popular programs on radio in Newfoundland were not those in which a creative person provided content for listeners to passively consume. The *Doyle News* and the *Barrelman* were examples of a folk process in which both the producer and the consumer shaped the culture – a characteristic similar to pre-existing methods of the oral transmission of culture.[5]

That raises a question that goes to the heart of a social history of broadcasting. To what extent did listeners affect the content of popular culture, or to what extent were they passive receptors? An ideological apologist for commercial radio might argue that listeners were in the driver's seat since they chose what to listen to and what to ignore, and business went along for the ride. An advocate for public broadcasting, on the other hand, might point to the limited range of commercial programming and the power that advertisers had over that content. He or she might see the state-owned radio station as representing the people. A more critical approach would suggest that listeners could choose only from the products that business provided for them and that the state agenda was not always synonymous with listeners' interests. In this historically specific case of a mixed commercial and state-owned station, listeners actively shaped programming though their correspondence and passively shaped the meaning of that programming through interpreting it in their own ways.

While many scholars now accept that listening is itself a creative act, in which the person sitting at home reconstructs what the programming means, that was not always apparent to observers in the past. During the Great Depression some North American and European intellectuals worried that the standardization of culture implicit in mechanical reproduction would destroy the genius of individual creativity in art.[6] Many also observed with horror the ways that Goebbels and Riefenstahl used broadcasting and film to mobilize the basest passions of the mob. Notwithstanding the case of Rwanda in 1994, in which a radio voice telling listeners to kill touched off a genocide, we have become less pessimistic that people are powerless to resist the messages of mass media. A British historian of radio broadcasting, Paddy Scannell, has argued that public broadcasting is by its nature democratic. He suggests that it creates nationwide communities of people who listen to the same programming and that events once witnessed by only the select few could now be listened to by people of all classes.[7] In Benedict Anderson's oft-used phrase, radio created 'imagined communities.'[8] The BCN played such a role in people's lives, encouraging Newfoundlanders to imagine themselves as part of a community. In this case, however, Scannell's observations about democratization must be set against the centralizing desire of the benign dictatorship of the Commission of Government and against the unequal access to radio receivers among listeners. Furthermore, that 'imagined community' could be mobilized by a nationalist intellectual such as Smallwood to reject the nation state and join another larger country – not the sort of outcome envisioned by many of those who employ Anderson's concept.

The government had created the BCN primarily as a tool to encourage the people to embrace the Commission's economic reconstruction agenda. This is not the place to assess the successes and failures of the Commission's economic and social policies, except to note that the gap between people's expectations of what the Commission would do and the material accomplishments of the government were apparent to all by the time of the BCN's inaugural broadcast. During its decade of operation, government radio propaganda did not enlist Newfoundlanders in supporting all of the Commission's schemes, nor did it prevent the growth of public criticism of the Commission. In those respects the BCN did not achieve the result the Commission intended. Listeners' perceptions were influenced more by the material reality of their lives than the imaginary Newfoundland created by broadcasters such as the Barrelman. The government also tried to restrict privately owned stations from building a national audience and limit access to alternative voices on VONF so that nothing would impede the state's use of radio to achieve its own goals. But such limits could not entirely contain the democratic uses of the medium by individual broadcasters and listeners. On the other hand, the government found broadcasting effective in mobilizing the nation for the war effort and then an effective way to advance the cause of political union with Canada. But in these cases the BCN provided a medium for non-government organizations to pursue goals consistent with the Commission's objectives. Programming devoted to recruitment of servicemen, air raid precautions, and mobilizing the home front were also all created and sponsored by groups that could claim to have come organically from the people of Newfoundland. Similarly, Joseph Smallwood's Confederate Association worked toward achieving the referendum outcome that the Commission secretly favoured but could not openly pursue.

The history of the Broadcasting Corporation of Newfoundland also shows some of the tensions in the Commission form of government itself. The Commission's two goals, reconstruction of the economy and balancing the budget, were not reconciled until wartime conditions made that second goal obsolete. So, too, the BCN programming exemplified the tension between public service and the revenue generation of commercial broadcasting. The commissioners and the Dominions Office officials were sensitive to the non-elected nature of the regime and did not want to give the impression they were dictating what people could hear on the radio. Yet they wanted to maintain control over access to the air.

The history of radio station VONF during the periods that it was privately owned and state-owned also suggests that the dichotomy between public and commercial radio was not as great as partisans on each side argued. On balance, the continuity between the period of 1932–9 and 1939–49 is more striking than the discontinuities. Under both private and state ownership, the station sometimes served as a propaganda apparatus for the state and embodied notions of public service that encouraged it to write off the cost of such things as public health broadcasts. Of most importance here, VONF produced the same sort of popular culture under both owners, with only some minor exceptions. The Dominion Broadcasting Corporation had known that the listeners it could attract and whose attention to the programming it could sell to advertisers had been disproportionately urban and wealthy. So it had catered to elite musical tastes that would realize that middle-class audience, while providing popular music for younger listeners. The Broadcasting Corporation of Newfoundland, under daily management of Galgay, Williams, Frazer, and Furlong, might have sometimes had notions of improving the public's musical taste similar to those within the BBC, but in practice they did little to affect public taste. The BCN provided its audience with a range of music, from hillbilly and swing to classical, because Galgay recognized that a demand for a range of musical styles existed. As a public broadcaster, the BCN played some music that it saw as an alternative to the mass music of America, but the requirement to keep listeners tuned in had ensured that VONF satisfied the 'jitterbug set' and avoided music that appealed to only elite tastes. Another factor mitigated against radical change in 1939: the Commission of Government had missed the opportunity to provide a BBC-style 'public' broadcasting system when it chose to continue to sell time on its station to commercial sponsors. That allowed the BCN to repay the loan the Commission had made when it established the Corporation, important since the overriding concern of the Commission was to return solvency to the government's finances, and it allowed the BCN to provide St John's–based businesses with the opportunity to advertise to a national audience.

Privately owned and state-owned radio had both brought music and other culture in from outside Newfoundland, and both had also invented an indigenous Newfoundland popular culture. That culture was not exclusively self-referential, but included forms from the international cultural community. That did not make it less authentic or less relevant to people's lives and tastes. And it was the commercial advertising that paid for a space for that cultural programming during both the period of private ownership and state ownership. Public broadcasting advocates might argue that commercial broadcasting eroded local culture in favour of American mass culture and that the state-owned broadcaster was a bulwark against crass American culture. But such an interpretation is not supported by the case of VONF. There was no great dichotomy between 'private' and 'public' broadcasting; advertising was a mechanism to generate revenue and pay for the production of programming during the whole of its history before 1949. Under both capitalist and state ownership, VONF served the local business community by providing a medium though which listeners could be made into consumers. R.J. Murphy used VONF to make a profit through the retail of listeners' attention to advertisers, and the Commission intended to use it as a tool to aid their reconstruction of Newfoundland – but these different agendas were not reflected in different programming. While the BBC tried to create 'public' broadcasting that was an alternative to broadcasting in which commercial considerations would dictate which content and forms were broadcast, the actual record of state-owned broadcasters did not always live up to that ideal. This finding is not surprising, in the Newfoundland case, since the Commission did not have an ideological commitment to promote an alternative to the North American mass culture. In fact, the state promoted commercial broadcasting to a level of market penetration that it would not have achieved in the hands of private enterprise, because it underwrote the capital costs of building a high-power transmitter.[9] Since the revenue from advertising fell far short of the cost of maintaining an island-wide audience for commercial programming, the BCN is an example of the state taxing listeners, through licence fees, and having these listeners subsidize the businesses that chose to advertise.

One charge often levelled against broadcast media is its tendency to homogenize culture right down to the level of encouraging privileged dialects of the metropolitan centre and the middle-class over other dialects. Furlong and Galgay had endeavoured to maintain a level of standard English pronunciation among the BCN broadcasters. They were often frustrated by both the local colloquialisms of Newfoundland non-standard English in the *Doyle News* and the more American-sounding fast-paced commercial-style radio persona adopted by some broadcasters. But they did not try to impose British accents upon broadcasters, unlike the Australian Broadcasting Commission, for example, which recruited broadcasters primarily for their English or near-English accents.[10] A dialect map of Newfoundland and Labrador of the 1940s would show large variation, and while broadcasting was undoubtedly one of the mechanisms that flattened out the extremes of local speech, it was not the only factor.

Broadcasting had another modernizing effect: the BCN was a secular cultural institution at a time when most Newfoundland cultural institutions were organized along denominational lines. Nineteenth-century Newfoundland, like the other colonies of British North America, had its sectarian divisions between Church of England and Roman Catholics and other Protestant denominations. Mutual suspicions had on occasion erupted into political conflict, and as we have seen, sectarian tension rose once more during the confederation debate of the 1940s. A denominational division of government patronage, including a state-funded church-run school system, had quieted open rivalry by institutionalizing sectarianism. As a counter-factual exercise one can imagine the United Church station VOWR and the Seventh Day Adventist station VOAR being joined by a Roman Catholic station and a Church of England station, and perhaps many more denominations. Much of the public sphere was conducted along these lines, such as the debating societies of the Methodist College Literary Institute and the Holy Cross Literary Association. The English members of the Commission of Government believed that such sectarianism was wasteful of scarce resources and made public administration poorer than it would have been if government appointments were based exclusively upon merit. It is not surprising that the Commission favoured a centralized state monopoly, for such a public institution would avoid demands for a division of the spoils of broadcast frequencies. In contrast to its failure to end the duplication of school systems, the Commission was able to create a secular broadcast system, because that was a new area, without an established jealous church presence, except for VOWR and VOAR. Not that the English commissioners were the only people favouring secular cultural institutions; progressive members of each of the major Christian denominations had come together to support the secular Memorial University College as a memorial to the Newfoundlanders of

220 The Voice of Newfoundland

all denominations who had died side by side during the First World War. Although it likely had not occurred to men such as Galgay, the BCN was a modernizing institution in that it was non-denominational.

Human agency is greater than the hegemonic cultural forms created by the state or determined by the logic of attempts by business to stimulate consumer exchange.[11] Within the public venue of radio broadcasting there was room for individual broadcasters to use the medium for their own agenda. Smallwood, for example, could proselytize for his vision of a new Newfoundland on both privately owned and state-owned radio. People used radio broadcasting for greater things than selling a particular brand of toothpaste or lectures from British civil servants justifying their policies. The broadcasts of the National Convention informed Newfoundlanders of the specific benefits of union with Canada, and they also provided a venue for the articulation of visions of the future of Newfoundland's civil society. Beneath the layers of partisan debate, radio broadcasting served as a public venue for the resolution of the differing views of Newfoundland's past and future. The responsible government advocates articulated a nationalist view of an independent Newfoundland. Meanwhile the confederates mobilized a populist rhetoric against the old political and economic elites, which they linked with the uncertainties of responsible government. Newfoundland broadcasters invented a Newfoundland popular culture and gave voice to the debates within the Newfoundland nation. That was true for privately owned commercial radio and state-owned radio, and made VONF into the Voice of Newfoundland.

Notes

Introduction

1 Lewis, *Empire of the Air*; McNeil and Wolfe, *Birth of Radio*.
2 Barnouw, *History of Broadcasting in the United States*. The equivalent in the United Kingdom is a multi-volume institutional history of the BBC by Asa Briggs. For an example, see Briggs, *History of Broadcasting in the United Kingdom*, vol. 3.
3 Peers, *Politics of Canadian Broadcasting*; Weir, *National Broadcasting in Canada*.
4 See the innovative books by Hilmes, *Radio Voices*; and Scannell and Cardiff, *A Social History of British Broadcasting*. Even Scannell and Cardiff's excellent study gives fifteen chapters of institutional history followed by chapter 16 on 'listening.' The book's institutional narrative of production is not fully integrated with the discussion of consumption.
5 Eagleton, *Literary Theory*, 74–90; Levine, *The Unpredictable Past*, 304.
6 Vipond, 'The Mass Media in Canadian History,' 2–4.
7 The best book on early Canadian radio is Vipond, *Listening In*. While this book is concerned primarily with state regulation, it moves the debate in the direction of examining programming and the social impact of radio. Unfortunately no comprehensive history of the Canadian Broadcasting Corporation has been written in the last forty years.
8 For examples of this literature see, on the resource economy, Ryan, *Ice Hunters*; on social relations, Cadigan, *Hope and Deception in Conception Bay*; on the development of the state, Bannister, *Rule of the Admirals*; and on the rise and fall of the nation state, see O'Flaherty, *Lost Country*.
9 See Wright, *A Fishery for Modern Times*.
10 Sider, *Culture and Class in Anthropology and History*.
11 For examples of this body of scholarship, see Hiscock, 'The Barrelman

Radio Programme'; Narváez, 'Joseph R. Smallwood'; Narváez, 'Folk Talk and Hard Facts'; and Rosenberg, 'The Gerald S. Doyle Songsters and the Politics of Newfoundland Folksong.'

12 The most famous statement on the many meanings of the word *culture* is by Williams, in *Key Words*, 87–93. The analytical categories of 'popular culture' and 'mass culture' are much debated among scholars. One tradition sees popular culture as symbolic acts of resistance to the mass culture that is produced by capitalist media enterprises. Popular culture or folk culture is seen as 'authentic' and democratic if not revolutionary, while mass culture is a set of commodities that are sold to people. Another tradition views 'popular culture' uncritically as what a mass of people like. This study examines radio programming, which cannot be understood except as a product of the mass media industry and may or may not be popular in the sense that a mass of people like it. Popular culture is also a set of symbolic commodities of which the meanings are in part determined by those who consume them. For discussions of the contested nature of culture, see Denning, 'The End of Mass Culture'; Levine, *Highbrow/Lowbrow*, 171–242.

13 Daniel Czitrom suggests that until the development of the mass media of film, cultural critics saw 'popular culture' as an oxymoron. Following Matthew Arnold, most people believed 'culture' was something one attained by virtue of elite education and superior taste. 'Popularity' was culture's antitheses. Only in the twentieth century did scholars begin to take the expressive culture of the mass of people as a subject of inquiry. See Czitrom, *Media and the American Mind*, 30–7. Also see Arnold, *Culture and Anarchy*. In a provocative essay James Overton has questioned the existence of a 'Newfoundland culture' separate from an ideological discourse on what that culture is. See Overton, 'A Newfoundland Culture?'

14 In a different context Ian McKay has shown how the government of Nova Scotia encouraged the perception that a pre-modern traditional folk existed into the twentieth century so that modern urban people could visit that society as a treatment for the ennui of life in urban centres. McKay has rightly criticized the existence of any such anachronistic culture. His comments in this regard apply equally to Newfoundland. See McKay, *Quest of the Folk*.

15 For a fascinating discussion of early modern consumption in Newfoundland and its place in the North Atlantic world, see Pope, *Fish into Wine*.

16 Harold Innis pioneered thinking about the effects of media of communication over time and space, although he said little on radio, and founded a body of scholarship that focused upon the medium rather than the content of the message. See Innis, *The Bias of Communication*.

17 Canadian historians have moved beyond refighting the public vs private radio debate. Michael Nolan redeemed private broadcasters from the condescending view that they were inferior to the public broadcaster, and Mary Vipond showed the formation of the public network to be less a radical restructuring of broadcasting than had been assumed. See Nolan, 'An Infant Industry'; Vipond, *Listening In*. Marc Raboy pointed out that the state-owned broadcaster served the administrative needs of the state, rather than the public. See Raboy, *Missed Opportunities*.

18 One tradition within cultural studies builds upon Gramsci's insight that the dominant class engages in a dialectical compromise with subordinate classes in order to form a culture to which both subscribe but which serves the long-term interest of the dominant class. See Gramsci, *Prison Notebooks*.

19 Thompson, *Ideology and Modern Culture*, 153.

20 The same point is also made for television-watching by Ang, *Desperately Seeking the Audience*, 161. Ang makes a persuasive case that scholars should not conceive of the audience using the analytical categories generated by the television and advertising industries. Although Newfoundland broadcasters undoubtedly had an idealized audience for their programming in mind, they did not conduct the sort of quantitative audience research that occurred in other countries.

21 Newfoundland's political history during the first half of the twentieth century is sketched in Noel, *Politics in Newfoundland*. The authoritative history of the Commission of Government is Neary, *Newfoundland and the North Atlantic World*, although this book says little about the Commission's broadcasting policy or the BCN. The literature upon merchant credit is voluminous. A helpful starting point is Hiller, 'The Newfoundland Credit System.'

22 Mary Vipond has made this point about Canadian historians as well. See Vipond, 'Mass Media in Canadian History,' 4–5.

23 McChesney, *Telecommunications, Mass Media and Democracy*, 27–8.

24 Smulyan, *Selling Radio*.

25 Prang, 'Origins of Public Broadcasting in Canada.'

26 Scannell and Cardiff.

27 For a discussion of the British elite's reaction to the overlapping commercial culture and American culture, see LeMahieu, *A Culture for Democracy*.

28 Anderson, *Imagined Communities*.

1. Career of Service

1 J.T. Downey, Sound Island Placentia Bay, to Arthur Mews, deputy colonial secretary, 9 November 1925, Special Subject Files 461, GN 2/5, Provincial

Archives of Newfoundland and Labrador (PANL). It seems from this letter that Downey was a member of the clergy, although I have not been able to determine who he was.

2 Smulyan, *Selling Radio*.

3 Arthur Mews, deputy colonial secretary, to J.T. Downey, 20 November 1925, Special Subject Files 461, GN 2/5, PANL.

4 Marc Raboy has made the useful distinction between state-owned broadcasters (which pursue the interests of the state) and genuine public broadcasters, which would serve the interests of the people. See Raboy, *Missed Opportunities*.

5 Vipond, *Listening In*, 110, 196–203; Fortner, *Radio, Morality, and Culture*, 164–71.

6 Fortner, 52–4, 120.

7 Arthur Mews, deputy colonial secretary, to A. Barnes, colonial secretary, 26 December 1928, GN 2/5 461, PANL.

8 Hugh LeMessurier to A. Barnes, colonial secretary, 27 December 1928, GN 2/5 461, PANL; Mansell, *Let Truth Be Told*, 4 and 8.

9 *Daily News*, 'Our Radio Station, 16 March 1931, 3. The members of the Radio Board were James F. Pike, president; James Howell, secretary; Earnest P. Nicholle, treasurer; and W.H. Pike, Andrew Goobie, Herbert Adey, and Frank Kinsman.

10 *Daily News*, 'A Busy Week for Our Station, 21 March 1931, 11.

11 *Daily News*, 'Broadcast Station of 5000 Watts Now Licensed to Operate, 12 December 1930, 3.

12 *Daily News*, 'Promotion and Plans New Radio Station,' 19 December 1930, 7.

13 Editorial, 'A Radio Association Is Indicated,' *Daily News*, 22 January 1931, 4.

14 *Daily News*, 'Radio Dealers Discuss Problem of Interference,' 24 January 1931, 3; 'Locate Two Sources Radio Interference,' 30 January 1931, 3.

15 Coherer, letter to the editor, *Daily News*, 14 April 1931.

16 Ibid.

17 M. Pelly, letter to the editor, *Daily News*, 8 April 1931, 8; Catswhiskers, letter to the editor, *Daily News*, 14 April 1931, 6; Outport, letter to the editor, *Daily News*, 25 April 1931, 5.

18 *Daily News*, 'Opening of Our First Broadcasting Station,' 2 May, 22; front page advertisement for VOAS, *Daily News*, 18 July 1931, 1.

19 Ash, 'The Story of Radio in Newfoundland,' 349.

20 *Daily News*, 'Radio Station VOGY, 8 May 1933, n.p.

21 *Daily News*, 'Budget Broadcast,' 29 June 1933, 3.

22 *Daily News*, 'Obituary, J.J. Murphy,' 5 August 1938, 3.

23 'Obituary William F. Galgay,' *Newfoundland Journal of Commerce* 33, no. 11 (November 1966): 51.
24 Hierlihy, *Memoirs of a Newfoundland Pioneer in Radio and Television*, 27–31.
25 Browne, *Eighty-Four Years a Newfoundlander*, 208; Minutes, 12 June 1933 to 5 April 1934, 1–21 November 1933, box 20, GN 5/2/A/1, PANL.
26 *Daily News*, 'New Studio Officially Opened,' 15 November 1932, 3.
27 Ibid. During the 1920s and 1930s there was a widespread sentiment that 'reproductions' were not as good as original performances. For a classic statement of that view, see Benjamin, 'The Work of Art in the Age of Mechanical Reproduction.'
28 Anderson, 'White Reception of Jazz in America'; LeMahieu, *A Culture for Democracy*, 91–4, 105, 116–17.
29 *Daily News*, 'New Studio Officially Opened,' 15 November 1932, 3.
30 Log book of radio station VONF, 14 November 1942 to 10 March 1934, Admiralty House Archives (AHA).
31 Neary, *Newfoundland in the North Atlantic World*.
32 See letter comparing the quality of local live musicians with the repetitive phonograph records. 'Mute Milton,' letter to the editor, *Daily News*, 2 January 1935.
33 John Reith, *Into the Wind* (London: Hodder and Stoughton, 1949), quoted in LeMahieu, 146.
34 *Daily News*, 'Stations VONF and VOGY to Be Amalgamated,' 26 September 1934, 3.
35 Memorandum to the Commission, 29 September 1934, file 1, GN 38 S7-1-1, PANL.
36 *Daily News*, 'Radio Stations to Operate Separately,' 5 January 1935, 3; 'Unification Broadcasting Is under Consideration,' 15 January 1935, 3.
37 Microfilmed Enumerator Returns of the Newfoundland Census, 1935, PANL.
38 Census – Radio Owners, file 5, S5-1-5, GN 38, PANL.
39 28 May 1938, 1.01.008, Barrelman Papers, Archives and Manuscript Division, Queen Elizabeth II Library, Memorial University of Newfoundland (AMD).
40 12 June 1939, 1.01.020, Barrelman Papers, AMD.
41 Hiscock, 'Folklore and Popular Culture,' 67.
42 C.G. Graves, 'Report on Broadcasting in Newfoundland,' 21 June 1935, Dominions Office Original Correspondence 35 (D035) 505/N1071/12, microfilm reel B-4947, Library and Archives Canada (LAC).
43 H.L. Kirke, 'Report on Technical Survey of Broadcasting Conditions in Newfoundland,' October 1935, DO 35/505/N1071/17, LAC; Extracts of

226 Notes to pages 30–4

Minutes of 110th Meeting of Commission of Government, 11 October 1935, PANL.

44 Editorial, 'The Radio Tax,' *Daily News*, 7 December 1935, 4.

45 Humphrey Walwyn, Newfoundland governor, to Malcolm MacDonald, secretary of state for dominion affairs, 12 November 1937, DO 35/738/ N118/8, LAC.

46 H.W.C. Bay Roberts, letter to the editor, *Daily News*, 9 January 1937. The *Purity Programme* was sponsored by Purity Factory, which manufactured candy, among other products. The word *purity* was not a reference to the morality of the program.

47 Thomsen, 'Jazz: From "Race" Music to "Art" Music?' 79.

48 C.G. Graves, 'Report on Broadcasting in Newfoundland.'

49 Cliffe, 'Note: Broadcasting in Newfoundland,' 2 February 1938, 9–10, DO 35/736/N118/10, LAC.

50 Frazer was seconded to the Newfoundland government in September 1936. *Daily News*, 'Major Harper Ends His Term of Office,' 22 September 1936, 3.

51 G.D. Frazer, 'Broadcasting,' file 6, S5-1-5, GN 38, PANL.

52 Governor to secretary of state for dominion affairs, 12 November 1937, microfilm reel B-5018, DO 35/738/N118/8, LAC.

53 W.H. Horwood, administrator, to Malcolm MacDonald, secretary of state for dominion affairs, 2 April 1938, 3–4, DO 35/738/N118/17, LAC.

54 Governor to secretary of state for dominion affairs, 6 January 1938, GN 38, S5-1-5, PANL.

55 J.H. Penson to secretary of commission, 20 July 1937, file 10, S5-1-5, GN 38, PANL.

56 J.H. Penson to Commission of Government, 3 November 1937, file 1, S5-1-5, GN 38, PANL.

57 Governor to secretary of state for dominion affairs, 21 June 1935, DO 35/ 505/N1071/12, microfilm reel B-4947, LAC.

58 Great Britain, *Newfoundland Royal Commission 1933* (Amulree Report); Neary, *Newfoundland*, 16.

59 Clutterbuck to Penson, 9 June 1938, DO 35/738/N118/17, microfilm reel B-5018, LAC.

60 *Daily News*, 'Committee for Broadcasting Nfld,' 9 July 1938, 3.

61 Minutes of first meeting of committee to draft broadcasting act, 18 July 1938, file 1939–1947, GN 6, PANL. Minutes of the meetings and drafts of the *Broadcasting Act* may be found in file 5, GN 150, PANL.

62 A copy of the *CBC Act* can be found in Bird, *Documents of Canadian Broadcasting*, 143–53.

63 C.L. Parkins, for example, unsuccessfully tried to enlist the Board of Trade in a campaign of opposition to the creation of a government-owned station, which he believed would stifle privately owned stations. C.L. Parkins to H.T. Renouf, 28 September 1937, file 17, box 32, MG 73 Newfoundland Board of Trade, PANL.

64 Meeting of Broadcasting Committee, 20 December 1938, file 1939–1947, GN 6, PANL.

65 Summary of meeting titled 'Re Proposed Act Respecting Broadcasting,' 20 January 1939, file 16, box 36, MG 73 Newfoundland Board of Trade, PANL.

66 'Analyst' warned that the controversy over who was permitted to broadcast on the CBC was going to be reproduced in Newfoundland. Letter to the editor, *Evening Telegram*, 2 February 1939.

67 L.R. Curtis, letter to the editor, *Daily News*, 7 December 1938.

68 Ibid.

69 'A Lover of Good Programmes the Second,' letter to editor, *Daily News*, 7 February 1939.

70 His move may have been prompted by concern that his career was not assured, had he remained at VONF. In 1935 H.L. Kirke, of the BBC, interviewed many Newfoundland broadcasters while preparing a report upon the feasibility of establishing a public broadcasting station. Kirke reported that Butler did not get along with others and thought him not a good engineer because he was 'too inclined to experiment.' H.L. Kirke Report, 11 November 1935, D035/505/N1071/18, LAC.

71 VOCM operated for awhile before the Colonial Broadcasting System Limited was incorporated on 30 April 1937. Joseph L. Butler is recorded as owning twenty-six shares, his wife Evelyn owned twenty-two, Walter B. Williams Sr owned twenty-five, and Walter B. Williams Jr owned twenty-four. Butler enhanced his ownership in 1949 when he invested money and the company issued additional shares, and the Williams family remained minority shareholders. 'Colonial Broadcasting System Limited,' file 01505, Registry of Companies, Government of Newfoundland and Labrador.

72 G.D. Frazer to commissioner of finance, 4 August 1937, file 58, Galgay Papers, AMD.

73 Governor to secretary of state for dominion affairs, 12 November 1937, DO 35/738/N118/8, microfilm reel B-5018, LAC.

74 W.H. Horwood, administrator, to Malcolm MacDonald, secretary of state for dominion affairs, 2 April 1938, D035/738/N118/17, microfilm reel B-5018, LAC.

75 General manager to governors, 4 October 1947, Subject – Comment on VOCM Correspondence, file 18, Galgay Papers, AMD.

76 Regulations for Broadcasting Stations made under the Newfoundland Broadcasting Act, chapter 2, 1939, file 1939–1947, GN 6, PANL.
77 Webb, 'Who Speaks for the Public?'
78 Report of Frazer's Visit to Montreal, Ottawa, Toronto, New York, 15 May 1939, file 42, Galgay Papers, AMD.
79 G.D. Frazer to J.S. MacGregor, Empire Service director, BBC, 22 December 1938, file 63, Galgay Papers, AMD.
80 MacLeod had been born in St John's in 1908 and was performing at dances and celebrations as well as working as an organist and choirmaster at Wesley United Church during the 1930s, the services of which were broadcast over the church-owned VOWR. He had frequently appeared as an accompanist in both live appearances and on the air. *Encyclopedia of Newfoundland and Labrador*, 'Robert Ferguson MacLeod,' 3:418–19.
81 G.D. Frazer, 20 January 1938, Memorandum on preparatory work carried out in connection with the Establishment of the Broadcasting Service of Newfoundland, file 1939–47, GN 6, PANL.
82 MacDonald had been born in Bonavista in 1911, started work for the United Towns Electric Company about 1930, and after 1932 began working as an unpaid sports announcer. He was later made part of the paid staff. Hiscock, 'Folklore and Popular Culture,' 14–18.
83 *Evening Telegram*, 'New Central Station Takes to the Air,' 14 March 1939, 5.
84 LeMahieu, 145–7.
85 Smallwood, 13 March 1939, 1.01.017, Barrelman Papers, AMD.

2. Addressing the Population at Large

1 2 November 1939, 1.01.024, Barrelman Papers, AMD.
2 Thompson, *Ideology and Modern Culture*, 255.
3 LeMahieu, *A Culture for Democracy*, 147.
4 On the corporatist ideology of the Commission, see Overton, 'Economic Crisis and the End of Democracy.'
5 Great Britain, *Newfoundland Royal Commission 1933*, 81.
6 McChesney, *Telecommunications*, 27–8.
7 Raboy, *Missed Opportunities*, xii–xiii.
8 Lodge, *Dictatorship in Newfoundland*, 4.
9 Draft telegram for secretary of state, file 845, GN 2/5, PANL.
10 G.D. Frazer to Galgay, 7 March 1939, 4, file 59, Galgay Papers, AMD; W.G. Horwood to William Galgay, 25 February 1939.
11 Vipond, *Listening In*, 62.
12 H.L. Kirke, 'Report on Technical Survey of Broadcasting Conditions in

Newfoundland,' October 1935, DO 35/505/N1071/17, LAC; Extracts of Minutes of 110th Meeting of Commission of Government, 11 October 1935.

13 G.D. Fraser to H.N. Stovin, 5 April 1939, Galgay Papers, collection 107, box 1, file 43, AMD.

14 The data up to 1936 reflect fiscal year ending 30 June, while the data after 1937 reflect year ending 31 December. Data added from Broadcasting Corporation of Newfoundland Annual Report for the year ending 31 December 1946, file 1939–1947, GN 6, PANL.

15 Tuck, 'The Newfoundland Ranger Force.'

16 Tizzard, *On Sloping Ground*, 337.

17 Ibid.

18 Ibid.

19 Wayfarer, 'Budget Day,' *Daily News*, 14 July 1942, 4.

20 A.B. Morine, 'Newfoundland Constitution: What's the Matter? What's the Cure?' *Daily News*, 5 August 1939, 3.

21 *Daily News*, '123 Operators Now on Strike in 93 Offices of Postal Telegraphs,' 2 December 1938, 2. Also 'One of the Public,' letter to the editor, 15 December 1938.

22 G.D. Frazer, 'Memoranda: Broadcast Programmes,' 31 March 193, file 1939–1947, GN 6, PANL.

23 A series of these can be found in 'Daily Radio Bulletin,' B9/14, GN 31/3A, PANL.

24 G.D. Frazer to William Galgay, 7 March 1939, file 59, Galgay Papers, AMD; John E. Bell *et al.* to David Fraser [*sic*], 14 December 1938.

25 *Daily News*, 'Radio Address Given by Mr K.M. Brown,' 9 December 1938, 2.

26 K.M. Brown, 29 April 1939, F27570/79-007 (CD887), Memorial University of Newfoundland and Labrador Folklore and Language Archive (MUNFLA).

27 J.B. Clark to Michael Barkway, 18 January 1946, Canadian Representative, 1946, file 2B, Countries: Canada, E1/509/3, BBC Written Archives Centre. I thank Len Kuffert for providing me with a copy of this correspondence.

28 Potter, 'The BBC, the CBC, and the 1939 Royal Tour of Canada'; Vipond, 'The Mass Media in Canadian History.'

29 F27267/79-007 (CD735) and F27267/79-007 (CD736), MUNFLA.

30 F27543/79-007 (CD873), MUNFLA.

31 F27268/79-007 (CD736), MUNFLA.

32 (CD751), MUNFLA.

33 F27540/79-007 (CD872), MUNFLA.

34 F27541/79-007 (CD872), MUNFLA.

35 Royal Visit Broadcasts, 17 June [?] 1939, file 80, Galgay Papers, AMD.

36 Great Britain, *Newfoundland Royal Commission 1933*.
37 Governor to secretary of state for dominion affairs, 12 November 1937, DO 35/738/N118/8, microfilm reel B-5018, LAC.
38 Browne, *Eighty-Four Years a Newfoundlander*, 235–42; *Daily News*, 'Official Statement on Leave of Absence,' 27 October 1939, 3.
39 Neary, *Newfoundland in the North Atlantic World*, 95.
40 Gorvin, *Papers Relating to a Long Range Reconstruction*, 2:24.
41 *Daily News*, 'First of a Series of Broadcasts Given Last Night,' 19 February 1937, 3.
42 *Evening Telegram*, 'Cooperation on the Air,' 7 January 1939, 5.
43 Assistant director for co-operation to acting secretary for rural reconstruction, 20 November 1939, file 'Radio Propaganda, Co-operative Division,' GN 31/3B MR1, PANL.
44 Laite had been born in Newfoundland in 1895 but had immigrated to the United States with his family in 1900. He was educated in public schools in Boston and served overseas in the Canadian Army. He took a bachelor of arts in music at Northwestern University in Illinois, after which Laite sang professionally with the Chicago Civic Opera and on radio. He returned to Newfoundland on vacation in 1937 and decided to remain. *Daily News*, 'Celebrated Singer Returns Home,' 18 March 1937, 3.
45 *Evening Telegram*, 'Variety Show on New Station,' 13 March 1939, 3.
46 Whitfield Laite to director of co-operation, n.d., file 'Radio Correspondence,' GN31/3A C3/12, PANL.
47 See correspondence from listeners, especially Gerald Brown, Bell Island, 21 January 1940, file 'Radio Correspondence,' GN 31/3A C3/12, PANL.
48 Charles White, Burin North, to Whitfield Laite, 6 May 1940, file 'Radio Correspondence,' GN 31/3A C3/12, PANL.
49 F27109/79-007 (CD656), MUNFLA.
50 F27539/79-007 (CD871), MUNFLA.
51 F27508/79-007, University Tape 121 (CD855–6), MUNFLA.
52 F27110/79-007 (CD657), MUNFLA.
53 Whitfield Laite to director of co-operation, n.d., file 'Radio Correspondence,' GN31/3A, C3/12 PANL.
54 Whitefield Laite to director of co-operation, n.d., file 'Radio Propaganda, Co-operative Division,' GN 31/3B MR1, PANL; Whitefield Laite to director of co-operation, 1 June 1940, 'Radio Scripts 1939–1940,' GN 31/3A C3/5, PANL.
55 F27110/79-007 (CD657), MUNFLA.
56 H.W. Quinton to commissioner of natural resources, 11 December 1939, file 'Radio Propaganda, Co-operative Division,' GN31/3B MR1, PANL.

57 H.W. Quinton to acting secretary of rural reconstruction, 4 February 1940; J.H. Gorvin to Quinton, 26 February 1940, file 'Radio Propaganda, Co-operative Division,' GN 31/3B MR1, PANL.

58 J.H. Gorvin to acting director of agriculture, 19 December 1939, file 'Radio Programmes, Agricultural Division,' GN 31/3A R95, PANL.

59 File 'Radio Programmes, Agricultural Division,' GN 31/3A R95, PANL.

60 *Daily News*, 'Farewell Party Tendered to Mr and Mrs Richardson,' 26 September 1940, 3.

61 Neary, *Newfoundland in the North Atlantic World*, 124.

62 *Daily News*, 'Co-op Officer Gets New Post,' 16 March 1943, 3.

63 The schedule of the 1943 series and scripts of addresses from 1944 can be found in GN 31/3B AR10, PANL.

64 Chief co-operative officer to secretary for rural reconstruction, 23 February 1942, file 'Radio Propaganda, Co-operative Division,' GN 31/3B MR1, PANL.

65 See radio scripts in file 'Radio Propaganda, Co-operative Division,' GN 31/3B MR1, PANL.

66 Steve O'Driscoll, Flowers Cove, to Neil MacNeil, 16 June 1942, file 'Radio Propaganda, Co-operative Division,' GN 31/3B MR1, PANL.

67 *Daily News*, 'Radio and Education,' 16 December 1946, 4.

68 Grace Sparkes to Galgay, 4 October 1948, file 120, Galgay Papers, AMD; Galgay to Sparkes, 7 December 1948.

69 *Daily News*, 'Children's Hour Program in War Savings Campaign,' 11 March 1942, 3.

70 *Evening Telegram*, 'Hello, Boys and Girls, This Is Your Savings Programme,' 27 October 1948, 2.

71 Ibid.

72 An extant recording of the *Children's Savings Programme* of 8 December 1945 consists of children singing popular tunes such as 'Meet Me in St Louis,' tap-dancing (which on radio lacks much entertainment value), and recitations. It also announced a new program of savings to encourage Junior Thrift Clubs in the schools and war savings stamps books. F27073/79-007 (CD638), MUNFLA.

73 *Daily News*, 'Widening Educational Horizons,' 4 November 1939, 9. A columnist in the *Evening Telegram* had proposed a Newfoundland 'school of the air' based upon the example created by the American Columbia Broadcasting Company before the inauguration of the BCN. See *Evening Telegram*, 'On Thinking It Over: School by Radio,' 7 February 1939, 6.

74 Radio Address, 17 April 1939, file 9, S-3-4-1, GN 38, PANL.

75 Clipping from *Western Star*, 29 January 1944, file 92, Galgay Papers, AMD.

76 C.W. Carter to secretary of education, 23 August 1948, file 108, Galgay Papers, AMD.
77 Hiller and Harrington, *The Newfoundland National Convention*, 2:121.
78 C.W. Carter, director adult and visual education, to secretary of education, 23 August 1948, file 108, Galgay Papers, AMD.

3. Entertainment and Enlightenment

1 2 March 1939, 1.01.017, Barrelman Papers, AMD.
2 I have adopted the concept of 'cultural intervention' from David Whisnant. He used it to describe folk culture popularizers who selected folk songs, for example, that supported a particular agenda, and then promoted a revival of those songs, thus intervening in the culture that they were ostensibly trying to preserve. See Whisnant, *All That Is Native and Fine*.
3 Vipond, *Listening In.*
4 'The Dominion Broadcasting Company Ltd.: Memo of Contracts Now in Force'; R.J. Murphy to G.D. Frazer, 7 August 1937, file 58, Galgay Papers, AMD.
5 G.D. Frazer to William Galgay, 7 March 1939, file 59, Galgay Papers, AMD.
6 *Encyclopedia of Newfoundland and Labrador*, 'O.L. Vardy,' 5:474; Confidential memo J.A. Winter to secretary of Commission, 16 February 1939, file 845, GN 2/5, PANL.
7 Newfoundland Governor Walwyn to Malcolm MacDonald, secretary of state for dominion affairs, 12 November, 1937, 10, DO 35/738/N118/8, LAC.
8 Hiscock, 'Folk Process in a Popular Medium,' 179, 182–3. Fifty-four years after the program ended, Tom Cahill, who remembered the program as a boy, adapted some of the original scripts and published them as a novel. Cahill, *The Adventures of the Irene B. Mellon.*
9 C.G. Graves as quoted in Scannell and Cardiff, *Social History*, 1:189.
10 Scannell and Cardiff, *Social History*, 1:191.
11 Graves, 'Report on Broadcasting in Newfoundland,' 20, 23, DO 35/505/N1071/12, LAC.
12 G.D. Frazer to chairman of BCN, 15 May 1939, file 1939–1947, GN 6, PANL.
13 Hilmes, *Radio Voices.*
14 *Daily News*, 'Beyond Reasonable Doubt,' 4 November 1943, 5. '*Beyond Reasonable Doubt* new radio serial, the first instalment of which was aired November 3rd over station VONF, has so far been proven one of the best and most engrossing combinations of thrilling mystery and powerful romance ever heard on the Newfoundland air waves … On the air Monday through Friday at 9:30 pm over VONF.'

15 Hugh D. Lilly, letter to the editor, *Evening Telegram*, 26 February 1948.
16 I thank the folk singer and scholar Anita Best for explaining the distinction to me.
17 'A Lover of Good Programmes the Second,' letter to the editor, *Daily News*, 7 February 1939,
18 LeMahieu, *A Culture for Democracy*, 105; M. Anderson, 'The White Reception of Jazz.'
19 'Mrs Fan de Radio,' letter to the editor, *Evening Telegram*, 11 March 1939.
20 The possible musicians he named were Stuart Godfrey, T. Howell, Basil Hutton, Margaret Kean, Whitefield Laite, Sandy Lawrence, Eleanor Mews, Shelia O'Neil, T. O'Neil, Ignatious Rumbolt, John Scurry, and John Power. G.D. Frazer, 'Memoranda: Broadcast Programmes,' 31 March 1939, file 1939–1947, GN 6, PANL.
21 See, for example, the schedules published in the *Daily News*, 17 April 1939 and 20 April 1939.
22 *Daily News*, 'Radio Programmes, 3 May 1939, 7.
23 *Daily News*, 'Radio Programmes, 27 May 1939, 6.
24 *Daily News*, 'Radio Programmes, 31 May 1939, 10.
25 *Daily News*, 'Radio Programmes, 29 November 1939, 4.
26 Thomsen, 'Jazz,' 79–83.
27 'The Radio Critics,' Lewisporte, letter to the editor, *Daily News*, 6 December 1940.
28 H.B., letter to the editor, *Daily News*, 18 January 1940.
29 'How about Joe Swing,' letter to editor, *Daily News*, 28 November 1941.
30 Wayfarer, 'Swing Is Tripe,' *Daily News*, 29 November 1941.
31 'Music Lover,' letter to the editor, *Daily News*, 29 November 1941.
32 'Another One,' letter to the editor, *Daily News*, 1 December 1941.
33 R.A. MacLeod to general manager, 8 December 1939, file 79, Galgay Papers, AMD.
34 J.J. Weed, Weed and Co., to Galgay, 19 December 1939, file 96, Galgay Papers, AMD.
35 C.O. Langois to G.D. Frazer, 11 January 1939, file 57, Galgay Papers, AMD.
36 'Report of Secretary GPO to BCN Chairman,' 15 May 1939, file 42, Galgay Papers, AMD.
37 G.D. Frazer to J.S. MacGregor, Empire Service director, BBC, 22 December 1938, file 63, Galgay Papers, AMD; Frazer, 'Broadcasting,' 16, file 6, S5-1-5, GN 38, PANL.
38 MacGregor to Frazer, 25 November 1938, file 63, Galgay Papers, AMD.
39 Frazer to MacGregor, 27 January 1939, file 63, Galgay Papers, AMD.

40 W.R. Baker to Frazer, 6 February 1939, Frazer to W.R. Baker, 24 March 1939, file 63, Galgay Papers, AMD.

41 Frazer to MacGregor, 24 March 1939, file 63, Galgay Papers, AMD.

42 Simon Frith points out that the BBC did not reject the notion that wireless programming was educational as opposed to entertaining. He suggests that Reith wanted to create entertainment by and for the 'cultured' so that listening in Britain would not be reduced to vulgar American mass culture. See Frith, *Music for Pleasure*, 41.

43 'List of Empire Transcriptions,' file 63, Galgay Papers, AMD.

44 Sam Heppner in *Radio Times*, 1936, as quoted in Scannell and Cardiff, *Social History*, 211.

45 Scannell and Cardiff, *Social History*, 221, 223. Some critics and musicians felt that music should not serve as an adjunct to dancing, but should itself be the centre of attention. Dance music was therefore not an art form, encouraging the development of music, which required a cultivated taste. See Thomsen, 'Jazz,' 79–101.

46 October 1944, file 12, Galgay Papers, AMD, first broadcast on 28 January at 3:30, with VOWN coming on the air especially for it. The BCN reported that the series was very popular with teachers, pupils, and the general public.

47 List of BBC Programmes, 7 July 1948, file 3, Galgay Papers, AMD.

48 Report on BBC Transcriptions, month of August 1948, file 31, Galgay Papers, AMD.

49 Report of Frazer's visit to Montreal, Ottawa, Toronto, New York, 15 May 1939, file 42, Galgay Papers, AMD.

50 Frazer to E.A. Weir, 9 February 1939, and Frazer to E.A. Weir, 13 April 1939, file 43, Galgay Papers, AMD.

51 Frazer to Storvin, 5 April 1939, file 43, Galgay Papers, AMD.

52 G.D. Frazer to G.T. Herbert, 25 May 1939, file 96, Galgay Papers, AMD.

53 Rosenberg, 'The Gerald S. Doyle Songsters and the Politics of Newfoundland Folksong.'

54 *Daily News*, 'New Feature in Local Broadcasting,' 10 January 1931, 3.

55 This analysis owes a debt to Hiscock, 'Folklore and Popular Culture,' 56–111.

56 Terranovan, 'Topics of the Day,' *Evening Telegram*, 18 October 1947, 6.

57 Memo on Preparations, signed GDF 20/1/38, file 1939–1947, GN 6, PANL.

58 Hiscock, 'The Public Despatch and the Doyle Bulletin.'

59 *Evening Telegram*, 'Bigger News Bulletin for Country,' 13 March 1939, 3.

60 Haig-Smith, Department of Posts and Telegraphs, to Galgay, 23 March 1943, file 112, Galgay Papers, AMD.

61 Haig-Smith to Gerald S. Doyle, 20 January 1944, file 105, Galgay Papers, AMD.
62 B. Anderson, *Imagined Communities*.
63 General manager to secretary, 18 March 1943, file 5, Galgay Papers, AMD.
64 Clayton Johnson, Grand Bank, personal communication.
65 *Gerald S. Doyle News Bulletin*, 1946 (CD848), MUNFLA.
66 G.D. Halley to chairman, 6 March 1946, file 1939–1947, GN 6, PANL; *Evening Telegram*, 'Libel Action over Radio Announcement,' 16 May 1947, 1.
67 General manager to chairman, 28 March 1946, file 42, Galgay Papers, AMD.
68 *Jones v. Great Eastern Oil and Import Co. Ltd* in *The Reports, 1941–1946 Decisions of the Supreme Court of Newfoundland* (St John's: Queen's Printer, 1956), 439.
69 Smallwood, *I Chose Canada*, 205.
70 NBC News Commentary by Al Vardy, 21 September 1939, (CD770), F27337/79-007, MUNFLA.
71 Another extant broadcast was similar. It was almost all war news, followed by items on Van Dies House Un-American Activities Committee and on the AFL/CIO struggle. It ended with the BCN announcer Evan Whiteway doing an advertisement for Green Label margarine. Al Vardy News, 7 March 1941 (CD 744), MUNFLA.
72 'News Fan,' letter to the editor, *Daily News*, 5 November 1943.
73 'Listener,' Bell Island, letter to the editor, *Daily News*, 8 November 1943.
74 'Another News Fan,' letter to the editor, *Daily News*, 22 November 1943. See also 'West Ender,' letter to the editor, *Daily News*, 5 April 1945.
75 Michael Barkway, BBC, to Galgay, 22 January 1948, file 4, Galgay Papers, AMD.
76 A.E. Poynter and J.C. Crosbie, Newfoundland Butter Company, to Newfoundland Broadcasting Corporation [*sic*], 20 May 1939, file 1939–1947, GN 6, PANL.
77 Frazer to Donald Manson, CBC, 25 May 1939, file 96, Galgay Papers, AMD.
78 Manson to Frazer, 16 June 1939, file 96, Galgay Papers, AMD.
79 F27277/79-007 (CD740), F27278/79-007 and F27278/79-007 (CD741), MUNFLA.
80 Galgay to governors, 20 November 1946, file 7, Galgay Papers, AMD.
81 David Brinkley report from Gander, 21 September 1946, RWB 4488 A5, National Broadcasting Corporation Radio Collection, Library of Congress.
82 Webb, 'Canada's Moose River Mine Disaster.'
83 'Why I Oppose Communism,' 7.02.001, J.R. Smallwood Papers, AMD.
84 *Daily News*, 'From the Masthead by the Barrelman,' 19 July 1937, 5.
85 Hiscock, 'The Barrelman,' 60, 68.

86 Contracts between F.M. O'Leary Ltd and J.R. Smallwood, 29 June 1938 and
30 June 1938, file 10, box 6, Leo Moakler Collection, AMD.

87 Smallwood, *I Chose Canada*, 206.

88 17 January 1938, 1.01.004, Barrelman Papers, AMD.

89 In April 2007 Wally Johnson checked this with his father, Clayton Johnson,
who remembered sending the letter of 18 January 1942 (now contained in
2.02.057, Barrelman Papers, AMD). The incident Johnson related had actually happened, but there had not really been thousands of woodpeckers
trapped in the stick. He reported that exaggeration was what was
expected of those to wrote to the Barrelman.

90 4 July 1938, 1.01.010, Barrelman Papers, AMD.

91 Interview with Ellen Carroll, 17 October 1941 (CD847), MUNFLA. There
had also been a broadcast the preceding year on 19 October 1940.

92 Narváez, 'Joseph R. Smallwood,' 52.

93 Hiscock 'The Barrelman.'

94 Paine, 'The Persuasiveness of Smallwood,' 59.

95 20 December 1939, 1.01.025, Barrelman Papers, AMD.

96 See, for example, letter from T.D. Carew taking issue with comment made
by Barrelman in broadcast. Letter to the editor, *Daily News*, 18 June 1938.

97 *Daily News*, 'Fogo Notes: Good Radio Reception,' 24 March 1939, 6.

98 Letter from 'Anonymous,' 2.02.020, Barrelman Papers, AMD.

99 Ben C. Keats to Barrelman, 22 February 1941, 2.02.045, Barrelman Papers,
AMD.

100 'Solomon,' letter to the editor, *Daily News*, 15 March 1941.

101 Razlogova 'True Crime Radio.'

102 Mike Kelly to Smallwood, 5 February 1939, 2.02.018, Barrelman Papers,
AMD.

103 Hiscock 'The Barrelman,' 105–10.

104 Paine, 'The Persuasiveness of Smallwood,' 63.

105 David Tait, Green's Island, to Smallwood, 17 March 1941, 2.02.046, Barrelman Papers, AMD.

106 October 1937, 1.01.001, Barrelman Papers, AMD.

107 On this ideological message in Depression-era radio programs in the
United States, see Levine 'American Culture and the Great Depression.'

108 June 1938, 1.01.009, Barrelman Papers, AMD.

109 'Old Harry,' Bonavista, letter to the editor, *Evening Telegram*, 13 July 1939.

110 28 February 1939, 2.02.018, Barrelman Papers, AMD.

111 Thomas Tuck, Bishop's Falls, to Smallwood, 3 May 1941, 2.02.048, Barrelman Papers, AMD.

112 7 May 1934, 1.01.008, Barrelman Papers, AMD.

113 Hiscock 'The Barrelman,' 311–14.

114 Ibid., 92–4.

115 Hilmes argues that American broadcasters created a split between male and female radio. Daytime was for women's programs, with its mass culture and advertisers manipulating women, while broadcasters used nighttime for men and thus by contrast it became elite culture. She argues that programming during the 1930s and 1940s was affected by a dialectic in which radio's 'Mass/private/feminine base [was] constantly threatened its "high"/public/masculine function.' Hilmes, *Radio Voices*, 152–3.

116 See Hiscock, 'The Barrelman,' 288–97.

117 *Daily News*, 'Charlie White's New Song to Be "Aired" Tonight'; 'Allied Forces to Be Guests Blondell Show,' 13 October 1942, 3.

118 2.02.071, Barrelman Papers, AMD. One listener reported hearing *Command Performance* and reported that both she and her family were insulted by Blondell's comments and song. Ruth Way, Grand Falls, 24 January 1943, to Smallwood. Other listeners did not feel that Blondell deserved the criticism she received. L.E. Pelley to Barrelman, 17 February 1943, 2.02.072, Barrelman Papers, AMD.

119 One reader wrote Smallwood, responding with indignation to a letter published in a US newspaper that questioned Newfoundlanders' work ethic and honesty. Max Forward, Carbonear, 25 February 1943, 2.02.072, Barrelman Papers, AMD.

120 Ewart Young, 'Reporter at Large: 60,000 Letters Feed Local Radio Program,' *Daily News*, 5 July 1943, 3.

121 Webb, 'Confederation, Conspiracy and Choice.'

122 Smallwood, *I Chose Canada*, 212.

123 See, for example, M.F. Harrington, 'Toast to Newfoundland,' *Daily News*, 27 October 1943, 5.

124 Compare Michael Harrington as the Barrelman at war's end, F27568/79-007 (CD886), MUNFLA, with Joseph Smallwood during December 1940, F27569/79-007 (CD886). The scripts of the program under Harrington's tenure are available in Harrington Collection, AMD.

125 For examples, see Thomas Noseworthy, Markland, 30 November 1943, 2.02.083, Harrington Collection, AMD, welcomed Harrington, but complained that the tall tales were 'not so hot.' Jean Gosse, Buchans, 6 November 1944, 2.02.096, suggested that a good children's radio program could undo damage done to children's morals by movies and comics. Mary Noseworthy, Harbour Grace, 2 November 1944, wrote that she liked the *Children's Savings Programme* with Bob Macleod 'because there is lots of Newfoundland songs and music sung and played by the children.'

238 Notes to pages 107–11

Dominic A. Lynch, Argentia, 23 October 1944, suggested a program of debates upon various subjects and a program of Newfoundland music. He later he thought could include not only songs and ballads of 'grit and endurance' but also 'humourous' music and 'jigs and reels.'

126 Faculty at Memorial University College judged the contest. Harrington read over the air the names of the winners and read the top award-winning poem. See 23 December 1944, 5.01.005, Harrington Collection, AMD. For examples of the hundreds of poems submitted by listeners, see those collected for November 1946 in 2.02.120, Harrington Collection, AMD.

127 Hiscock, 'The Barrelman Radio Programme.'

128 My count underestimates the letters from men, since I excluded the many letters signed by initials for the first name, which was a device that I think men were more likely to use than women. Women seem to have been more likely to prefix their names with 'Miss' or 'Mrs' than men were to use 'Mr.' I know that correspondents such as J.J. Peckford was a man, but I excluded him from my count for consistency of method.

129 David Tait, Green's Island, to Smallwood, 17 March 1941, 2.02.046, Barrel-man Papers, AMD.

130 *Evening Telegram*, 'Broadcasting Corporation of Newfoundland,' 11 April 1939, 1.

131 *Evening Telegram*, 'A New Type of Program for Nfld Listeners,' 31 August 1946, 12.

132 *Evening Telegram*, 'Palmolive's "Happy gang" Variety Show to Air on VONF,' 29 November 1947, 3.

133 A.E. Poynter, Harvey-Brehm Ltd, to Galgay, 19 April 1947, file 70, Galgay Papers, AMD; Galgay to governors, 21 April 1947, file 5, Galgay Papers, AMD.

134 Galgay to A.E. Poynter, 27 May 1948, file 70, Galgay Papers, AMD.

135 *Evening Telegram*, 'A New Radio Personality,' 26 April 1947, 2; 'St John's Woman to Broadcast Daily on Station VONF,' 30 May 1947, 8; *Daily News*, 'Young Nfld Lady Has Bright Future in Field of Radio,' 25 April 1947, 5.

136 Galgay to A.E. Poynter, 27 May 1948, file 70, Galgay Papers, AMD.

137 Charles R. Bell (Brokers, Importers, and Manufacturers Agents) to Frazer, 19 August 1939, file 96, Galgay Papers, AMD.

138 *Daily News*, 'Green Hornet over Station VONF,' 15 February 1945, 6.

139 Smallwood, *I Chose Canada*, 208.

140 Tizzard, *On Sloping Ground*, 338–9.

141 Smallwood, *I Chose Canada*, 212.

4. Gibraltar of North America

1 Brown, *Manipulating the Ether*, 192.
2 Horten, *Radio Goes to War.*
3 On Edward R. Murrow, see Barnouw, *The Golden Web*, 76–83, 140–2.
4 F27106/79-007 (CD655), MUNFLA; F27106/79-007 (CD655), MUNFLA.
5 Nicholas, *The Echo of War*, 220.
6 Major General J.B. Brooks, commanding general, Newfoundland Base Command, to George D. Hooper, US consul general, St John's, 7 October 1943, file 874, box 57, Foreign Service Posts, Consul General St John's Newfoundland, RG 84, National Archives, College Park, MD, (NARA).
7 *Daily News*, 'Ottawa to Give CBC Monopoly on Radio News,' 8 July 1940, 6. C.D. Howe announced that the CBC would be given monopoly in news, and Trans-Radio News Service would have its permit to distribute news cancelled 1 July.
8 F27106/79-007 (CD655), MUNFLA; F27106/79-007 (CD655), MUNFLA.
9 Mansell, *Let Truth Be Told*, 188–95 (quotation on 188).
10 *BBC Handbook, 1942*, 15, as quoted in Briggs, *The History of Broadcasting in the United Kingdom*, 3:403.
11 F27430/79-007 (CD817), MUNFLA.
12 *Hello Newfoundland*, 23 January 1941 (CD 752), MUNFLA.
13 Halper, *Invisible Stars.*
14 Nicholas, *The Echo of War*, 52; Briggs, *The History of Broadcasting*, 316, 492–4.
15 Introduction in Knight, ed., *Calling Newfoundland.*
16 *Daily News*, 'Girlfriends of the Empire,' 31 March 1942, 3.
17 Ibid.
18 *Daily News*, 'Calling Newfoundland,' 14 September 1942, 3.
19 Hilmes, *Radio Voices*, 130–50.
20 Matthews, Morris, and March to Smallwood, 6 July 1941, 2.02.050, Barrelman Papers, AMD.
21 For example, 'Hello Newfoundland' (CD645), MUNFLA/CBC.
22 *Hello Newfoundland*, 24 August 1942, F27631/79-007 (CD917), MUNFLA.
23 For example, 'Hello Newfoundland' (CD645), MUNFLA/CBC.
24 *Hello Newfoundland*, 8 September 1943 (CD846), MUNFLA.
25 *Calling Newfoundland*, 4 June 1945 (CD783), MUNFLA.
26 *Hello Newfoundland*, 24 December 1945, F27634/79/79-007 (CD919), MUNFLA.
27 H. Rooney Pelletier to Galgay, BBC, 6 January 1948, file 17, Galgay Papers, AMD.
28 *Hello Newfoundland*, 15 September 1947, F27255/79-007 (CD729), MUNFLA.

29 *Encyclopedia of Newfoundland and Labrador,* 'Margo T. Davies,' 1:595.
30 'Salute to Canada,' 3 September 1942, F27631 79-007 (CD917), MUNFLA.
31 F27634/79-007 (CD919), MUNFLA.
32 *Daily News,* 'Commissioner to Broadcast Address,' 20 November 1939, 3.
33 *Daily News,* 'War Savings Broadcasts This Week,' 12 May 1941, 7.
34 *Daily News,* 'Newfoundland's Part in Present War,' 25 November 1939, 3.
35 F27106/79-007 (CD655), MUNFLA.
36 Ibid.
37 (CD 801), MUNFLA.
38 *Daily News,* 'Newfoundland's War Effort,' 11 December 1939, 3. See also 'Novelty Broadcast by GWVA Monday Night,' 16 February 1940, 3: 'An attractive arrangement of war-time songs and choruses has been made, with the leads taken by prominent city artistes, and as has always been the case when War Vets are "on the air" the numbers should go with a swing.'
39 *Daily News,* 'Nfld's Effort Is Broadcast,' 2 October 1940, 3.
40 Nicholas, *The Echo of War,* 42.
41 *Daily News,* 'Nfld's Effort in Response to Britain's Need,' 3 July 1940, 3.
42 *Daily News,* 'Many Copies of Marching Song Are Purchased,' 21 November 1940, 3. The song 'Marching Together' composed by W.H. Barter and tune composed by his brother Bombardier Barter has been published and dedicated to the Newfoundland Heavy Regiment Royal Artillery. Copies of the sheet music were also on sale in St John's.
43 *Daily News,* 'Tonight's Broadcast from VONF,' 20 January 1942, 9.
44 *Daily News,* 'Future Recruiting Programmes,' 22 November 1940, 3.
45 *Daily News,* 'Recruiting Broadcasts,' 27 March 1941, 3.
46 *Daily News,* 'Tonight's broadcast from VONF,' 20 January 1942, 9.
47 *Daily News,* 'Recruiting Programme Brought Good News,' 13 February 1942, 12.
48 Haig-Smith at Rotary Club, from Ballroom at Newfoundland Hotel, 29 February 1940, F27434/79-007 (CD819), MUNFLA.
49 W.A. Thomson, staff officer (Intelligence), St John's, Canadian Department of National Defence, Naval Service, to Galgay, 30 November 1943, file 64, Galgay Papers, AMD.
50 J.T. Meaney, letter to editor, *Daily News,* 7 August 1941.
51 Editorial, 'Censorship,' *Daily News,* 23 January 1942, 4.
52 F.W. Heakes, air commodore, RCAF, to Broadcasting Corporation, 14 January 1943, file 64, Galgay Papers, AMD.
53 F.W. Heakes, air commodore, RCAF, to Broadcasting Corporation, 9 January 1943, file 64, Galgay Papers, AMD; F.V. Heakes, air vice marshal, to manager, 16 February 1944, file 67, Galgay Papers, AMD.

54 *Daily News*, 'USS "Edmund B. Alexander" Berths at Southside Pier Ending an Historical Voyage,' 30 January 1941, 3.

55 F27111/79-007 (CD657), MUNFLA.

56 L.O. Clark, Newfoundland Base Contractors, to Galgay, 13 April 1942, file 64, Galgay Papers, AMD.

57 For example, air raid precautions talk by Raymond Gushue, 26 June 1942 (CD 744), MUNFLA.

58 Advertisement, 'Your Health: Radio Service of the Department of Health and Public Welfare over Station VONF Tuesdays and Saturdays at 8pm,' *Daily News*, 18 September 1935, 5.

59 F27255/79-007 (CD729), MUNFLA.

60 Neary, *Newfoundland*, 347.

61 *Daily News*, 'Your Health,' 15 November 1938, 5. Public health broadcast over VONF referring to syphilis as 'an increasingly important, an ever-present crippling, killing disease in Newfoundland.'

62 'Is Silence Golden,' 22 November 1941, file 6, GN38 S-6-5-2, PANL.

63 'The Great Imitator,' 23 November 1942, file 6, GN38 S-6-5-2, PANL.

64 General manager to secretary, 10 August 1943, file 105, Galgay Papers, AMD.

65 Galgay to Furlong, 10 August 1943, file 1939–1947, GN 6, PANL.

66 For a biography of Leonard Miller, see Martin, *Leonard Albert Miller*.

67 Galgay to Furlong, 10 August 1943, file 1939–1947, GN 6, PANL.

68 Leonard Miller to secretary for public health and welfare, 23 July 1943, file 1939–1947, GN 6, PANL.

69 H.M. Mosdell to R.S. Furlong, 29 July 1943, file 1939–1947, GN 6, PANL.

70 Galgay to Furlong, 10 August 1943, file 1939–1947, GN 6, PANL.

71 J.C. Puddester to R.S. Furlong, 2 September 1943, file 1939–1947, GN 6, PANL.

72 Galgay to governors, 16 March 1948, file 71, Galgay Papers, AMD.

73 Leonard Miller to Galgay, 19 February 1948, file 71, Galgay Papers, AMD.

74 Galgay to Furlong, 16 March 1948, file 1939–1947, GN 6, PANL.

75 George Williams to Galgay, 24 March 1948, file 71, Galgay Papers, AMD.

76 The chapter draws upon Webb, 'VOUS.'

77 *Daily News*, 'Soldiers Present Their Third USO Radio Program,' 22 October 1942, 3.

78 *Daily News*, 'Armistice Day Skit Heard on USO Show,' 12 November 1942, 2.

79 *Daily News*, 'Local Young Lady Is Featured on USO Broadcast,' 8 January 1943, 3; 'Comedy Featured in Broadcast,' 14 January 1934, 7.

80 *Daily News*, 'Radio Show of US Soldiers Again on the Air,' 4 February 1943, 3.

81 *Daily News*, 'Canadian Forces on Radio Program,' 27 February 1943, 5.
82 *Daily News*, 'Canadian Show on Nfld Radio,' 13 January 1944, 6.
83 Major Harford W.H. Powell, special service officer, to commanding general, Foreign Service Posts, Consul General St John's, Newfoundland Base Command, 1 October 1943, file 000.77, box 57, RG 84, NARA.
84 Powel, to commanding general, Newfoundland Base Command, 1 October 1943, file 000.77, box 57, RG 84, NARA.
85 Ibid.
86 Ibid.
87 Ibid.
88 *Evening Telegram*, '"Beyond Reasonable Doubt" on VONF,' 1 November 1943, 4.
89 Powel, to commanding general, Newfoundland Base Command, 1 October 1943, file 000.77, box 57, RG 84, NARA.
90 Major John H. Doughty, staff judge advocate, to commanding general, Newfoundland Base Command, 6 October 1943, file 676.3, box 57, RG 84, NARA.
91 Major General J.B. Brooks, commanding general, Newfoundland Base Command, to George D. Hooper, US consul general, St John's, 7 October 1943, file 874, box 57, RG 84, NARA.
92 Major Harford W.H. Powel, special service officer, to commanding general, Newfoundland Base Command, 1 October 1943, file 000.77, box 57, RG 84, NARA.
93 Major General John B. Brooks to J. Haig-Smith, 9 October 1943, file 676.3, box 22, decimal file 1943, Newfoundland Base Command, RG 338, NARA.
94 Webb, 'The Origins of Public Broadcasting.'
95 J. Haig-Smith to Major General John B. Brooks, 9 November 1943, file 676.3, box 22, decimal file 1943, Newfoundland Base Command, RG 338, NARA.
96 The War Department preferred that the Newfoundland station use an American call sign, WXLU, and that the station's frequency and power not be registered with the Inter-American Radio Office in Havana, since it was for a military purpose and not subject to the international treaty that governed civilian broadcasting. The Newfoundland Base Command reported that the Newfoundland Government had requested the station continue to use 'VOUS' and that the first five months of operation had not resulted in any interference with other broadcasters. Adjutant general, War Department, to commanding general, Eastern Defence Command, 11 March 1944, file 676.3, box 44, RG 338, Newfoundland Base Command, NARA; Newfoundland Base Command to commanding general, Eastern Defence Command, 3 April 1944.

97 Once the station was established, military officials expanded its operations to better cover the distant bases in Placentia Bay and the island's west coast. In the spring of 1944 a relay transmitter was built at Fort McAndrew to better serve the base at Argentia. In August 1944 the Commission granted permission for the operation of another American station, VOHF, at the base at Stephenville, which was delayed since the nearby VOWN provided Harmon Field with adequate coverage of AFRS programming, but opened in March 1945. See A.J. Cuamy, Department of Posts and Telegraphs, to Lieutenant Colonel H.H. Maxwell, 21 August 1944, file 676.3, box 77, decimal file 1945, Newfoundland Base Command, RG 338; Newfoundland Base Command to commanding officer, 1388th AAF Base, 4 August 1944, file 676.3, box 44, decimal file 1944, RG 338, NARA.

98 Harford W.H. Powel to Colonel John R. Reitemeyer, 14 February 1945, file 676.3, box 47, decimal file 1945, Newfoundland Base Command, RG 338, NARA.

99 *Evening Telegram*, 'VOUS Provides Day Long Service,' 19 February 1949, 3.

100 F.J. Mathews to William Galgay, 23 November 1945, file 90, collection 107, Galgay Papers, AMD; Roy Owen, Information Service Section, Fort Pepperrell, to William Galgay, 14 January 1946; assistant general manager, BCN, to Roy Owen, 19 January 1946.

101 Posen and Taft, 'The Newfoundland Popular Music Project.'

102 See 'Newfoundlander,' letter to the editor, *Evening Telegram*, 3 October 1945.

103 General manager to chairman, 18 March 1944, file 42, Galgay Papers, AMD.

104 General manager to governors, 18 May 1948, file 71, Galgay Papers, AMD.

105 Horten.

106 Webb, 'VOUS.'

107 Draft of radio address for Home Affairs and Education, file 9A, S-3-2-1, GN 38, PANL.

108 Memorandum titled 'Programs,' 6 September 1947, file 6, Galgay Papers, AMD.

5. Most Important Work

1 Joseph Smallwood, quoted in McNeil and Wolfe, 34.

2 Webb, 'Confederation, Conspiracy and Choice.'

3 Day, *The Radio Years*, 1:214–15.

4 For a more detailed discussion of the National Convention, see Webb, 'Newfoundland's National Convention.' An edited transcript of the convention proceedings has been published: consult Hiller and Harrington, eds. *The Newfoundland National Convention, 1946–1948*. For an examination of Canadian and British government policies, see MacKenzie, *Inside the North Atlantic Triangle*, and Neary, *Newfoundland*.

5 R.B. Job's proposal is discussed in an editorial, 'A National Conclave,' *Daily News*, 20 March 1943, 4. The Board of Trade called for a royal commission to determine the popular will on the future form of government. See *Daily News*, 'Meeting Calls for Royal Commission,' 30 March 1943, 3.

6 Memorandum, N.A. Roberston to prime minister, 25 September 1945, in Bridle, ed., *Documents on Relations*, 2:169–71.

7 Lord Addison to Cabinet, 18 October 1945, DO 35/1347/N402/54, LAC.

8 General manager to chairman, 10 January 1946, file 42, Galgay Papers, AMD. Examples of political letters that Harrington read over the air a year earlier can be found in January 1945, 5.01.006, Harrington Collection, AMD.

9 General manager to chairman, 10 January 1946, file 42, Galgay Papers, AMD.

10 Log book of Radio Station VONF, 14 November 1932 to 10 March 1934, AHA.

11 Chairman to Galgay, 22 May 1945, file 25, Galgay Papers, AMD.

12 General manager to chairman, 23 May 1945, file 1939–1947, GN 6, PANL.

13 Chairman to Galgay, 22 May 1945, file 23, Galgay Papers, AMD.

14 Galgay to chairman, 1 June 1945, file 23, Galgay Papers, AMD.

15 Galgay to W.J. Carew, secretary of home affairs, 23 June 1945, file 23, Galgay Papers, AMD.

16 Radio Address by Peter J. Cashin on the future political and economic situation of Newfoundland, file 23, Galgay Papers, AMD.

17 Editorial, *Grand Falls Advertiser*, 9 June 1945, file 23, Galgay Papers, AMD.

18 Second address by Peter Cashin, file 23, Galgay Papers, AMD.

19 Galgay to chairman, 18 June 1945, file 68, Galgay Papers, AMD.

20 Third address by Peter Cashin, file 23, Galgay Papers, AMD.

21 Ibid.

22 Avalon, letter to the editor, *Daily News*, 7 December 1945.

23 General manager to governors, memo re Ordinary Report, 25 September 1947, file 1939–1947, GN 6, PANL.

24 Cashin, *Address on National Affairs*, 9.

25 H.E. Governor McDonald, 21 May 1946, F27280/79-007 (CD742), MUN-FLA.

26 Broadcast for the Benefit of Returning Officers Explaining the Terms of the National Convention Act Pertaining to the Election Procedures, 9 September 1946, F27633/79-007 (CD918), MUNFLA.

27 VONF Broadcast to the Electors of Bay Roberts District, 19 June 1946, by W.E. Mercer, candidate to the National Convention, file 78, Galgay Papers, AMD.

28 *Daily News*, 'Broadcasts and Politics,' 22 June 1946, 4.

29 *Daily News*, 'Broadcasting the Convention,' 6 September 1946, 4.

30 Governor to Dominions Office, January 1946, file 5, S2-1-22, GN 38, PANL.

31 Horace MacNeil, St Anthony, to Gerald S. Doyle, copy published in *Evening Telegram*, 27 March 1946, 6.

32 E.D.C. Hiscock, letter to the editor, *Evening Telegram*, 10 April 1946.

33 General manager to governors, 'National Convention,' 17 August 1946, file 23, Galgay Papers, AMD.

34 George Williams to Galgay, 31 August 1946, file 7, Galgay Papers, AMD.

35 Hiller and Harrington, 46.

36 Summary of debate on Steering Committee Report, 20 September 1946, file 123, Galgay Papers, AMD.

37 BCN Annual Report for the Year Ending 31 December 1946, file 1939–1947, GN 6, PANL.

38 Ibid.

39 Michael Harrington, 'A personal memoir,' in Hiller and Harrington, 1:xxiv.

40 Webb, 'Newfoundland's National Convention,' 65–6.

41 BCN Annual Report for the Year Ending 31 December 1946, file 1939–1947, GN 6, PANL.

42 Galgay to governors, 20 November 1946, file 7, Galgay Papers, AMD.

43 Williams to Galgay, 23 November 1946, file 7, Galgay Papers, AMD.

44 George Williams to Galgay, 27 December 1946, file 7, Galgay Papers, AMD.

45 J.R. Smallwood (5 January 1948) quoted in Hiller and Harrington, 1:1044.

46 Horwood, *Joey*, 79–80.

47 Programs, 6 September 1947, file 6, Galgay Papers, AMD.

48 Hiller and Harrington, 1:345–6.

49 English, 'The Judges Go to Court,' 355–89.

50 Ibid., 377.

51 Judge Dunfield's address to the jury appeared in *Daily News*, 'Judge Dunfield's Address to Jury in Cashin Libel Trial,' 19 April 1947, 5.

52 Galgay to F.G. Bradley, 18 April 1947, file 68, Galgay Papers, AMD.

53 Hiller and Harrington, 1:499–502.

54 Francis J. Ryan, assistant secretary, to Galgay, 19 April 1947, file 68, Galgay

Papers, AMD; general manager to governors re Ordinary Report, 21 April 1947, file 1939–1947, GN 6, PANL.

55 George Williams to Galgay, 27 May 1947, file 4, Galgay Papers, AMD.
56 Draft memo, general manager to governors, 22 July 1947, file 70, Galgay Papers, AMD.
57 Ibid.
58 Hiller and Harrington, 1:737.
59 Ibid., 738, 755.
60 Malcolm Pelley, Smith's Sound, letter to the editor, *Daily News*, 23 December 1946.
61 Ranger W. Walsh to chief ranger, 10 January 1948, S-2-5-2, GN 38, PANL; Ranger G. Fitzpatrick to chief ranger, 26 December 1947.
62 Ranger C. Parsons to chief ranger, 22 December 1947, S-2-5-2, GN 38, PANL.
63 Ranger C. Matthews to chief ranger, 13 December 1947, S-2-5-2, GN 38, PANL.
64 Ranger A. Stevens to chief ranger, 7 November 1947, S-2-5-2, GN 38, PANL.
65 Ranger C. Strong to chief ranger, 2 December 1947, S-2-5-2, GN 38, PANL.
66 Ranger J.J. Hogan to chief ranger, 3 January 1948, S-2-5-2, GN 38, PANL.
67 Ranger J. Coffin to chief ranger, 7 January 1948, S-2-5-2, GN 38, PANL.
68 Ranger J.F. Luscombe to chief ranger, 7 October 1947, S-2-5-2, GN 38, PANL.
69 Ranger S.M. Christian to chief ranger, 8 October 1947, S-2-5-2, GN 38, PANL.
70 Galgay to F.M. O'Leary, 6 April 48, file 29, Galgay Papers, AMD; Williams to Galgay, 12 April 1948.
71 George Williams to Galgay, 26 June 1948, file 3, Galgay Papers, AMD.
72 Smallwood to R.L.M. James, 29 June 1948, S7-1-3, GN 38, PANL.
73 R.L.M. James to Commission Government, 29 June 1948, S7-1-3, GN 38, PANL.
74 J.B. McEvoy to Galgay, 6 May 1948; Galgay to McEvoy, 7 May 1948, file 32, Galgay Papers, AMD.
75 *Evening Telegram*, 'Application to Broadcast Is Refused Mr John B. McEvoy,' 8 May 1948, 2.
76 CBC, 'Political and Controversial Broadcasting Policies and Rulings,' 'Paragraphs (3), (4) and (5) of Section 22 of the Act of 1936 read as follows: (3) Dramatized political broadcasts are prohibited,' file 29, Galgay Papers, AMD.
77 W.L. Collins, RGL, to G.R. Williams, 27 September 1948, file 21, Galgay Papers, AMD.

78 Broadcast of RGL, 9 October 1948, defending petition to overturn referendum, file 21, Galgay Papers, AMD.
79 P.J. Cashin to Galgay, 10 August 1948; Galgay to P.J. Cashin, 11 August 1948, file 21, Galgay Papers, AMD.
80 Frederick W. Marshall, RGL, letter to the editor, *Evening Telegram*, 11 October 1948.
81 W.L. Collins, RGL, letter to the editor, *Evening Telegram*, 12 October 1948.
82 F.W. Marshall to R.L.M. James, 1 November 1948, and James to Commission of Government, 8 November 1948, S7-1-3, GN 38, PANL.
83 W.L. Collins, secretary, RGL, to Galgay, 24 November 1948, file 120, Galgay Papers, AMD.
84 Galgay to Collins, 7 December 1948, file 120, Galgay Papers, AMD. See also the published correspondence between the secretary of state for dominion affairs and the Responsible Government League. *Evening Telegram*, 'Correspondence regarding Radio Broadcast,' 3 November 1948, 3.
85 Day, 1:214–15.
86 'Terranovan, 'Topics of the Day: Local Broadcasting,' *Evening Telegram*, 23 February 1948, 6.
87 W.V. Parsons, letter to the editor, *Evening Telegram*, 19 January 1949.
88 Galgay to governors, 12 June 1948, file 3, Galgay Papers, AMD.
89 Note on broadcast of the convention, file 36, Galgay Papers, AMD.
90 General manager to governors, re Ordinary Report, 21 April 1947, file 1939–1947, GN 6, PANL.
91 For a comment upon the number of listeners, see Terranovan, 'Topics of the Day: Convention Resuming,' *Evening Telegram*, 7 January 1947, 6.

6. Personal and Intimate Character

1 Seventh Annual Report, year ending 31 December 1945, file 9, Galgay Papers, AMD.
2 General manager to secretary, 16 June 1943, file 89, Galgay Papers, AMD.
3 Galgay to governors, 25 September 1947, file 69, Galgay Papers, AMD.
4 Galgay to chairman, 12 April 1946, file 77, Galgay Papers, AMD.
5 Broadcasting Corporation of Newfoundland Annual Report for the Year Ending 31 December 1946, file 1939–1947, GN 6, PANL.
6 Hiscock, 'Folklore and Popular Culture,' 52.
7 *Daily News*, 'The Church Radio Service,' 15 January 1946, 4.
8 Terranovan, 'Topics of the Day: The Radio Tax,' *Evening Telegram*, 15 January 1946, 6.

9 Mrs Caleb Pye, Brooklyn Bonavista Bay, 31 October 1944, 2.02.096, Barrelman Papers, AMD.

10 Terranovan, 'Topics of the Day: Radio Fare below Par,' *Evening Telegram*, 23 May 1946, 6; see also Terranovan, 'Topics of the Day: Broadcasting Probe,' 10 April 1947, 6; Terranovan, 'Topics of the Day: Radio Conference,' 13 June 1947, 6.

11 Cyril D.B. Knight, letter to the editor, *Evening Telegram*, 15 March 1946.

12 R.S. Furlong to J.S. Currie, 11 June 1945, and memo on programs, file 1939–1947, GN 6, PANL.

13 Memo on programs, 11 June 1945, file 1939–1947, GN 6, PANL.

14 Ibid.

15 'Culture,' letter to the editor, *Daily News*, 6 March 1945.

16 'Critic,' letter to the editor, *Daily News*, 8 March 1945.

17 Ibid.

18 Scannell and Cardiff, *A Social History*, 365.

19 K.W., letter to the editor, *Daily News*, 8 March 1945.

20 'Another Listener,' *Daily News*, 6 April 1945.

21 Memo on programs, 11 June 1945, file 1939–1947, GN 6, PANL.

22 Ibid.

23 Ibid.

24 MacKay, 'Being Beastly to the Germans,' 520–1; Briggs, *History of Broadcasting in the United Kingdom*, 2:110–11.

25 Michael Barkway speech to Rotary Club 1947, University Tape 97, F27412/79-007, (CD 808), MUNFLA.

26 R.S. Furlong to G.W. Williams, 1 March 1946, file 1939–1947, GN 6, PANL.

27 The BCN recovered about two thirds of the cost of Reuters' service through its sales. Seventh Annual Report, year ending 31 December 1945, file 9, Galgay Papers, AMD.

28 Cyril Conner to Galgay, 21 June 1948, file 3, Galgay Papers, AMD.

29 Galgay to governors 21 April 1947, file 5, Galgay Papers, AMD.

30 Galgay to Furlong, 17 January 1941, file 30, Galgay Papers, AMD.

31 Galgay to governors, 25 September 1947, file 4, Galgay Papers, AMD.

32 Galgay to governors, 21 April 1947, file 5, Galgay Papers, AMD; George Williams to Galgay, 13 May 1947.

33 Memorandum, 'Programs,' 6 September 1947, file 6, Galgay Papers, AMD.

34 Ibid.

35 This chapter draws upon Webb, 'Who Speaks for the Public?'

36 General manager to governors, 27 December 1945, file 42, Galgay Papers, AMD.

37 R.B. Herder, *Evening Telegram*, to W.S. Roddis, secretary of posts and tele-
    graphs, 20 March 1946, file 47, Galgay Papers, AMD.

38 Roy Thomson, of the Thomson group of newspapers, had apparently vis-
    ited St John's in 1944, a visit that Galgay believed had been suggested by a
    relative, Captain F.R. Davies, who had been the public relations officer for
    the Canadian Army in Newfoundland. Handwritten note, file 47, Galgay
    Papers, AMD.

39 General manager to governors, Subject: *Sunday Herald* Application, 13 Jan-
    uary 1947, file 15, Galgay Papers, AMD.

40 Even at this late date, Galgay was not certain if such regulations should be
    made by the Corporation or by the Department of Posts and Telegraphs,
    and suggested that he would discuss the issue with the secretary of posts
    and telegraphs, W.S. Roddis. Roddis had replaced Haig-Smith when the
    latter had returned to Britain. General manager to governors, 19 March
    1946, file 111, Galgay Papers, AMD.

41 L.R. Curtis to Galgay, Memorandum re Proposed Regulations to Be Made
    under the Newfoundland Broadcasting Act, Chapter 2 1939, 1 June 1946,
    file 13, Galgay Papers, AMD.

42 Ibid.

43 Ibid.

44 McChesney, *Telecommunications, Mass Media and Democracy.*

45 Peers, *The Politics of Canadian Broadcasting*, 284–6, 444–5; Weir, *The Struggle
    for National Broadcasting in Canada*, 241–6.

46 L.R. Curtis to Galgay, Memorandum re Proposed Regulations to Be Made
    under the Newfoundland Broadcasting Act, Chapter 2 1939, 1 June 1946,
    file 13, Galgay Papers, AMD.

47 Report for the commissioner, September 1946, file 6, Galgay Papers,
    AMD.

48 Draft memo, general manager to governors, 22 July 1947, file 70, Galgay
    Papers, AMD.

49 G.R. Williams to Galgay, 31 August 1946, file 7, Galgay Papers, AMD.

50 J.L. Butler to R.L.M. James, commissioner of finance, 2 August 1947, file 18,
    Galgay Papers, AMD.

51 Memorandum to commissioner for finance re Colonial Broadcasting Sys-
    tem Radio Station VOCM, file 18, Galgay Papers, AMD.

52 Report for the commissioner, Licensing of New Stations and Power
    Increases, 6 September 1947, file 6, Galgay Papers, AMD.

53 Ibid.

54 Memorandum of the Governors of the Broadcasting Corporation of New-
    foundland with Reference to a Application for Increased Power and Exten-

sion of Broadcast Facilities by the Colonial Broadcasting System Ltd [1947], file 1939–1947, GN 6, PANL.

55 Yet it must be noted that despite the daily tensions between the state-owned and privately owned stations, some cooperation continued. Important public events and some other programming were broadcast over both VOCM and VONF, requiring the two broadcasters to coordinate their activities. For example, the documentary on 'House of Bowring,' 10 February 1949, was presented over VOCM, VONF, VONH, and VORG. F27630/79-007 (CD917), MUNFLA.

56 Hiller and Harrington, 2:121–2.

57 Hiller and Harrington, 1:200–204.

58 Ibid., 218.

59 Ibid., 850.

60 McChesney; Godfried, WCFL.

61 General manager to governors, memo re VOCM, 4 October 1947, file 1939–1947, GN 6, PANL.

62 Ibid.

63 University Tape 121, (CD855), F27506/79-007, MUNFLA; and F27486/79-007 (CBC845), MUNFLA.

64 Overton, 'Engaging the Enemy Within,' 81–97.

65 Weir.

66 Galgay to governors, 26 June 1947, file 72, Galgay Papers, AMD.

67 General manager to governors, 4 October 1947, Subject – comment on VOCM correspondence, file 18, Galgay Papers, AMD.

68 Ibid.

69 General manager to governors, 17 August 1948, file 31, Galgay Papers, AMD.

70 Hiller and Harrington, 1:849–50.

71 Ibid., 850.

72 Ibid., 889.

73 Ibid.

74 Manson to general manager, 30 August 1948, file 23-1-7-1, vol. 405, RG 41, LAC.

75 Manson to Galgay, 27 August 1948, file 23-1-7-1, vol. 405, RG 41, LAC.

76 Ibid.

77 Donald Manson to R.A. MacKay, 20 September 1948, file 23-1-7-1, vol. 405, RG 41, LAC.

78 Galgay to Manson, 7 September 1948, file 23-1-7-1, vol. 405, RG 41, LAC.

79 Extract from Minutes of Board of Governors, 24 September 1948, file 23-1-7-1, vol. 405, RG 41, LAC.

80 Frigon to Chief Engineer Keefer, 4 November 1948, file 23-1-7-1, vol. 405, RG 41, LAC.
81 Newfoundland Broadcasting: Responsibilities of Corporation in Connection with Newfoundland's Entry into Confederation, file 23-1-7-1, vol. 405, RG 41, LAC.
82 Radio Broadcasting System, file 23-1-7-1, vol. 405, RG 41, LAC.
83 Ibid.
84 Hugh Palmer to E.L. Bushnell, 23 November 1948, file 23-1-7-1, vol. 405, RG 41, LAC.
85 Ibid.
86 'Loyal Confederate,' St John's, letter to the editor, *Evening Telegram*, 30 July 1948.
87 'Loyal Newfoundlander,' letter to the editor, *Evening Telegram*, 31 July 1948.
88 'Victor,' letter to the editor, *Evening Telegram*, 3 August 1948.
89 E.L. Bushnell to Hugh Palmer, 29 November 1948, file 23-1-7-1, vol. 405, RG 41, LAC.
90 'Re Brief Submitted to Canadian Government by Newfoundland Delegation: Comments by Canadian Broadcasting Corporation re Portion of Brief Dealing with Broadcasting in Newfoundland,' file 23-1-7-1, vol. 405, RG 41, LAC
91 Statements on questions raised by the Newfoundland Delegation during the negotiations for the union of Newfoundland with Canada, 11 December 1948, file 103, Galgay Papers, AMD.
92 Anon., 15 July 1944, file 123, Galgay Papers, AMD.
93 Geo Williams to Galgay, 31 August 1946, file 7, Galgay Papers, AMD.
94 General manager to governors, 18 May 1948, file 71, Galgay Papers, AMD.
95 General manager to governors, 28 September 1948, file 20, Galgay Papers, AMD.
96 For a discussion of Newfoundland's participation in the North American Regional Broadcasting Conference at Havana, see general manager to governors, 8 December 1947, file 1, GN 150, PANL.
97 General manager to chairman, 28 December 1948, file 120, Galgay Papers, AMD.
98 Galgay to governors, 25 September 1947, file 69, Galgay Papers, AMD.
99 Galgay to governors, 22 March 1949, file 50, Galgay Papers, AMD.
100 CBT Grand Falls Opening, 1 July 1949, F27067/79-007 (CD79-007), MUNFLA. The inaugural program was carried on the network. It included re-enactments of events in Newfoundland history such as Cabot Landfall and Marconi's reception of a message from UK.

101 Dick O'Brien to general manager, 21 January 1949, Subject: CBC Revision of Programmes, file 100, Galgay Papers, AMD.

102 Ibid.

103 'Listener,' letter to the editor, *Evening Telegram*, 20 October 1948.

104 Terranovan, 'Topics of the Day: When CBC Takes Over,' *Evening Telegram*, 5 January 1949, 6.

105 Herbert D. White, letter to the editor, *Evening Telegram*, 1 December 1948.

106 'Good Music Lover,' letter to the editor, *Evening Telegram*, 7 December 1948.

107 Terranovan, 'Topics of the Day: CBC Taking Over,' *Evening Telegram*, 26 March 1949, 6.

108 Hugh Palmer to J. Howes, 16 November 1948, file 23-1-7-1, vol. 405, RG 41, LAC.

109 A. Frigon to Chief Engineer Keefer, 4 November 1948, file 23-1-7-1, vol. 405, RG 41, LAC.

110 E.L. Bushnell to W.E.S. Briggs, 8 November 1948, file 23-1-7-1, vol. 405, RG 41, LAC.

111 Galgay to staff, 4 February 1949, file 68, Galgay Papers, AMD.

112 N.R. Olding to Maritimes regional engineer, 1 February 1949, file 23-1-7-1, vol. 405, RG 41, LAC.

113 'Canadian Broadcasting Corporation: Tentative Outline of Informational Programmes Concerning Newfoundland,' file 23-1-7-1, vol. 405, RG 41, LAC.

114 F27382/79-007 (CD793), MUNFLA.

115 Terranovan, 'Topics of the Day: Informing Canadians,' *Evening Telegram*, 8 March 1949, 6.

116 D.C. McArthur, CBC, to Galgay, 8 February 1949, file 100, Galgay Papers, AMD.

117 Ibid.

118 Galgay to governors, 22 March 1949, file 50, Galgay Papers, AMD.

119 Secretary of state for external affairs to high commissioner for Canada in Newfoundland, 24 March 1949, file 102, Galgay Papers, AMD.

120 G. Williams to Galgay, 24 March 1949, file 50, Galgay Papers, AMD.

121 Williams to Galgay, 17 February 1949, file 101, Galgay Papers, AMD.

122 Galgay to governors, 22 March 1949, file 50, Galgay Papers, AMD.

123 High commissioner for Canada in Newfoundland to secretary of state for external affairs, 5 March 1949, file 102, Galgay Papers, AMD.

124 High commissioner for Canada in Newfoundland to secretary of state for external affairs, 7 March 1949, file 102, Galgay Papers, AMD.

125 Paul A. Bridle to Galgay, 25 March 1949, file 102, Galgay Papers, AMD.

126 Galgay to governors, 22 March 1949, file 50, Galgay Papers, AMD.

Epilogue

1 Blake, *Canadians at Last*, 39–40.
2 For an example, see his use of radio broadcasting to suppress a labour dispute. Paine, 'The Mastery of Smallwood and Interlocutory Rhetoric.'
3 A useful synopsis of his long and varied career accompanies his papers. Harrington Collection, AMD.
4 Papers of the *Great Eastern* Radio Show, AMD.
5 Wellman, *The Broadcast*.
6 Pocius, 'The Mummers Song in Newfoundland,' 57, 71, 73–5.
7 Ted and Dora Russell Collection, AMD.
8 Narváez, 'Folk Talk and Hard Facts,' 156–61.
9 Neil Rosenberg, 'Omar Blondahl's Contribution to the Newfoundland Folksong Canon.'

Conclusion

1 Film and television have attracted much more attention from scholars interested in content analysis of mass media than has radio. For a recent exception, see Hilmes and Loviglio eds., *Radio Reader*.
2 I borrow this phrase from George Lipsitz, 'Listening to Learn and Learning to Listen,' 624.
3 On a Canadian, liberal, nationalist intellectual who argued for public broadcasting, see Nolan, *Foundations: Alan Plaunt*.
4 This analysis owes a debt to Thompson, *Ideology and Modern Culture*, 256–8.
5 Hiscock, 'Folklore and Popular Culture in Early Newfoundland Radio Broadcasting'; Hiscock 'Folk Process in a Popular Medium'; Hiscock 'The Barrelman Radio Programme'; and Narváez, 'Joseph R. Smallwood, "The Barrelman."'
6 Benjamin, 'The Work of Art in the Age of Mechanical Reproduction,' 217–51.
7 Paddy Scannell, 'Public Service Broadcasting and Modern Public Life,' as quoted in Kate Lacey, 'Radio in the Great Depression: Promotional Culture, Public Service and Propaganda,' in Hilmes and Loviglio, eds., 34.
8 Anderson, *Imagined Communities*.
9 I have made the same point about the operation of the Canadian Radio Broadcasting Commission and the CBC. The Canadian state-owned broad-

caster also extended the penetration of commercial advertising. See Webb, 'The Invention of Radio Broadcasting in Newfoundland and the Maritime Provinces,' 124–57.

10 K.S. Inglis, *This is the ABC*, 22–3.

11 Gramsci, *Prison Notebooks*.

Bibliography

Primary Sources

Admiralty House Museum and Archives (Mount Pearl)
   Official Log Book of radio station VONF, 14 November 1942 to 10 March 1934
Archives and Manuscript Division, Queen Elizabeth II Library, Memorial University (St John's)
   Barrelman Papers
   John Higgins Papers
   Leo Moakler Collection
   Joseph R. Smallwood Papers
   Michael Francis Harrington Collection
   Papers of the *Great Eastern* Radio Show
   Ted and Dora Russell Collection
   William Galgay Papers
Government of Newfoundland and Labrador (St John's)
   Registry of Companies
Law Library (St John's)
   Jones v. Great Eastern Oil and Import Co. Ltd in *The Reports, 1941–1946 Decisions of the Supreme Court of Newfoundland* (St John's: Queen's Printer, 1956)
Library and Archives Canada (Ottawa)
   DO 35, Dominions Office Original Correspondence
   RG 41, Records of the Canadian Broadcasting Corporation
Library of Congress (Washington DC)
   RWB 4488 A5, National Broadcasting Corporation Radio Collection
Memorial University Folklore and Language Archive (St John's)
   Recordings of the Broadcasting Corporation of Newfoundland ('University Tapes')

National Archives (Washington DC)
  RG 84, Foreign Service Posts
  RG 338, Newfoundland Base Command
Newspapers
  Daily News, 1929–49
  Newfoundland Gazette, 1939–49
  Evening Telegram, 1939–49
Provincial Archives of Newfoundland and Labrador (St John's)
  GN 2/5 Colonial Secretary's Office
  GN 5 Supreme Court, Central District
  GN 6 Royal Commissions
  GN 31 Department of Natural Resources
  GN 38 Commission of Government
  GN 150 Broadcasting Corporation of Newfoundland
  Newfoundland Board of Trade Collection, MG 73, PANL
  Peter Cashin Papers
  William Browne Papers

Secondary Sources

Anderson, Benedict. *Imagined Communities: Reflections on the Origins and Spread of Nationalism.* London: Verso, 1991.

Anderson, Maureen. 'The White Reception of Jazz in America.' *African American Review* 38, no. 1 (Spring 2004): 135–45.

Ang, Ien. *Desperately Seeking the Audience.* London: Routledge, 1991.

Arnold, Mathew. *Culture and Anarchy and Other Writings.* Cambridge: Cambridge University Press, 1993.

Ash, Earnest. 'The Story of Radio in Newfoundland.' In *The Book of Newfoundland*, edited by J.R. Smallwood, 1:339–50. St John's: Newfoundland Book, 1937.

Bannister, Jerry. *The Rule of the Admirals: Law, Custom, and Naval Government in Newfoundland, 1699–1832.* Toronto: University of Toronto Press, 2003.

Barnouw, Erik. *A History of Broadcasting in the United States.* Vols. 1 and 2. New York: Oxford University Press, 1966.

Benjamin, Walter. 'The Work of Art in the Age of Mechanical Reproduction.' In *Illuminations*, edited by Walter Benjamin, 217–51. New York: Schocken Books, 1968.

Bird, Roger, ed. *Documents of Canadian Broadcasting.* Ottawa: Carleton University Press, 1988.

Blake, Raymond B. *Canadians at Last: Canada Integrates Newfoundland as a Province.* Toronto: University of Toronto Press, 1994.

Bridle, Paul, ed. *Documents on Relations between Canada and Newfoundland.* Vol. 2, *1940–49.* Ottawa: Department of External Affairs, 1984.

Briggs, Asa. *The History of Broadcasting in the United Kingdom.* Vol. 2, *The Golden Age of Wireless.* London: Oxford University Press, 1961.

– *The History of Broadcasting in the United Kingdom.* Vol. 3, *The War of Words.* London: Oxford University Press, 1970.

Brown, Robert J. *Manipulating the Ether: The Power of Broadcast Radio in Thirties America.* Jefferson, NC: McFarland, 1998.

Browne, William J. *Eighty-Four Years a Newfoundlander.* St John's: Dicks, 1981.

Cadigan, Sean T. *Hope and Deception in Conception Bay: Merchant–Settler Relations in Newfoundland, 1785–1855.* Toronto: University of Toronto Press, 1995.

Cahill, Tom. *The Adventures of the Irene B. Mellon.* St John's: Cuff, 1995.

Cashin, Peter. *Address on National Affairs Delivered by Major Peter J. Cashin over Radio Station VOCM St John's, Newfoundland, on January 12 1946.* St John's: Manning and Rabbitts, n.d.

Czitrom, Daniel J. *Media and the American Mind: From Morse to McLuhan.* Chapel Hill: University of North Carolina Press, 1982.

Day, Patrick. *A History of Broadcasting in New Zealand.* Vol. 1, *The Radio Years.* Auckland: Auckland University Press, 1994.

Denning, Michael. 'The End of Mass Culture.' *International Labor and Working-class History* 37 (Spring 1990): 4–18.

Eagleton, Terry. *Literary Theory: An Introduction.* Minneapolis: University of Minnesota Press, 1983.

Encyclopedia of Newfoundland and Labrador. 5 vols. St John's: J.R. Smallwood Heritage Foundation, 1981–1994.

English, Christopher. 'The Judges Go to Court: The Cashin Libel Trial of 1947.' In *Essays in the History of Canadian Law.* Vol. 9, *Two Islands: Newfoundland and Prince Edward Island,* edited by Christopher English, 355–89. Toronto: University of Toronto Press, 2005.

Frith, Simon. *Music for Pleasure: Essays in the Sociology of Pop.* New York: Routledge, 1988.

Fortner, Robert S. *Radio, Morality, and Culture: Britain, Canada, and the United States, 1919–1945.* Carbondale: Southern Illinois University Press, 2005.

Godfried, Nathan. *WCFL, Chicago's Voice of Labour, 1926–78.* Urbana: University of Illinois Press, 1997.

Gorvin, J.H. *Papers Relating to a Long Range Reconstruction Policy in Newfoundland.* Vol. 2. St John's: Queen's Printer, 1938.

Gramsci, Antonio. *Selections from the Prison Notebooks of Antonio Gramsci*. London: Lawrence and Wishart, 1973.

Great Britain. *Newfoundland Royal Commission 1933 Report* (Amulree Report). Command paper 4480. London: His Majesty's Stationery Office, 1934.

Halper, Donna L. *Invisible Stars: A Social History of Women in American Broadcasting*. Armonk, NY: Sharpe, 2001.

Hierlihy, Oscar. *Memoirs of a Newfoundland Pioneer in Radio and Television*. St John's: Breakwater Books, 1995.

Hiller, James K. 'The Newfoundland Credit System: An Interpretation.' In *Merchant Credit and Labour Strategies in Historical Perspective*, edited by Rosemary Ommer, 86–101. Fredericton: Acadiensis, 1990.

Hiller, James K., and Michael Harrington, eds. *The Newfoundland National Convention, 1946–1948*. 2 vols. St John's: Montreal and Kingston: McGill-Queen's University Press, 1995.

Hilmes, Michele. *Radio Voices: American Broadcasting, 1922–1952*. Minneapolis: University of Minnesota Press, 1997.

Hilmes, Michele, and Jason Loviglio, eds. *Radio Reader: Essays in the Cultural History of Radio*. New York: Routledge, 2002.

Hiscock, Philip. 'Folklore and Popular Culture in Early Newfoundland Radio Broadcasting: An Analysis of Occupational Narrative, Oral History and Song Repertoire.' MA thesis, Memorial University of Newfoundland, 1986.

– 'Folk Process in a Popular Medium: The "Irene B. Mellon" Radio Programme, 1934–1941.' In *Studies in Newfoundland Folklore: Community and Process*, edited by Gerald Thomas and J.D.A. Widdowson, 177–90. St John's: Breakwater Books, 1991.

– 'The Public Despatch and the Doyle Bulletin: Two Early Newfoundland News Services.' In *Beyond the Printed Word: The Evolution of Canada's Broadcast News Heritage*, edited by Richard Lochead, 115–22. Kingston: Quarry, 1991.

– 'The Barrelman Radio Programme, 1937–1943: The Mediation and the Use of Folklore in Newfoundland.' PhD diss., Memorial University of Newfoundland, 1994.

Horten, Gerd. *Radio Goes to War: The Cultural Politics of Propaganda during World War II*. Berkeley: University of California Press, 2002.

Horwood, Harold. *Joey: The Life and Political Times of Joey Smallwood*. Toronto: Stoddart, 1989.

Inglis, K.S. *This Is the ABC: The Australian Broadcasting Commission, 1932–1983*. Melbourne: Melbourne University Press, 1983.

Innis, Harold A. *The Bias of Communication.* Toronto: University of Toronto Press, 1971.

Knight, G. Wilson, ed. *Calling Newfoundland: Poems 1940–41 by Margot Davies.* St John's: Memorial University Press, 1981.

LeMahieu, D.L. *A Culture for Democracy: Mass Communication and the Cultivated Mind in Britain between the Wars.* Oxford: Clarendon, 1988.

Levine, Lawrence W. 'American Culture and the Great Depression.' *Yale Review* 74 (January 1985): 196–223.

– *Highbrow/Lowbrow: The Emergence of Cultural Hierarchy in America.* Cambridge: Harvard University Press, 1988.

– *The Unpredictable Past: Explorations in American Cultural History.* New York: Oxford University Press, 1993.

Lewis, Tom. *Empire of the Air: The Men Who Made Radio.* New York: HarperCollins, 1991.

Lipsitz, George. 'Listening to Learn and Learning to Listen: Popular Culture, Cultural Theory, and American Studies.' *American Quarterly* 42, no. 4 (December 1990): 624.

Lodge, Thomas. *Dictatorship in Newfoundland.* London: Cassell, 1939.

MacKay, Robert. 'Being Beastly to the Germans: Music, Censorship and the BBC in World War Two.' *Historical Journal of Film Radio and Television* 20, no. 4 (2000): 513–25.

MacKenzie, David. *Inside the Atlantic Triangle: Canada and the Entrance of Newfoundland into Confederation.* Toronto: University of Toronto Press, 1986.

Mansell, Gerard. *Let Truth Be Told: 50 Years of BBC External Broadcasting.* London: Weidenfeld and Nicolson, 1982.

Martin, John R. *Leonard Albert Miller: Public Servant.* Markham, ON: Associated Medical Services, 1998.

McChesney, Robert. *Telecommunications, Mass Media and Democracy: The Battle for Control of U.S. Broadcasting, 1928–1935.* New York: Oxford University Press, 1993.

McKay, Ian. *The Quest of the Folk: Antimodernism and Cultural Selection in Twentieth-Century Nova Scotia.* Montreal and Kingston: McGill-Queen's University Press, 1994.

McNeil, Bill, and Morris Wolfe. *The Birth of Radio in Canada: Signing On.* Toronto: Doubleday, 1982.

Narváez, Peter. 'Joseph R. Smallwood, "The Barrelman": The Broadcaster as Folklorist.' In *Media Sense: The Folklore–Popular Culture Continuum,* edited by Peter Narváez and Martin Laba. Bowling Green: Bowling Green State University Popular Press, 1987.

- 'Folk Talk and Hard Facts: The Role of Ted Russell's "Uncle Mose" on the Fishermen's Broadcast.' In *Studies in Newfoundland Folklore: Community and Process*, edited by Gerald Thomas and J.D.A. Widdowson, 191–212. St John's: Breakwater, 1991.

Neary, Peter. *Newfoundland in the North Atlantic World, 1929–1949*. Montreal and Kingston: McGill-Queen's University Press, 1988.

Nicholas, Siân. *The Echo of War: Home Front Propaganda and the Wartime BBC, 1939–45*. Manchester: Manchester University Press, 1996.

Noel, S.J.R. *Politics in Newfoundland*. Toronto: University of Toronto Press, 1971.

Nolan, Michael. *Foundations: Alan Plaunt and the Early Days of CBC Radio*. Toronto: CBC, 1986.

- 'An Infant Industry: Canadian Private Radio 1919–36.' *Canadian Historical Review* 70, no. 4 (1989): 496–518.

'Obituary William F. Galgay.' *Newfoundland Journal of Commerce* 33, no. 11 (November 1966): 51.

O'Flaherty, Patrick. *Lost Country: The Rise and Fall of Newfoundland, 1843–1933*. St John's: Long Beach, 2005.

Overton, James. 'A Newfoundland Culture?' *Journal of Canadian Studies* 23, nos. 1 and 2 (1988): 5–22.

- 'Economic Crisis and the End of Democracy.' *Labour/Le Travail* 26 (Fall 1990): 85–124.

- 'Engaging the Enemy Within: The Problem of the Jehovah's Witnesses in Newfoundland during World War II.' In *Engaging the Enemy: Canada in the 1940s*, edited by Andrew Hiscock and Muriel Chamberlain, 81–97. Llandybie, Wales: University of Wales Canadian Studies Group, 2007.

Paine, Robert. 'The Persuasiveness of Smallwood: Rhetoric of *Cuffer* and *Scoff*, of Metonym and Metaphore.' *Newfoundland Studies* 1, no. 1 (Spring 1985): 57–76.

- 'The Mastery of Smallwood and Interlocutory Rhetoric.' *Newfoundland Studies* 2, no. 2 (Fall 1986): 191–212.

Peers, Frank W. *The Politics of Canadian Broadcasting, 1920–1951*. Toronto: University of Toronto Press, 1969.

Pocius, Gerald L. 'The Mummers Song in Newfoundland: Intellectuals, Revivalists and Cultural Nativism. *Newfoundland Studies* 4, no. 1 (Spring 1988): 57–85.

Pope, Peter E. *Fish into Wine: The Newfoundland Plantation in the Seventeenth Century*. Chapel Hill: University of North Carolina Press, 2004.

Posen, I. Sheldon, and Michael Taft. 'The Newfoundland Popular Music

Project.' *Canadian Journal for Traditional Music* (1973), http://cjtm.icaap.org/
content/1/v1art4.html.

Potter, Simon J. 'The BBC, the CBC, and the 1939 Royal Tour of Canada. *Cultural and Social History* 3, no. 4 (2006): 424–44.

Prang, Margaret. 'The Origins of Public Broadcasting in Canada.' *Canadian Historical Review* 46, no. 1 (1965): 1–31.

Raboy, Marc. *Missed Opportunities: The Story of Canada's Broadcasting Policy.* Montreal and Kingston: McGill-Queen's University Press, 1990.

Razlogova, Elena. 'True Crime Radio and Listener Disenchantment with Network Broadcasting, 1935–1946.' *American Quarterly* 58, no. 1 (March 2006): 137–58.

Rosenberg, Neil. 'The Gerald S. Doyle Songsters and the Politics of Newfoundland Folksong.' *Canadian Folklore canadien* 13, no. 1 (1991): 45–58.

– 'Omar Blondahl's Contribution to the Newfoundland Folksong Canon.' *Canadian Journal for Traditional Music* (1991), http://cjtm.icaap.org/content/19/v19art4.html.

Ryan, Shannon. *The Ice Hunters: A History of Newfoundland Sealing to 1914.* St John's: Breakwater Books, 1994.

Scannell, Paddy, and David Cardiff. *A Social History of British Broadcasting.* Vol. 1, *1922–1939, Serving the Nation.* Oxford: Blackwell, 1991.

Sider, Gerald S. *Culture and Class in Anthropology and History: A Newfoundland Illustration.* Cambridge: Cambridge University Press, 1986.

Smallwood, Joseph R. *I Chose Canada: The Memoirs of the Honourable Joseph R. Smallwood.* Toronto: MacMillan, 1973.

Smulyan, Susan. *Selling Radio: The Commercialization of American Broadcasting, 1920–1934.* London: Smithsonian Institution Press, 1994.

Thomas, Gerald, and J.D.A. Widdowson, eds. *Studies in Newfoundland Folklore: Community and Process.* St John's: Breakwater Books, 1991.

Thompson, John B. *Ideology and Modern Culture: Critical Social Theory in the Era of Mass Communications.* Stanford: Stanford University Press, 1990.

Thomsen, Christen K. 'Jazz: From "Race" Music to "Art" Music? When Jazz Was "Popular" Music; Incorporation and Transformation.' *Storia Nordamericana* 7, no. 2 (1990): 79–101.

Tizzard, Aubrey M. *On Sloping Ground: Reminiscences of Outport Life in Notre Dame Bay, Newfoundland.* St John's: Memorial University Press, 1979.

Tuck, Marilyn. 'The Newfoundland Ranger Force, 1935–1950.' MA thesis, Memorial University of Newfoundland, 1983.

Vipond, Mary. *Listening In: The First Decade of Canadian Broadcasting, 1922–1932.* Montreal and Kingston: McGill-Queen's University Press, 1992.

– 'The Mass Media in Canadian History: The Empire Day Broadcast in 1939. *Journal of the Canadian Historical Association* n.s. 14 (2003): 1–21.

Webb, Jeff A. 'Newfoundland's National Convention, 1946–48.' MA thesis, Memorial University of Newfoundland, 1987.

– 'The Origins of Public Broadcasting: The Commission of Government and the Creation of the Broadcasting Corporation of Newfoundland.' *Acadiensis* 24, no. 2 (Autumn 1994): 88–106.

– 'The Invention of Radio Broadcasting in Newfoundland and the Maritime Provinces, 1922–1939.' PhD diss., University of New Brunswick, 1995.

– 'Canada's Moose River Mine Disaster (1936): Radio-Newspaper Competition in the Business of News.' *Historical Journal of Film, Radio and Television* 16, no. 3 (October 1996): 365–76.

– 'Confederation, Conspiracy and Choice: A Discussion.' *Newfoundland Studies* 14, no. 2 (1998): 169–87.

– 'VOUS – Voice of the United States: The Armed Forces Radio Service in Newfoundland.' *Journal of Radio Studies* 1, no. 1 (June 2004): 87–99.

– 'Who Speaks for the Public? The Debate over Government or Private Broadcasting in Newfoundland, 1939–1949. *Acadiensis* 35, no. 1 (Autumn 2005): 74–93.

Weir, E. Austin. *The Struggle for National Broadcasting in Canada.* Toronto: McClelland and Stewart, 1965.

Wellman, Jim. *The Broadcast.* St John's: Creative Book Publishing, 1997.

Whisnant, David E. *All That Is Native and Fine: The Politics of Culture in an American Region.* Chapel Hill: University of North Carolina Press, 1983.

Williams, Raymond. *Key Words: A Vocabulary of Culture and Society.* London: Fontana, 1976.

Wright, Miriam. *A Fishery for Modern Times: The State and the Industrialization of the Newfoundland Fishery, 1934–1968.* Don Mills: Oxford University Press, 2001.

Index

musical taste of, 73; National Convention, broadcast of proceedings, 143, 156–9, 159–61, 167–8; political broadcasts, 147–51, 162, 165, 168; potential libel, 90–1, 160–1; public service, view of, 170, 172; royal tour broadcast, 55–7; sexually transmitted diseases, broadcasts on, 128–9; style of broadcasting, 53; US servicemen, broadcast of arrival, 126; view of private broadcasters, 181–6, 188–9, 212–13, 249n40; war effort, 122,140–1; women's programming, 76

Gambo, 100, 163

Gander, 94, 168, 172, 196

Ganou, Penelope, 25

gender, broadcasters' use of, 104, 117–19, 237n115; listeners' preference, 51, 75–6, 108–10, 238n128

Gerald S. Doyle News Bulletin, description of, 84–7, 91, 89–90, 205; inaugural broadcast, 25; listeners, 109–111, 155; news on, 62, 174; role in creating popular culture, 107–7; social role of, 71, 88–90, 215

Godfrey, Stuart, 78

Goodman, Benny, 79

Goose Bay, 125

Gorvin, John H., 59, 62–3, 68–9

Grand Falls, 10, 172, 190, 194–6, 251n100

Graves, C.G., 29–31, 74

Great Eastern Oil Company, 90–1

Great Eastern, 208

Green Hornet, 110, 176

Green Label News, 174. *See also* Vardy, O.L.

Grenfell, Wilfred, 58

Guards Band, 78

Haig-Smith, J., 87–8, 125

Halley, Gordon, 39

Halton, Matthew, 114

Hancock, George, 102–3

Happy Gang, 109

Harper, E.E., 28

Harrington, Michael F., as Barrelman, 105–6, 147, 174, 237n125; career of, 105–6, 205, 207–8; in National Convention, 154, 158

Hawkins, Helen, 109–10

Heakes, F.W., 125

Hello Newfoundland. See Calling Newfoundland

Hickman, Edgar, 187

Hierlihy, Clifford, 171

Hierlihy, Oscar, 23, 39

Hill Billy Music. *See* country music

Hilmes, Michele, 75, 119

Hiscock, E.D.C., 156

Hiscock, Philip, 73, 95–7

Historians, view of broadcasting, 4–5, 7–8; view of Newfoundland, 5, 10–11

Hollett, Malcolm, 187

Holyrood, 55

Horwood, Harold, 160

Horwood, William, 40

Howie Wing, 110

Hunt, Charles E., 38, 158, 184

Hymns from Home, 132

Inskip, Thomas, 40

International Bible Students Association. *See* Jehovah's Witnesses

Irene B. Mellon, 73, 203, 232n8

Jackman, Ignatius, 187

Jacques Fountain, 97

James, R.L.M., 165, 184